HEARING THE VOICE
OF THE MARKET

HEARING THE VOICE OF THE MARKET

Competitive Advantage through Creative Use of Market Information

Vincent P. Barabba
Executive Director, Market Research
and Planning, General Motors Corporation

and

Gerald Zaltman
The Albert Wesley Frey Distinguished Professor of Marketing,
University of Pittsburgh

HARVARD BUSINESS SCHOOL PRESS
Boston, Massachusetts

Library of Congress Cataloging-in-Publication Data

Barabba, Vincent P., 1934-
    Hearing the voice of the market : competitive advantage through creative use of market information / by Vincent P. Barabba and Gerald Zaltman.
      p. cm.
    Includes bibliographical references and index.
    ISBN 0-87584-241-0 (hard : acid free paper) :
    1. Decision-making. 2. Industrial management. 3. Marketing research. 4. Competition. I. Zaltman, Gerald. II. Title.
HD30.23.B358 1990
658.8'02--dc20   90-44491
                                                    CIP

To my mother and brother who made it possible for me to learn about and listen to the voice of the market (VPB)
and
To Ann, whose voice is always worth hearing (GZ)

Contents

Preface

The phrase "knowledge is power" is often used out of context to imply that the person who controls knowledge also controls power. As is so often the case, Sir Francis Bacon had an entirely different concept in mind when he first used the phrase in 1597. In fact, he never actually said, "Knowledge is power." Instead, in a parenthetical comment on the relationship of the knowledge of God to God's power, he said, "For knowledge itself is power."

Bacon used the term in the context of the sixteenth-century view that knowledge is the power through which mankind can create a better life here on earth. There is much insight to be gained by returning to the basic premise of Bacon's phrase; that is, the power of knowledge is a resource that enables other things to happen.

The purpose of this book is to help managers and market researchers in private and public sector organizations improve their collaborative as well as independent efforts to acquire and use information as a resource through which beneficial things will happen to customers, the organization, and society. Although we use private sector examples, the basic tools and concepts we introduce are fully appropriate to public sector agencies.

An important premise of the book is that even small improvements in learning about the marketplace and in making creative use of market information can have a major effect in eliciting more favorable responses to the firm's offerings. A second important premise is that there is no organization of any size or nature that cannot substantially improve its use of information in order to develop and deliver goods and services that reflect both customer needs and the organization's capabilities and constraints. Improved use of market information benefits society as a whole as much as it does the organizations serving society's diverse constituent groups.

It is difficult to think of a topic that is more basic to the conduct of human affairs than the use of information. The use, nonuse, misuse, and abuse of information is about as fundamental and pervasive a social and psychological process as one can find. It is as essential to such a complex, dynamic setting as "Europe 1992" as it is to a "new moon" market day in Chala, Nepal, where living standards for months may be determined by a single day's market activity. How information about the marketplace in Europe or Chala is or is not used is of great consequence to customers, just as it is to huge multinational corporations and individual entrepreneurs.

A topic of this importance and pervasiveness cannot avoid being a complicated one. At the same time, making improvements in the use of market information is not necessarily complicated or difficult. It can be made difficult, of course. An interesting paradox is that many simple things can be done to substantially improve how market information is used. Because of the complexity of the topic many theories and ideas are interrelated and thus recur in different chapters. That is the nature of the beast. Perhaps the reader will find it helpful.

We have been students of the information-use process throughout our careers. We have learned by participating, often through trial and error as well as through deliberate experimentation, as employees and/or consultants in a diverse array of private and public organizations. Because we have a deep curiosity about the process, we have also studied information use, nonuse, and misuse from the perspectives offered by practitioners and scholars who also have a strong interest in the topic.

We offer our insights not so much as diagnostic tools or prescriptive guidelines, but as probes to thinking. It is important, of course, to ask such questions as, "Does this issue apply to me?" "Would this solution work here?" "Do I agree with this position?" But it is more important to ask, "Does this issue exist here in this or another form? If it doesn't, should it? How could I adapt this solution or develop one suitable for my circumstances? Why do I agree or disagree with their position?" We intend to be both helpful and provocative and to encourage the reader to approach our observations and prescriptive guidelines as "thinker toys," as tools or devices to focus attention on current practices and thinking, and to examine the reasons why they should or should not be continued or modified.

Finally, we must point out that a topic of such importance, diversity, and complexity as information use is studied in many different ways. Each of the perspectives has merit and a tradition of productive thinking. We are eclectic in "perspective taking." This, in itself, is a perspective. It has the advantage of offering the reader a sampling of approaches to the subject of information use, along with our own experiences and those of various practitioners. But it involves a trade-off. It does not do full justice to any one approach. Thus, important issues such as corporate culture, organizational memory, human information processing, ethics, and the design of management information systems are necessarily underdeveloped. We have, however, provided the reader with direction in finding more complete treatments of these and other relevant topics.

We hope you find our trade-off an acceptable one, that the cost of underdeveloping or even neglecting a topic you feel merits more attention is offset by the value of having a greater variety of "thinker toys" to play with. Many of the ideas we raise are not available or easy to find in the published literature or from specialist organizations. This is another reason we felt our more eclectic approach would be of special value to the reader. It was, in fact, the primary reason we chose to write this book. We believe this book to be the first to advocate a disciplined approach to the gathering, management, and application of market knowledge and to demonstrate the linkage between decision process quality and market information process quality.

Vincent P. Barabba
Capitola, CA

Gerald Zaltman
Owl's Head, ME

Acknowledgments

A large number of people contributed in a correspondingly large number of ways to the development of this book. We first extend our deepest gratitude to the following colleagues who were our "voice of the market": Meera Buck (Shell Oil Company), Dean H.J. Zoffer, Michael McCarthy, and M.L. Chan (University of Pittsburgh), George Day and Alden Clayton (Marketing Science Institute), Daniel Dennehy (Ramm Metals, Inc.), Rohit Deshpande (Dartmouth College), Deborah Dougherty (University of Pennsylvania), Richard Luecke and Natalie Greenberg (Harvard Business School Press), Ann Gove and Kjell Gronhaug (Norwegian School of Economics and Business Administration), Steve Haeckel (IBM Corporation), Ajay Kohli (University of Texas), Bill Lawton and Herb Blitzer (Eastman Kodak Company), Jack Osborn (Brannon Cottage Inn), and Christine Moorman (University of Wisconsin).

The same level of gratitude is extended to colleagues who made direct contributions to the book: Michael Kusnic (General Motors Corporation) and Dan Owen (Decision and Risk Analysis, Inc.) for input to the Introduction— Dan Owen also contributed significantly to Chapter 12; John Albers, Mickey Barnhart, Wayne Brannon, James Christian, Katherine Frohardt-Lane, Alice Hayes, Robert Kleinbaum, Gerald Lieberman, Patrick Martin, Kevin Reilly, and Donald Thomas (General Motors Corporation), Robert Groves and W. Allen Spivey (University of Michigan), David Marker (Westat, Inc.), Vithala Rao (Cornell University), Alan Shocker (University of Minnesota), Richard Smallwood (Applied Decision Analysis, Inc.), and especially Barbara Richardson (Richardson and Associates) all contributed to Chapter 4; and Marc Itzkowitz (General Motors Corporation) to the Appendix.

Although they are too numerous to list here, we would like to thank the three groups of MBA students at the University of Pittsburgh who took a

course focusing on the subject matter of the book and whose work experiences provided us with valuable insights and whose critical reading of the
manuscript improved the presentation of material.

We particularly want to thank the many managers, researchers, and
consultants in a wide variety of organizations who, over a period of years,
provided us with the raw material for fashioning the ideas in this book. These
people, several hundred in the span of several projects, gave generously of
their time and, most important, extended their trust in sharing with us their
ideas and experiences so openly. We hope that all of them and their colleagues
will find this book of value and accept that as our way of saying, "Thank you."

The physical production of the manuscript required a special tolerance of
the authors' idiosyncrasies and a high level of professional skill among those
responsible for the preparation of numerous and, to them, seemingly endless
drafts. We were very fortunate to have found people with both qualities and
want to express our deep appreciation to Annette Brining, Margaret Jonnet,
Denise Magee, and Laura Manko.

While those individuals mentioned above are, in a sense, invisible co-
authors, we accept responsibility for any errors. We did not always follow
their advice, although we tried hard to practice what we preach—to listen to
the voice of the market (represented by the many reviewers) and to balance
their advice with our own sense of what was feasible, given our objectives.
Our book is substantially better than it might have been had we not had the
benefit of their articulate voices.

Introduction

Indeed it has been said that we are now living in a second industrial revolution; but instead of steam, the new revolution is being propelled by *information*. And, as in the first revolution, relative success will be determined by the ability to handle the propelling force .... There can be little doubt that the need today is for conceptual skills, that is, the ability to process information and make judgments.[1]

Robin M. Hogarth
Judgement and Choice

INFORMATION USE IN TODAY'S WORLD

We now live in an increasingly complex world, one characterized by Alvin Toffler as "future shock": Toffler said, "By future shock I mean the disorientation and decision overload produced by high-speed change ... [which] sometimes leads to a breakdown of our capacity for rational decision making."[2]

Millions of men and women are now in the situation predicted by Toffler. The decisions they face come faster and faster, decisions that affect more people, money, land, and resources than ever before. One of the effects of the increased tempo is that the time available to check the accuracy of information has been shortened. Often the demand for action is so great that data are hastily assembled, used, and assumed to be adequate. Unfortunately, the data are often outdated, or incorrect, or both. In today's world all decisions, whether domestic household, corporate headquarters, or federal or local government, need to be timely, confident, and based on accurate information. Thus, in recent years, there have been major changes in the general information environment.

1

A number of private and public entities have experienced Toffler's future shock:

The Xerox Corporation. For Xerox, one of the world's fastest growing and most profitable major corporations, future shock came when customers throughout the world began replacing their large Xerox copiers with several small Japanese copiers. Though it considered the possibility of that purchasing pattern, top management at Xerox did not believe it would actually occur. Also, Eastman Kodak began development of a competitive large-volume copier, something Xerox had not anticipated.

Eastman Kodak. Here the story is somewhat different. Kodak was stunned in the late 1970s by an unprecedented increase in the price of silver, a major raw material in the manufacture of film. The greatest shock, however, was a continuing erosion of market share in amateur film, photo-finishing print paper, and commercial films for X-ray and printing to Fuji and private label brands. Kodak lost less market share than Xerox because it believed the information identifying its problems sooner.

General Motors. GM had a very successful lineup of large and powerful products. Like Kodak, it also faced change because of an unprecedented increase in the price of a basic commodity—petroleum. That crisis coincided with another, the availability of small, high-quality Japanese cars. GM also faced formidable competition from European vehicles, many of which offered excellent mileage and value, due, in part, to favorable exchange rates.

The United States Census Bureau. A new era in the history of the Census Bureau began in September 1980 when a federal judge in Detroit ruled on behalf of the city and against the bureau. Although significant change had been taking place over the 190-year period of U.S. census taking, it was always evolutionary, and seldom of such a nature as to suggest that new ways of counting the population would ever be required. The court's decision shocked the bureau with the realization that the driving force and direction for change was to be imposed from the outside.

The bureau found itself trying to satisfy many stakeholders whose needs and demands appeared to be contradictory. At the heart of the controversy was the issue of whether or not to adjust the census count, given an expected undercount of minorities. On the one hand there were forces insisting that established statistical practices be consistently applied. On the other hand was the demand for equity. By not being counted, minorities would be under-represented in Congress—because of redistricting—and shorted on the funds distributed through population-driven allocation formulae. The issue was put most succinctly by then Atlanta mayor Maynard C. Jackson: "There are only two itty-bitty things at stake here: money and votes."

Having information available does not ensure that it will be used to make good decisions. The organizations mentioned above had considerable information about the market well before they had to face the changed environments. Despite this, much of their decision making was driven by analyses of sales data and internal records. When a firm dominates the market it tends to think that by understanding its own sales and trends it is understanding the entire market (e.g., the Census Bureau found out it had defined its environment much too narrowly). It believed it was sufficient to understand the citizens who would be required to fill out the census questionnaire. Instead, it found that other powerful parties were also interested in how the census was making a count that would affect their constituents.

The experiences of these four large organizations are typical of organizations of all sizes and in all goods and services settings. What follows is just a small sample of the conditions that now make it imperative for managers in all kinds of organizations to understand how to use information to improve the quality of their decision making. As we will find, competitive advantage resides increasingly in how information is used rather than in who has information.

Fewer options. In a competitive domestic and international marketplace where traditional boundaries are becoming blurred, there are often fewer available strategies or actions than in the past.

Too much unhelpful data. Managers have lots of information that is not very relevant, timely, or useful. Although technically sound, the data may be addressing the wrong problem, or may be in a form that makes their translation into action difficult.

Overload. The sheer volume of analyses is often overwhelming. This can lead to a reaction against the use of *any* information—paralysis by analysis.

The trick 'em approach. This occurs when the managers in one group anticipate how the managers in another group will respond to their analysis, and then change that analysis so that when the second group adjusts the first group's report, the final analysis will come out the way the first group wanted it to in the first place.

The silo effect. This occurs when major functional areas do not talk to one another in situations where they should. They simply exist side by side like isolated silos. This effect is symptomatic of what we call the new marketing myopia (the old marketing myopia is defining one's market too narrowly)— the perception that it is primarily the marketing function that does marketing, when in fact virtually all groups make decisions that affect how customers and others view the firm's offerings.

More frequent surprises. Virtually all markets are changing more rapidly than in the recent past. Thus, the period of time for which a decision may remain appropriate is getting shorter. This leads to greater amounts of uncertainty surrounding important decisions. Uncertainty, more than competitors and resource constraints, is becoming the arch enemy of many managers.

These conditions are of concern not only to managers but also to the researchers and consultants with whom the managers often must work in order to improve quality in the decision process, which, in turn, requires improving quality in the process of using market information.

The Viewing Lens

It is important to recognize that a viewing lens is often used by decision makers and others to understand the voice of the market, that is, what the market says it wants and is willing to pay for. By viewing lens we mean a frame of reference: the assumptions, expectations, and rules used to evaluate and respond to a situation. The viewing lens has two sides through which to view the marketplace. Managers view the marketplace through one side; researchers often view it through the other. These different frames of reference create asymmetrical surfaces on either side of the lens. In effect, two different viewing lenses are used for evaluating and responding to the same data.

These different views may create different behaviors. For example, because of uncertainty, the information provider may present managers with more data and more analyses. Managers, on the other hand, may respond to uncertainty by demanding less information having greater value. By "greater value" managers usually mean information (a) that is clearly placed in a decision context, (b) that is in a form that facilitates their making better judgments, and (c) that is easily synthesized with their other knowledge. The two groups may even interpret the voice of the market differently.

The important point to keep in mind, when data are viewed differently, is that neither party is right or wrong. Rather, one must understand why the two parties—the information users and the information providers—differ. It is this kind of understanding, when arrived at in constructive ways, that leads to better insight about the marketplace among all parties. This, in turn, increases the likelihood of finding the "right" answer.

It is our basic position that insufficient attention has been given to increasing the quality of the information process as well as the decision process. As a result, the mutual dependence of quality decision processes and quality market information processes has also been ignored.

QUALITY IN THE DECISION PROCESS

Managers everywhere now know how critical quality is to their products and services. They have learned that quality cannot be an afterthought, that is, "inspected in" at the end of the production line. It must be intrinsic to the whole production process.

Unfortunately, few managers have applied this same insight about quality to their decision making. In fact, many are unaware of the process they are actually using to make decisions. When asked how they make decisions they might say, "I weigh the facts," "I balance costs and benefits," "I look at the down side," or "I list strengths and weaknesses." However, if pressed with, "What is the sequence of steps that you go through in order to assure quality in your decisions?" few managers can articulate them.

The significance of managers' inability to articulate the process of decision making is that without a clear procedure in mind, improving and maintaining quality in decisions are both difficult. Instead of initially building quality into the decision process, most managers try to inspect it in later. For example, the recommendations of a task force on a $400-million acquisition were reviewed by senior management in a two-hour meeting, and a decision was made. Its review consisted of asking specific questions and, apparently, judging the quality of the recommendations by the quickness and depth of the response. The senior managers were inspecting quality into the decision process. It is hard to see how they could have gotten a feel for the issues in such a brief session. It is hard to see how the analysis team could have accurately anticipated all of the issues that the senior managers needed to address.

Fundamental Concepts

Definition of a quality decision. A quality decision can only be meaningfully defined as a decision which is irrevocably tied to allocations of resources, including capital and operating budgets, personnel, time, and so forth. The critical element is the tight connection between the decision and the resource allocation. By this definition, a decision to "increase market share," "improve quality," or "manufacture great appliances" has not been made until the concomitant resources have been identified and allocated.

Two very practical implications emerge from this definition. First, by defining decisions in terms of resource allocations, the implementation of the decision is facilitated and accountabilities are established. If the decision to increase market share is defined by specific resource allocations to price reduction, increased advertising, and improved product features, the implementation of the decision can be monitored and particular managers held accountable. Without this precise definition of resources, each manager will be able to show that whatever he or she wants to do supports the decision implementation. Hence, senior managers lament, "We keep deciding to change, but nothing ever happens."

A second practical implication is that defining decisions by resource allocations forces managers to resolve conflict. If the resource requirement is a part of the definition of the decision to increase market share, then the source of those resources must be identified. Will the resources come from slowing down or stopping other projects, from cash flow, or from additional financing? If the decision to go for increased market share comes for free, it's hard to be against it. If it requires resources, there may be some conflict about where they will come from. Decision makers must resolve such conflicts to ensure implementation. If conflict is left for lower-level managers to resolve, the status quo will be a formidable barrier to change.

Decisions and uncertainties. Managers control their resources, but there are other uncontrollable factors that influence decision outcomes. Competitive action, government regulation, and customer preferences are largely uncontrollable, but they all influence the ultimate result of a resource allocation. Some of these will also be relatively uncertain. Identifying uncertain uncontrollable factors is critical, because they contribute to the overall risk associated with each possible decision or resource allocation.

Risk and return. Unfortunately, the decision alternatives that have the highest expected return often carry the greatest risk. Consequently, identifying the critical uncertainties and quantifying their relative contribution to overall risk are important, because doing so permits

- side-by-side comparison of risk and return for each alternative, which facilitates making the decision;
- identification of those uncertainties on which information-gathering activities should be focused; and
- identification of those uncertainties over which managers should strive for control through resource allocation, thus creating new, more valuable decision alternatives which have less risk.

Hence, a critical element of decision quality is information quality; not only accurate facts and numbers, but also a clear statement of the uncertainty about those facts and numbers.

The Organization as a Network of Decisions

Viewing organizations as decision networks is a valuable way of understanding the interaction between decision quality and information quality. Decisions made in one area of a firm frequently affect and are affected by decisions made in another area. For example, Exhibit I-1 illustrates the strategies chosen by different business units within a firm. It shows the amount of resources allocated to areas of activity, in this case, marketing, technology, manufacturing, and finance, for each unit. Of course, in each area, total resources are allocated among appropriate subdivisions. For example, the

Exhibit I-1
The Firm as a Network of Decisions Or Resource Allocations

	Areas of Resource Allocation			
	Marketing	Technology	Manufacturing	Finance
Business Unit 1	$$$$$	$	$	$$$
Business Unit 2	$$$	$$$	$$$	$$$
Business Unit 3	$	$$$$$	$$$$$	$$$

total marketing resource allocation might be divided into allocations for product, price, promotion, and delivery.

Quality in decision making requires that the resource allocations that comprise the business unit strategies complement each other. That is, they must work together to move each business unit in its strategic direction. Clearly, defining strategies and decisions in terms of resources facilitates attainment of complementary decisions. If the firm profiled in Exhibit I-1 has made quality decisions, there is an appropriate rationale for the marketing emphasis of Business Unit 1 and for the technology and manufacturing emphasis of Business Unit 3. If we look at the columns rather than the rows, we see the functional strategies of the firm. The capital allocation to each business unit is roughly the same, while the technology strategy emphasizes resource commitments to Business Unit 3.

Most organizations manage to gain reasonable complementarity in one direction, but not the other. When organized by business units, the decisions that comprise business strategies are more complementary than the decisions that make up functional strategies. When organized by functional activities, the decisions that comprise functional strategies are more complementary than the decisions that comprise the business strategies. Quality in decision making requires complementarity in both directions, but attainment of complementarity may be impeded by the silo effect.

As we mentioned above, within each functional area are appropriate subdivisions of resource allocation, such as product, price, promotion, and delivery for marketing. The resource allocations to the subdivisions must be not only complementary to, but also consistent with the business unit strategy. Similarly, the resource allocations that comprise the distribution strategy for Business Unit 1 must be consistent with the marketing strategy for Business Unit 1. Quality in decision making within the firm requires that lower-level resource allocations be consistent and nested within higher-level, consistent resource allocations. These notions of consistency and complementarity are

Exhibit I-2
Decision and Risk Analysis Process

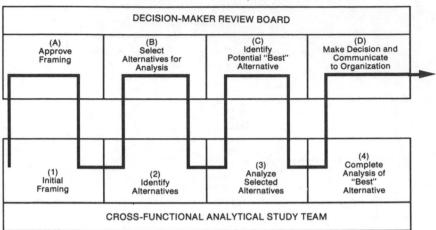

important elements of our framework and are discussed in more detail in Chapter 10.

Decision and risk analysis. Decision and risk analysis, a process for ensuring quality in decision making, is essentially a structured dialogue between a decision-maker review board and a cross-functional analytical study team (see Exhibit I-2). The review board consists of those who are responsible for the resource allocations. Often these decision makers will be from different business units or functional areas across which decision complementarity is important and difficult. During the time the team is assembled to work on a specific assignment it will (a) approve the framing of the problem, (b) select alternatives for analysis, (c) identify (create if necessary) the "best" potential alternative, and (d) make and communicate the required decisions.

The cross-functional analytical study team brings to bear high-quality information, analytic tools that assist in the proper treatment of uncertainties, and a logically consistent analytical framework. While they serve on the team, members (1) provide the initial framing definition, (2) identify alternative solutions, (3) analyze selected alternatives, and (4) conduct a thorough analysis of the best alternative.

The highly interactive dialogue that takes place between the two groups focuses, first, on the proper framing of the problem (activities 1 and A). By framing we mean identification and organization of all critical issues that must be included in the decision process. These issues include decisions, uncertainties, values, objectives, and facts.

A second dialogue determines which alternative strategies should be

Exhibit I-3
Two Dimensions of Decision Process Quality:
The Decision Maker's View

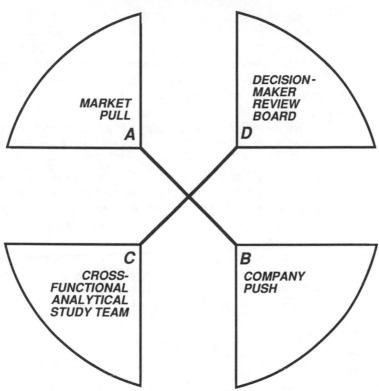

considered and evaluated (activities 2 and B). As an example, one alternative strategy might consist primarily of resource allocations that are responsive to the voice of the market, a second to the voice of the company. Other strategies may strike a balance between the two voices, but employ different approaches to achieving that balance. Our experience identifies this dialogue as a key stage for potential creative interaction between the worlds of the user and provider.

The third dialogue focuses on the insight into the sources of value in each alternative (activities 3 and B) that the analysis brings. This activity is important because with most complex problems, the best strategy usually cannot be identified at the outset. It is developed as a composite of alternative strategies based on the insight gained during the analysis.

A final dialogue (activities 4 and D) includes a thorough evaluation of the best strategy, an agreement among members of the review board that the decision has been made, and the development of a plan to communicate the decision to the rest of the organization as well as to begin implementation planning.

Obviously, engaging in this structural dialogue takes management's time, and that time is limited. Senior managers must, therefore, choose those decisions for which they will take active responsibility. Other decisions, for which there is not enough time, must be delegated to other managers who follow the same process model. In this way, a management team committed to total quality uses the time commitment required for decision quality, not as an excuse to make judgment calls but as a criterion for delegation of decisions.

The two dimensions of this decision quality process, from the view of the decision maker, are shown in Exhibit I-3. One dimension concerns balance between market pull (A) and company push (B). The other dimension is the dialogue between the cross-functional analytical study team (C) and a decision-maker review board (D) which takes place as the two groups attempt to achieve the appropriate balance between market pull and company push. From the decision maker's perspective, an appropriate balance needs to be attained along both dimensions in order to have quality in decision making.

There are five steps in achieving this balance (see Exhibit I-4):

Step 1. *Hearing the voice of the market.* This step is positioned between market pull and decision-maker review board and signifies the need for the board to explicitly commit to decision-making procedures that are market-based.

Step 2. Identify *alternative market requirements.* This is positioned between market pull and the cross-functional analytical study team. This positioning signifies the need to assess market forces and identify different combinations that create viable alternative bundles of market needs and requirements.

Step 3. Identify *alternative company offerings.* This step is positioned between the cross-functional analytical study team and company push to signify the need to identify appropriate combinations of company offerings from the internal capabilities of the firm.

Step 4. *Understanding the voice of the market.* This step relates steps 2 and 3, focusing on creatively harmonizing what the company is capable of providing with the wants and needs of the market. This step signifies the need for the appropriate level of management to meet its commitment to develop market-based decisions.

Step 5. *Decision process quality.* This step is positioned at the center of both environmental dimensions and the previous four steps because it evaluates the quality of the decision process. It is at this step where learning takes place.

QUALITY IN THE MARKET INFORMATION PROCESS

There are two elements to information process quality. One has to do with the psychological, sociological, and other organizational dynamics af-

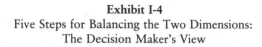

Exhibit I-4
Five Steps for Balancing the Two Dimensions:
The Decision Maker's View

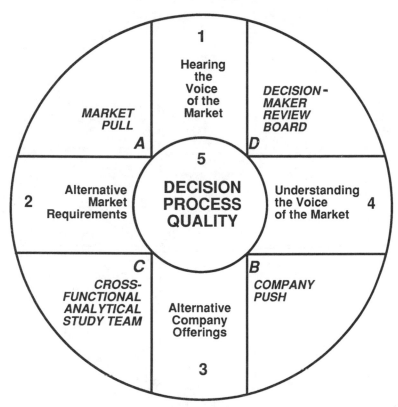

fecting information use. The second has to do with the collection and treatment of data in technically sound and appropriate ways. While each element is important, it is far more likely that a problem will exist with the behavioral element. The technologies for data collection—storage, retrieval, and statistical analyses—are well developed. The technology for putting data into use, however, is in its infancy. This is partly because the conversion of data into applicable knowledge is an inherently human process. A computer cannot do it alone. As a process it is often difficult to deal with and hence is given little attention.

There is a framework for addressing quality in the market information process which is similar in structure to the framework discussed earlier for addressing quality in the decision process. This framework is more fully described in Chapter 4.

Exhibit I-5
Two Dimensions of Market Information Process Quality:
The Information Provider's View

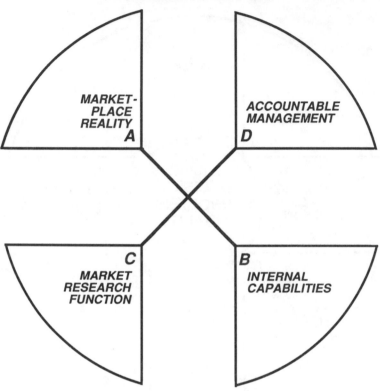

The two dimensions of the market information quality process from the view of the information provider are shown in Exhibit I-5. One dimension is achieving balance between marketplace reality (A) and internal capabilities (B). The second dimension is the dialogue between the market research function (C) and accountable management (D) as they attempt to achieve the appropriate balance between the realities of the marketplace and the internal capabilities of the firm. From the information provider's perspective, an appropriate balance needs to be attained along both dimensions in order to provide quality market information.

To help achieve this balance, five steps must be taken (see Exhibit I-6):

Step 1. *Assess market information needs.* This step is positioned between marketplace reality and accountable management. This positioning signifies the need for the appropriate managers to involve themselves in the early phases of the market research process to make sure the firm *measures the right things.*

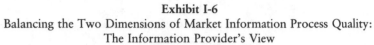

Exhibit I-6
Balancing the Two Dimensions of Market Information Process Quality:
The Information Provider's View

Step 2. *Measure the marketplace.* This step is positioned between market-place reality and the market research function. This positioning signifies the acceptance that market research's professional and technical skills are sufficient to measure things right.

Step 3. *Store, retrieve, and display data.* This step is positioned between the market research function and internal capabilities to signify the need to ensure that the correctly collected information is stored so that the market information is easily related to the firm's internal capabilities to meet (or hopefully, exceed or lead) market requirements.

Step 4. *Analyze and describe market data.* This step deals with analyzing the information collected in step 2 and stored in step 3 with primary focus on creatively identifying competitive advantages. It is appropriately positioned between internal capabilities and accountable management.

Step 5. *Market information process quality.* This step is positioned at the center of both environmental dimensions and the previous four steps to

Exhibit I-7
Balancing the View of the Decision Maker and the Information Provider

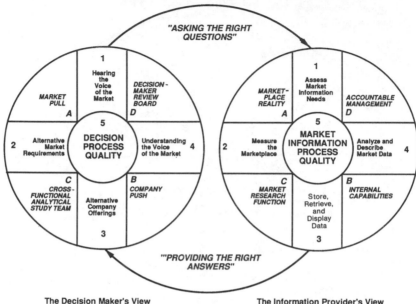

The Decision Maker's View   The Information Provider's View

evaluate the quality of the market information collection and use process. It is at this step where learning takes place.

The best way to improve quality in the market information process is to focus on the behavioral factors that enhance and/or impede the acquisition, processing, and application of information in the decision-making process. This involves understanding better how to manage the interactions between accountable management and the market research function, that is, those accountable for the reliability and validity of information provided to accountable management. It also involves learning how better to balance the internal capabilities of the firm (what it is willing and able to do) with the reality of the marketplace (what the market says it wants and is willing to pay for). Thus, improving total corporate performance requires that everyone in the firm understand how the balancing of the firm's internal capabilities with marketplace reality is affected by the behavioral dynamics (1) within accountable management groups, (2) within the market research function, and especially (3) between accountable management and the market research function.

BALANCING DECISION MAKER AND INFORMATION: THE PROVIDER'S VIEW

Since the viewing lens of the decision maker is different from that of the information provider, improved decision quality will only be achieved when both parties understand that these are real differences, and learn to appreciate the alternative point of view. The ultimate objective is to achieve a harmonious balance between the two views (see Exhibit I-7). When the two views are in balance, it is expected that the decision makers will be better positioned to "ask the right questions."

The information providers, working within the two dimensions and following the five steps, are better positioned to "provide the right answers." How the two views come together is more fully described in Chapters 2, 4, and elsewhere in the book.

Among those who provide information there is a tenet which states:

The respondents of questionnaires
give us our wherewithal.
But the users of information
give us our purpose.

However, there is also a message for users who seek knowledge to assist them in making wiser decisions. To them the message is equally simple and important:

You are not required
to do all the work
to acquire knowledge;
however,
you cannot
acquire knowledge
without doing
some of the work.

Notes

1. Robin M. Hogarth, *Judgement and Choice*, 2d ed. (New York: John Wiley, 1987), p. 3.
2. Alvin Toffler, in an interview in J. Walter Thompson house organ *JWT World*, 1985.

PART 1

THE PROBLEM OF MARKET INFORMATION AND DECISION MAKING

It is increasingly important for firms to use the voice of the market, that is, what customers want and are willing to pay for. Using the voice of the market goes far beyond the simple acquisition of data. It requires that the data be integrated into the decision process that determines what the firm is capable of and willing to present to the market. The decisions represent, in effect, the voice of the firm. A market-based firm is created when decision making throughout the company is based on the reconciliation of differences between the two voices. Spending money to develop ideas originating largely within the firm and later learning that customers are unlikely to pay for them is a gross misuse of R&D and market research resources. Chapter 1 discusses some of the central issues a firm must address in becoming market-based. In fact, addressing these issues well is possibly the single most important challenge facing companies today.

Chapter 2 introduces the concept of an inquiry center. In a broad sense, an inquiry center is the ideal state of mind within a company for effectively and efficiently reconciling the voice of the market with the voice of the firm. All firms, of course, have inquiry centers, but we describe the inquiry center in its ideal form so that readers may compare and assess their own system for making market-based decisions. Both Chapters 1 and 2 recognize that managers throughout a firm are the inquiry center's constituency. This topic is developed more fully in Chapter 3.

Before proceeding we would like to share briefly the results of an important empirical study conducted recently for the Marketing Science Institute involving 140 strategic business units of a large forest products firm.[1] The units fell into three categories: commodity, distribution, and specialty businesses. The study assessed the impact on profitability of having (and not having) a market orientation. Narver and Slater treated market orientation essentially as we view being market-based. It reflects: (a) the degree of understanding of buyers' preferences and a unit's continuous focusing on activities that increase the perceived value among customers of its offerings; (b) the extent to which there is an ongoing assessment of the business unit's offerings and capabilities relative to the competition; and (c) the degree of interfunctional coordination, i.e., the degree to which "information on buyers and competitors is shared throughout the business, decisions are made interfunctionally, and all functions contribute to the creation of the buyer value."

The study contains many important insights, all of which cannot be detailed here. One, however, is the finding that the degree of market orientation, that is, the degree to which the voice of the market is or is not used throughout a business unit, is strongly related to profitability. Overall, business units that are clearly market-based are significantly more profitable than those that are not, precisely because market-based activities and attitudes have a direct impact on the quality of thinking within a unit. This, in turn, affects the quality of decision making, which subsequently impacts customer perceptions of the relative value of a firm's offerings.[2]

Notes

1. John C. Narver and Stanley F. Slater, *The Effect of Market Orientation on Business Profitability* (Cambridge, MA: Marketing Science Institute, Report No. 89-120, December 1989).
2. For an excellent discussion of the antecedents and consequences of being market-based, see Ajay K. Kohli and Bernard J. Jaworski, "Market Orientation: The Construct, Research Propositions, and Managerial Implications," *Journal of Marketing*, vol. 54 (April 1990), pp. 1–18.

CHAPTER 1

When Customers Speak and Firms Don't Hear

THE NEW SOURCE OF COMPETITIVE EDGES

There is a basic concern shared by many in the business community: the creation of an environment in which managers throughout the firm are inquisitive about their markets, can satisfy their curiosity with appropriate market knowledge, and can make decisions rooted in this knowledge. It is our belief—and a central assumption of this book—that competitive edges are to be found more in knowing how and when to use information rather than in simply having it. As we shall show, knowledge about the "how" of information use is inadequately developed and poorly applied in very nearly all private and public sector organizations.

The effective use of information requires two special competencies. The first we call "competent curiosity." It is an inquisitiveness about the happenings in its markets that are of current and future importance, coupled with the ability to satisfy that curiosity with timely, relevant, accurate, and cost-effective information. The second competence we call "competent wisdom." It concerns the ability to translate information into effective action by doing the right thing and doing it right. Mr. Burton's letter on the following page reflects his worry that his firm is becoming less and less competent in both dimensions. The two competencies are closely linked: Competence in one requires competence in the other. Poor information (e.g., collecting the wrong data or collecting the right data the wrong way) cannot be used wisely, nor can good information compensate for poor judgment or deficient wisdom.

The inability to use information well is the Achilles' heel in most decision-making processes. This book describes several problems firms commonly experience in using information and presents solutions to them. Insights about these problems and ways of dealing with them were enriched by a three-year project in which nearly 300 key people in a broad array of product and service

Global Technologies

1990 Century Blvd., Los Angeles, California 91342

Ms. Mary L. Reynolds
Knowledge Use Consultants
123 Main Street
Jonesville, MI 48224

Dear Ms. Reynolds:

I enjoyed reading a summary of the recent speech you presented
to our senior management group. It has continued to stimulate
considerable discussion.

I was intrigued by two of your comments in particular. You reported that a private study by your firm shows that companies
having an effective system for hearing, understanding, and using market information throughout all functions are three times
more likely to be among their industry leaders than companies
that do not. Naturally, I'm curious to know more about how you
define an effective system so that we might determine whether we
have one.

Your reference to the "New Marketing Myopia"--the belief that
marketing is done primarily by the marketing function and only
when it needs market information--has stimulated much heated
discussion. This suggests you hit upon an important issue for us
to understand better.

We have very capable and dedicated managers, including a small
but highly competent market research staff. However, our overall market performance has become sluggish. For the first time
in my twenty-three years with the company, we have had five con-
secutive quarters in which sales have been essentially flat despite industrywide growth.

I am not convinced that our problems are related to how we go
about hearing and using what you call the "voice of the market"
in decision making. Still, it might be very worthwhile for us to
formally assess how we learn about our markets and how well we
use that information. How do we make a preliminary diagnosis of
whether that could be part of our problem? What are the indicators that a problem of this sort might exist?

Perhaps we could speak by phone at your convenience to discuss
this issue.

Sincerely,

George Burton, President

KNOWLEDGE USE CONSULTANTS

Mr. George Burton
President
Global Technologies
1990 Century Blvd.
Los Angeles, CA 91342

Dear Mr. Burton:

I enjoyed our phone conversation. As you requested, I am listing several questions for you to think about.

If your answers to the first two questions are "no," then you probably have a problem.

> Has senior management communicated clearly that market information should be used in major decisions throughout the firm? Do you, in fact, have such a commitment? Has it been demonstrated?

> Would you send your children to an educational institution that is comparable in quality to the system your managers use to learn about market events and to prepare themselves to deal with those events? That is, do you have a quality "instructional" system throughout the firm that facilitates, encourages, and even demands aggressive learning, thinking, and planning within a dynamic environment?

If your answers to even two of the following questions are "yes," then you probably have a problem.

> Does the majority of your market research focus on short-term, tactical issues? Is thinking almost exclusively developed to address operational issues and to put out fires rather than prevent them?

> Does most of your market research end up only in the marketing organization?

Is your market research generally perceived as supporting the perspective of the marketing organization?

Does the information you collect confirm what you already know or are inclined to do anyway? Is there relatively little research to develop ideas for new concepts, strategic planning, or defining alternative actions?

Is your research staff dependent on the program managers for their entire budgets? Are they able to work only on projects of immediate concern to managers?

Does your research tend to be used as report cards on managers rather than as learning material for them?

Do you focus largely on how well an action worked rather than on why it did or did not work? Do basic assumptions and decision rules need to be changed?

Do your nonmarketing staffs, such as those from engineering, manufacturing, human resources, and so forth, have access to important customer information? Are they unsure about how they themselves affect customer perceptions? Do they know what customer information they need?

Would your managers have difficulty explaining their roles in making your firm market-based or even explaining what being market-based means?

Please do not hesitate to call upon me if I may be of further assistance.

Sincerely,

Ms. Mary L. Reynolds

companies, and the research firms, consulting organizations, and advertising agencies with whom they often work, were interviewed.[1] The interviews explored the many factors affecting the use, nonuse, and misuse of information and the special techniques successful managers and researchers have developed to make more and better use of information. In addition, three extensive mail surveys and personal interviews involving more than 500 participants with whom similar issues were explored in a somewhat different way provided another important source of insight.[2] We also drew on the growing body of published research on information use. Our own experiences, together with those of many thoughtful managers and researchers, have provided the kinds of insights and suggestions that Reynolds might share with Burton.

The remainder of this chapter addresses the need for better information use and some of the factors that discourage it.

A MANAGEMENT DILEMMA

Our complex and competitive world is creating two significant and conflicting conditions. On the one hand, throughout all functional areas, firms have a growing need to be more sensitive to the voice ᴏf the market, especially to customers and competitors. This is essential for guiding corporate actions. On the other hand, traditional forces, often based on negative experiences in using market information, inhibit either the acquisition of information or its effective use. These forces exist despite burgeoning information and improved technologies for its use. The conflicting conditions have created a classic "we-should-but-don't" paradox: Managers in all functional areas are acutely aware that they should be making more frequent and much better use of market information but, in fact, are often doing the opposite.

The Need for Better Information Use

The need for more frequent and more effective use of information is stimulated by several factors:

- Improvements in the availability of quality, timely data are causing essentially the same information to become available at the same time to all competitors.
- The marketplace is increasingly characterized by a growing number of types of stakeholders (e.g., more diverse customers) that are changing more frequently. This means that a broader array of information may have to be used and that standard ways of interpreting information may no longer be adequate.
- The time available for reaching decisions is getting shorter as firms are

better able to bring new products to market sooner and to enter new markets more quickly than in the past.

- The half-life of information (i.e., the average time for which it is valid) is shrinking as changes in the marketplace occur more and more often. This means that what is true today is less and less likely to be true tomorrow. Managers not only need to examine market conditions more often but must be prepared to translate data into action much more frequently.
- Firms frequently have many attractive options. More careful use of market research is necessary for determining what the right thing to do is and how to do it right. This means that more exploratory or developmental market research is needed, even at the expense of confirmatory research, which now accounts for most of the research budget in all but a few firms.

Other factors making it necessary to better use information include the blurring of market boundaries, fragmenting market structures, and globalizing markets. The need for better use of market information does not mean that firms should be guided solely by that information. In fact, if that were the case, and assuming all firms were equally competent in using market information, a firm would not differ significantly from its competitors, which are also responding only to market needs.

Factors Discouraging Better Information Use

Despite incentives to do so, many practices and trends inhibit the collection of information and its effective use. These are just a few:

- The 90-day syndrome. This describes the tendency to confine thinking to the current quarter. As a senior researcher in a consumer package goods firm put it, "90 days is charitable, most of our brand managers are 30-day thinkers." An industrial products executive pointed out the consequences of this approach: "Much of today's fire fighting is a result of [management's] failure yesterday to look ahead to tomorrow. Today *is* yesterday's tomorrow." Formal research tends to focus on issues of current tactical relevance with little sensitivity to critical signals provided by the marketplace today about tomorrow.
- Manager turnover. Few organizations are able to develop institutional memory. When a key manager leaves, little of that person's accumulated experience is left behind to benefit his or her replacement. This results in the loss of an important source of market knowledge, what some call "walking the floor" (i.e., direct observation of what key stakeholders such as customers, dealers, suppliers, and so forth are doing). These observations become part of a manager's experience and are the bases for educated guesses, hunches, or intuition. They may even be the primary source of information used in making most decisions.
- Timing of research. Research is frequently done when a project is nearing

a launch date to verify that it was a good idea, rather than early to find out whether the idea was worthy of investment in the first place.

- Information technology. Major changes in the technology of information management have improved managers' ability to access and process information enormously. But this has sometimes led to less use and often greater misuse of information. One expert commented on the increased opportunity for misuse of information resulting from a manager's ability to access data directly:

> Brand managers are better able to use data directly without going through the research department. However, they can use data in more biased ways. So while the research department shouldn't be policemen, they may have to. The issue of who controls the data is critical and is going to change how research departments function.

- The changing status of the research function. More and more, firms contract out for research expertise rather than maintain a research staff. Researchers in some firms thus tend to be purchasing agents for the research activity. This deprives firms of an important in-house environmental scanning function which understands the business and is trusted by managers. In other instances, traditional research departments or groups may play a major role in ensuring the collection of valid, timely data but lack the internal stature that would enable them to play a more important role in decision making. As one seasoned executive observed,

> Research people are not trusted enough to handle such serious issues as strategic planning or thinking . . . . It's important for [client] researchers to have at least a token budget of their own. But the research director may not be skilled enough politically to get the money. It takes a lot of skill to build the consensus necessary to get the budget. The research department doesn't really have a power base.

- Marketing versus market research. There are many stakeholders in the marketplace whose actions are relevant to engineering, finance, human resources, manufacturing, corporate planning, and so forth. Yet most internal market research staffs largely serve the needs of only the marketing organization. Relatively little attention is given to market information needs existing elsewhere in the firm (see Chapter 3). All functional areas need to develop sensitivity to the voice of the market. Indeed, many outside groups such as customers and competitors are relevant to most functional areas and to most levels of planning, not just marketing. By focusing market research on marketing organization issues only, firms run the serious risk of not obtaining timely, relevant, and quality information for most of their key decisions.

Other inhibiting factors include the difficulty in justifying market research expenditures, impediments created by the different worlds of users and researchers, and the often unfounded assumption that because we live in a market we understand it and need not study it further. All these factors lead to the following dialogue between an information user and an information provider. In reality it is not a dialogue at all, but two position statements existing side by side.

> Provider: I'm being helpful to decision makers because I'm providing all this meaningful information. It is really frustrating, however, when the decision makers don't even know what information they want. Sometimes they respond to my question of "What do you need?" with "What do you have?"

> User: Don't you see that you make things more complicated than they need to be? Based on my experience and seasoned judgment, I understand the situation and I'm willing to take the responsibility and make the decision. All these studies you want to do—and the precision you're striving for—just add complexity to the situation. You're causing paralysis by analysis—all this research isn't worth the time or cost because it slows down the decision-making process. You raise everybody's expectations about reducing uncertainty and then simply add to the confusion because you bring in conflicting and surprising findings. No wonder we can't make timely and consistent decisions around here.

Thus, although there are a variety of factors that are making it more necessary for firms to improve their sensitivity to the voice of the market, there are other factors that are interfering with their doing so. Traditional research functions, where they exist at all, are generally unable to solve this dilemma. As in Hans Christian Andersen's story, "The Emperor's Clothes," there is a kind of "pretending" about how information is used.

There are two oft told tales about information use. The first concerns the dangers of letting market research lead to unsuccessful product concepts or get in the way of new and creative ideas. The second is an idyllic account of the entire process from recognizing the need for information, to its acquisition, and on to its decision application.

A Tale of Market Research Folly

Our first tale concerns the conventional wisdom among managers of not doing market research. It describes the disasters wrought by market research and the "successes" its absence can create. It is the story of the Edsel.

An article on the use of market research in the automotive industry in the May 31, 1989 issue of *Investor's Daily* reminded us of the almost legendary example of market research failure: "Then again, the infamous Edsel was the most heavily researched vehicle of its day. Yet it turned out to be perhaps the auto industry's biggest bomb."[3]

While attending a meeting of the Sacramento, California, Advertising Club in 1957, one of this book's authors listened to Fairfax Cone, of Foote, Cone and Belding, explain how his agency had access to research on every aspect of the Edsel's entry into the market, down to developing a long list of names for the car, and how we would soon be witnessing one of the world's most successful new-product introductions.

The facts, of course, are that after three years (1960) the Edsel, kept alive through two model changes, was allowed to pass into extinction (except for a few automobile collectors). Some people have concluded that inasmuch as the Edsel's development was so thoroughly "market researched," its failure must be related in some way to the failure of market research to provide timely and accurate information.

A review of the literature on the Edsel's failure leaves open the question of exactly how much research was actually conducted and how well it was used. John Brooks, in a revealing two-part series in *The New Yorker*, pointed out that the only research completed before the introduction of the Edsel was on its name. The conclusions were ignored by the Ford Executive Committee. The research included two interview studies, each involving 800 consumers, conducted in Peoria, Illinois, and San Bernardino, California, probing people's feelings about many different types of cars.[4] What research was done seemed sound. William Reynolds, a former market research manager at Ford, writing in *Business Horizons* in 1967 stated,

> If one goes through the bound volumes of Edsel research in the Ford archives, one is struck—after a somewhat eerie feeling is overcome— by the sophistication of the techniques used and the perspicacity of the findings. No styling research was conducted, but, as noted at the time, no one in the industry was doing such research. Otherwise, the research was comprehensive in the areas of market delineation, product characteristics and image, competition, copy strategy, and other aspects of the marketing plan.[5]

If there is any disagreement between these two authors on how much market research was actually done, there is little question between them about the extent to which it was used. Brooks made the point quite clearly:

> For although the Edsel was supposed to be advertised, and otherwise promoted, strictly on the basis of preferences expressed in polls, some old-fashioned snake-oil-selling methods, intuitive rather than

scientific, crept in. Although it was supposed to have been named in much the same way, science was curtly discarded at the last minute and the Edsel was named for the father of the Company's president, like a nineteenth-century brand of cough drops or saddle soap. As for the design, it was arrived at without even a pretense of consulting the polls, and by the method that has been standard for years in the designing of automobiles—that of simply pooling the hunches of sundry company committees. The common explanation of the Edsel's downfall, then, under scrutiny, turns out to be largely a myth, in the colloquial sense of that term.[6]

Reynolds confirmed Brooks's conclusion. He pointed out that, following the failure of the Edsel,

Ford learned to use marketing research. In part, this was a consequence of fear. Ford managers, if a mistake were made, wanted to be able to point to the research that had caused it. Ford researchers underwent the curious experience of a management that placed more confidence in research findings than the researchers did themselves. The result, however, was healthy. Ford management, partly because of the lack of confidence caused by the Edsel, is immunized against believing that their own preferences are identical to those of the public.[7]

Hence, we have two myths concerning the failure of market research on the Edsel. First, press reports identified market research contributing to an error of the first type (i.e., the product was right when it was wrong). Second, reports identified market research contributing to an error of the second type (i.e., the product was wrong when it was right). It is interesting that, for each perspective, there were other more detailed contradictory reports.

It is interesting, at least to those who report what's going on in car companies, that twenty years after Reynolds's assessment of the status and role of market research, the Edsel lesson appears to be losing some of its value. In the February 12, 1990 edition of the *Detroit Free Press*, business writer Rick Ratliff, discussing the role of car designers in the future of the Big Three domestic manufacturers, rekindled the vision of the market research failure from a slightly different perspective:

Telnack (vice president of design at Ford) led the team that shaped the Ford Taurus, a car that has reaped many international design awards, spawned a host of imitators and helped Ford become the most profitable manufacturer of the Big Three. *This came despite early research which indicated some would react violently against the car's design. Telnack stood his ground, and was rewarded.* Today, he believes the future belongs to cars that carry forth new variations of Taurus' so-called "aero look" with smoother corners, low hoods and high trunk areas.[8] (our emphasis)

Again, there appears to be another side to the story! In a 1988 book *Reinventing the Wheels* authors Alton Doody and Ron Bingaman support the notion that there was some negative reaction to the Taurus aero design:

Ford researchers also knew that a certain percentage of the American driving population would adamantly dislike the Taurus styling. These would be the types of people . . . who are almost always unreceptive to anything new or different. Ford designers labeled them "Johnny Lunchbuckets" and, for all practical purposes, these customers were written off as being unreachable—at least for the first model year or two.[9]

The authors also identified specific actions taken to improve the product. For example, in April 1981, more than a year after development had begun, the overall size of the car was drastically changed. As one Ford executive put it, "We scrapped the whole car . . . the car was re-engineered to be bigger than originally intended, and this was done because of a perceived change in the targeted market . . . . The small prototype of Taurus was expanded in all dimensions. Its wheelbase was enlarged, its track was widened, and its overall volume was increased."[10]

Reinventing the Wheels also pointed out, however, that market research not only uncovered the problem but also identified information that supported action plans to overcome it.

Marketing research would go beyond its customary bounds in ferreting out existing consumer attitudes and preferences. It would actually assist in rationalizing attitudes and in changing preferences. In short, the market was to be educated, briefed, and conditioned to appreciate the Taurus and Sable for what they really were, instead of what they merely seemed to be . . . . Before the Taurus finally reached the market, Team Taurus would disregard or override certain consumer likes and dislikes, even when those likes and dislikes were explicitly revealed through marketing research. Far from reflecting the arbitrariness and arrogance of "old" Detroit, however, these decisions were part of a calculated effort to improve the customers' understanding and appreciation of automotive quality, to build the very best mid-market car that anyone could build. This meant creating a rationally conceived, coherent, functioning piece of equipment; it did *not* mean tacking together an assortment of features to satisfy any and all of the perceived wants and whims that might emanate from the marketplace . . . . In short, the marketing research role within the team transcended traditional research techniques and parameters. The objective was not merely to "give the lady what she wants," but to tell the lady why she might want to change her viewpoint or consider an alternative.[11]

A variant of this tale of market research folly concerns product "successes" without benefit of market research. In a 1980 article in the *Harvard Business Review* titled "Managing Our Way to Economic Decline," authors Robert Hayes and William Abernathy stated,

> In the past 20 years, American companies have perhaps learned too well a lesson they had long been inclined to ignore: business should be customer oriented rather than product oriented. Henry Ford's famous dictum that the public could have any color automobile it wished as long as the color was black has since given way to its philosophical opposite: "We have got to stop marketing makeable products and learn to make marketable products." At last, however, the dangers of too much reliance on this philosophy are becoming apparent. As two Canadian researchers have put it: "Inventors, scientists, engineers and academics, in the normal pursuit of scientific knowledge, gave the world in recent times the laser, xerography, instant photography, and the transistor. In contrast, worshippers of the market concept have bestowed upon mankind such products as newfangled potato chips, feminine hygiene deodorant, and the pet rock . . . ."[12]

The authors were obviously biased in their selection of market-based examples. However, they did present two interesting examples of the necessity of market research in the development of technology.

The invention of xerography. There is no question that Chester Carlson's invention of xerography presented society with a great tool for distributing information. Still, many observers would give equal credit to Xerox CEO Joseph Wilson, who was also the marketer of xerography, and who fit the product into a market that was not aware it was in need of it. In a 1958 report, which led to IBM's decision not to acquire the rights to distribute xerographic copiers, a major consulting firm listed thirteen major assumptions, most untested by market research. The most critical one stated, "Machines will be offered for sale only. Lease option would not significantly affect the market size." It was Wilson's clear understanding of the market situation—derived in part through market research that caused him to consider selling copies (through a lease program) instead of machines—that led to Xerox's (then the Haloid Corporation) incredible success in the utilization of xerography. The absence of market research was far more apparent than real.

Two points can be made about instant photography. First, photography was a very mature industry well before Land introduced instant photography. It seems naive to assume that Land was not privy to at least cursory information about the large segment of customers who were concerned about the time and resources required to process their own film or send away for processing. Second, assuming not only that Land was capable of "knowing" what was possible but also that he could design and develop what was possible in such a way to make it commercially viable, then one needs to explain why he failed to bring instant movies (Polavision) to the market successfully.

The notion that knowing what is possible has more weight than knowing what the customer wants has been stated most eloquently by Akio Morita, the founder of Sony: "Our plan is to lead the public to new products rather than ask them what they want. The public does not know what is possible, but we do." Of course, a statement like this made by the founder of a firm that has made so many great applications of the transistor, carries much weight. But would Sony have been better off if it had listened to the market—which, at the time, knew little of transistors and magnetic tape technology—and found out whether the market was willing to trade off the attributes of the Sony Beta format for those of the VHS format?

The VideoDisc. Another example of how technology cannot stand on its own, no matter how advanced, is provided by RCA's $580-million VideoDisc venture.[13] R&D made a major technological breakthrough that had many technical merits, such as a higher-quality (relative to VCR technology) means for watching movies at home; yet, because of improper analysis of the desires of the market, the venture failed. Ironically, videodisc technology is now making a comeback with the help of companies that have done the proper marketing research, a lesson learned from RCA's failure. A marketing manager was quoted as saying, "I got the feeling that they [RCA] were not in touch with the consumer. They wanted to do something new and exciting."[14] However, doing something new and exciting often requires rethinking existing assumptions and testing their adequacy for a new course of action. The importance of this approach is illustrated by the following excerpt.

> RCA's VideoDisc strategy had been heavily dependent on a few key assumptions: that the traditional mass-market customer would prefer a low price to more features, that dealers could clear up any consumer confusion about multiple formats, that VCR producers could not substantially reduce the price gap between their players and disc players, that dealers would welcome disc systems as they had VCRs, and that consumers would want to own video programming just as they owned LP records and audio tapes.
>
> There had been no public discussion within RCA of what might happen if the key assumptions failed to hold, or what would be done if other factors that had not been considered influenced the market.

If key RCA executives involved in VideoDisc's introduction recognized the uncertainty of their position, that the statements made with such apparent assurance could be arbitrary choices between unknowable alternatives, they did not acknowledge it. Had they understood their position better, they might have provided for contingencies, as Japanese videoplayer makers had when they tried repeatedly during the 1970s to make a go of video cassette recorders. Major innovation had not been a feature of RCA life since the days of David Sarnoff, however, and few understood how to approach it. The people who were chosen to manage it, all heavy hitters in the established business, chose an approach that had only two possible outcomes—complete success or complete failure.

In fact, the outcome quickly revealed that most of the key [traditional] assumptions on which RCA had based its VideoDisc strategy were no longer valid . . . . Had the plan been for a stable product in a familiar business, it would have been well-conceived and well-executed, but for an innovative product in a marketplace destabilized by changing technologies, it was an approach that allowed little room for adjustment and no second chances.[15]

A Tale of the Textbook-Perfect Project

The second tale is the stuff of which textbooks are made. Although fictional, it accurately describes events that are not altogether uncommon in real life. A product management team wanted to reassess its positioning strategy in the wake of a competitor's unexpected success with a new product. The team did not feel pressured to make an immediate decision but wanted to have a well-developed option to consider when they next reviewed their product positioning strategy. They already had considerable relevant information. Most of the managers had experience in similar situations. Additional insights about the desirability of a change and what it might be had been provided by research conducted by the firm's advertising agency. Other information was available from tracking studies, distributors, and the trade press. However, the product team decided it would be helpful to have a more precise picture of how customers perceived a variety of competing products, including their own, on a number of product attributes or features. This analysis would also enable the team to identify potential new market positions for the product.

The firm's market research director, already familiar with the issue, and in anticipation having brought together existing information relevant to the problem, was asked to develop a research proposal and budget. With adequate lead time available, a proposal was developed and approved which, taking advantage of existing information, did not require unusual costs, and which addressed accurately most of the important research questions. The market research director and product team had worked together on a variety of projects. Consequently the managers had a good understanding of what research could and could not do and what was involved in the research process. The market research director understood how the managers usually made decisions and what their information needs were. The director also had great confidence in three outside research firms. They were asked to bid on the project, and the firm with the best design proposal was selected to do the data collection and basic tabulation. On schedule, the research supplier delivered the information to the market research director who prepared an initial draft of a report. Highlights of the report were circulated in draft form to the members of the product team and a meeting was scheduled for a full presentation of the results. Considerable discussion occurred during the meeting, disagreements about what the data meant were ironed out, and the management team felt it had a number of important new insights about its positioning strategy, including a fundamental change in direction. There was no need for a discussion about the reliability and validity of the research.

A few weeks later the managers reached a decision based upon the research and other information. The research alone did not dictate the decision, but it did contribute significantly to the team's conviction that the decision was a good one. Without it, confidence in this particular decision might have been much less, and the chances of arriving at another, probably poorer, decision would have been higher. The research was also important because it reinforced and, in its own way, validated other information used by the team. Had it been asked later, the team would have said that the cost of the research was more than justified as a kind of insurance against a wrong decision. That is, the research was designed in such a way that valid data suggesting that the action ultimately taken would be a mistake would have shown up if the data were really out there.

This description of how things ought to be carries a number of assumptions. A few of them are:

1. There is enough time to conduct accurate and reasonably priced research.
2. Relevant existing information is brought to managers' attention early so that they can assess their information needs well in advance of a decision.
3. The need for research is conveyed to researchers early enough for a quality research effort to be mounted.
4. Managers and researchers fully understand what is involved in both the decision-making and research processes, and good personal rapport exists between managers and researchers.
5. Differences in viewpoints among decision participants can be reconciled effectively. The research helps evaluate alternative viewpoints.
6. Research results are unambiguous in supporting a particular decision, and nearly all available information supports a particular decision.
7. The most attractive decision is also feasible to implement.

8. Uncertainty and risk are understood.

The list of assumptions could be extended considerably. These assumptions are valid most often with respect to relatively routine decisions. When even just one assumption is compromised, however, others are, too, in a domino effect. For example, if the need for research is not identified and conveyed to researchers early enough, accuracy may be lost as a project is implemented hurriedly. The market researcher is sometimes forced to say, in effect, "I can get it to you fast, accurate, and inexpensively . . . but you can only pick two!" This, in turn, may impede the development of a consensus as to what the information really means and lessens confidence in the effectiveness of particular decision options. This may have the further effect of eroding personal rapport between managers and researchers. The ideas in this book are particularly helpful in enabling researchers to provide information that is fast, accurate, and inexpensive—a difficult but essential task.

Because of the ease with which such domino effects can occur, patterns of information use very different from our storybook version are not uncommon, even for routine decisions. They develop when decisions

- are not routine,
- have a high degree of uncertainty and risk,
- involve different groups within a firm,
- have major long-term consequences for the firm,
- involve substantial current financial outlays,
- are urgent, and
- do not have the benefit of much existing information.

These patterns are also a good deal more challenging for managers and researchers to control. They involve important sociological and psychological processes which are commingled with the straightforward mechanics of doing research and making decisions. Moreover, these behavioral processes can be a source of significant value to the firm, even if they are sometimes a headache to researchers and managers. For example, someone with a very different perspective on an issue may be a source of conflict and delay a decision. But his or her participation may make less likely a decision based on a key but incorrect assumption; for example, imagine the value that would have accrued to RCA if someone had been able to challenge its key assumptions successfully. The task for research and the management team is to make sure that different perspectives are shared and examined in ways that will enhance the decision process. This increases the prospects of both doing the right thing and doing it right.

CONCLUSION

There is a tension between the need to make better use of market information and the many factors that discourage better information use. The management of this tension is perhaps the single most important challenge facing companies today. In one way or another, virtually all other significant challenges involve the task of orchestrating the voice of the market with the voice of the firm. In order to make better use of market information throughout the firm, it is necessary to recognize and address the myriad behavioral processes that add spice to the otherwise static storybook tales of how information is used.

Notes

1. For a brief report of some of these interviews, see Gerald Zaltman, "The Use of Developmental and Evaluative Market Research" (Cambridge, MA: Marketing Science Institute, Report No. 89-107, March 1989).
2. Gerald Zaltman, "Knowledge Transfer in Mental Health Services," final report to the National Institute of Mental Health, Department of Health and Human Services (Washington, DC, 1984); Rohit Deshpande and Gerald Zaltman, "A Comparison of Factors Affecting the Use of Marketing Information in Consumer and Industrial Firms," *Journal of Marketing Research*, vol. 24 (February 1989), pp. 114–118; Rohit Deshpande and Gerald Zaltman, "A Comparison of Factors Affecting Researcher and Manager Perceptions of Market Research Use," *Journal of Marketing Research*, vol. 21 (February 1984), pp. 32–38; and Rohit Deshpande and Gerald Zaltman, "Factors Affecting the Consumption of Market Research: A Path Analysis," *Journal of Marketing Research*, vol. 19 (February 1982), pp. 14–31.
3. Paul A. Eisenstein, "Car Makers Fine-Tune Market Research Use," *Investor's Daily*, May 31, 1989.
4. John Brooks, "The Edsel" (Annals of Business), *The New Yorker*, November 26, 1960, p. 57 and December 3, 1960, p. 199.
5. William Reynolds, "The Edsel Ten Years Later," *Business Horizons* (Fall 1967), p. 39.
6. Brooks, "The Edsel," p. 201.
7. Reynolds, "The Edsel Ten Years Later," p. 39.
8. Richard Ratliff, *Detroit Free Press*, February 12, 1990, p. 29.
9. Alton F. Doody and Ron Bingaman, *Reinventing the Wheels* (Cambridge, MA: Ballinger, 1988), p. 111.
10. Ibid., p. 120.
11. Ibid., p. 117.
12. Robert H. Hayes and William J. Abernathy, "Managing Our Way to Economic Decline," *Harvard Business Review* (July–August 1980), pp. 67–77.
13. Margaret B.W. Graham, *RCA and the VideoDisc: The Business of Research* (Cambridge, MA: Harvard University Press, 1986).
14. *BusinessWeek*, April 23, 1984, p. 90.
15. Graham, *RCA and the VideoDisc*, p. 88.

CHAPTER 2

The Inquiry Center

We have stressed the need to use the voice of the market, to understand the voice of the firm, and to reconcile these voices. Some firms do it well but many others do it poorly. A newly appointed director for strategic planning in a major chemicals firm remarked,

> The only reason we are one of the leading companies is that our competitors are even less adept at understanding what's happening in the marketplace and what that might mean for them. For example, [a major competitor] spends much more money on market research than we do but is even more constipated than we are with it if you can believe that—as far as knowing what to do with it.... My greatest concern now is to get our act together before [a set of major competitors] do. I know a few of my counterparts are trying to rattle their cages, too.

This particular planner has, in fact, made considerable progress in implementing a system which has improved how his firm understands and reconciles the voice of the market with the voice of the firm. He began with a thorough evaluation of the strengths and weaknesses of the largely informal system that was in place when he was hired. Using this assessment, he developed a consensus among key managers about what a preferred system would be and how best to narrow the gap between the existing and the preferred system. Much of the system is still informal and does not have a new or specific label. His firm has begun to develop an inquiry center.

THE INQUIRY CENTER AS A KNOWLEDGE LOOM

About 1939 Edna St. Vincent Millay wrote a poem entitled "Huntsman, What Quarry?." It quite poignantly pointed out that although there were

37

many ills facing society, there existed no "loom" to weave the "meteoric shower of facts . . . [that] lie unquestioned uncombined" into a usable fabric of wisdom.[1]

The inquiry center can be considered the knowledge loom of the 1990s. It can weave together—in a meaningful pattern—all information from a variety of sources leading to wise decisions, thus partially filling the void identified by Edna St. Vincent Millay over fifty years ago. In this chapter we provide a blueprint for building a knowledge loom. With it those responsible for developing an inquiry center can begin to make more effective use of knowledge in general, and market knowledge in particular, in their organization's decision-making process.

We use the term "inquiry center" to describe the "ideal state of mind within a company for effectively and efficiently reconciling the voice of the market with the voice of the firm." We have chosen not to define precisely what we mean by an inquiry center because we believe that ideas are more likely to be adopted if they can be easily adapted to the real lives of those who will use them.[2] In Chapter 11, we describe the mechanics of improving those formal and/or informal inquiry centers that are already in place.

The inquiry center describes a particular way of learning about the marketplace and using the resultant knowledge. While the term "center" denotes an organizational unit, it is as much an attitude, ethic, or creed as it is a formal entity. Of course, all firms and their divisions or departments and individual employees have ways of learning about their markets and of using the information; but few take the trouble to check how well their learning systems work and whether they can be improved. The inquiry center concept fosters the development of a corporatewide attitude essential in becoming a market-based organization. We shall comment later on the differences between an inquiry center and the market research functions found in most companies.

Exhibit 2–1 contains a set of definitional statements about the purpose of an inquiry center. These were provided by some of the nation's leading experts on the use of information at a recent conference on the concept. These statements will give the reader a good idea of the many different perspectives people have of the concept. They all share a common denominator: the need to bring together various sources of information about the marketplace and to make sure they are available and used throughout a company as a condition for making more effective market-based decisions.

In this chapter we show the relationship between the two special competencies identified in Chapter 1: competent curiosity and competent wisdom. We address this relationship by answering the question: How do we bridge the gap between facts and wisdom? The first step in answering the question is to understand where and how information fits into the process that leads to decision making.

Exhibit 2–1
Inquiry Center Definitions

1. To improve on and then institutionalize, an ongoing process for drawing upon various sources of information, knowledge, data, and wisdom in order to bring them to bear on important decisions about the business (more than just vehicles).

2. Premise: The IC will define itself.

Steps for implementation—Broad goals for employees: take responsibility for the success of the entire corporation.

• find the right people (good inquirers/change agents)
• give them broad goals
• let them go
• figure out what they did
• institutionalize it

3. The purpose of the IC is to build expertise and provide assistance to facilitate improved thinking, decisions, and actions.

4. The purpose of the Inquiry Center is to break down the barriers between functions and foster/accelerate systemic thinking that is needed to produce quality, innovative products that are necessary in order to compete successfully in international markets.

5. The purpose of the IC is to increase the problem-setting and problem-solving capacity of managers by acquiring, synthesizing, developing, evaluating, and disseminating information.

6. The purpose of the IC should be as advocate for the customer. This should involve raising consciousness of customer needs through all levels of thinking about the marketplace. The latter includes helping managers ask better questions (where "better" is defined in terms of "how might a customer react to this?") and also to answer the questions faster.

7. An IC challenges or makes managers aware of what:

• they think they know
• they think they need to know
• they expect to happen given certain decisions
• assumptions they hold about the if-thens regarding decisions

Finally, an IC is a safe haven for exploring possibilities, dreams, visions, and fears.

8. Providing a center of continuously growing expertise in data management (getting and managing information) and analytical techniques to help people throughout the corporation identify and surpass the world's best practice in all functions, and help them do so with increasing effectiveness and efficiency (i.e., it has as an important part of its mandate the diffusion of relevant expertise and it does this in part by moving high-potential people through the function on short-term assignments). *(continued)*

Exhibit 2-1 *(continued)*

9. The primary purpose of the inquiry process is to reach quality decisions (clearer actions) (better thinking) at all levels. This requires a systematic process for asking the right (and often difficult) questions and finding good answers. The purpose of knowledge development centers is to build ever-improving answering systems for broadly defined and interrelated knowledge domains.

   Drop the term IC, rather focus on the inquiry process and knowledge development center.

10. The purpose of the Marketing Inquiry Center is to support a corporate goal for making better products that reflect marketplace conditions and consumer desires. The IC will do so by developing a body of corporate marketing knowledge that will help managers in creative thinking about the outcomes of the market, in consumer sensitive planning for new and improved models, and decision making, and implementation that is consistent with consumer-driven marketing. The ultimate corporate benefit for the IC will be an enhanced worldwide competitive position and hence improved profitability.

FROM DATA TO WISDOM—AN INFORMATION HIERARCHY

About the time Edna St. Vincent Millay wrote "Huntsman, What Quarry?," T.S. Eliot wrote "The Rock." In it, he asked,

Where is the wisdom we have lost in knowledge?
Where is the knowledge we have lost in information?[3]

Had T.S. Eliot been writing about decision making in organizations, rather than about man's relation to God, perhaps he would have added three additional lines, with some slight modification, and developed an information hierarchy.

Where is the WISDOM we have lost in knowledge?
Where is the KNOWLEDGE we have lost in intelligence?
Where is the INTELLIGENCE we have lost in information?
Where is the INFORMATION we have lost in data?
Where are the DATA we have lost in ignorance?

The concept of an information hierarchy is not new. It has been illustrated in the familiar information pyramid shown in Exhibit 2-2.

The pyramid indicates that many facts—normally generated from transactions—are distilled into information which is eventually used to develop

Exhibit 2-2
Traditional Information Pyramid

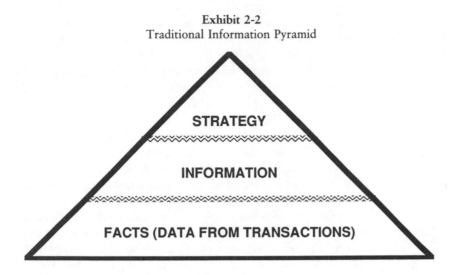

strategy. The potential flaw in this concept is taking the relationships illustrated in the pyramid literally, because the pyramid implies that strategy and information come together automatically, and that strategic information can be created in the absence of policy direction. There is strong evidence that these implications are not correct, because there are complex interrelationships that exist throughout the hierarchy. Knowledge creation, dissemination, and application are themselves not separable processes. Their integration is further complicated by the assumptions, truth tests, expectations, and rules about decision making that make up a viewing lens through which managers and researchers, or information users and information providers, view the marketplace differently.

The Law of the Lens

Effective providers of information are well aware of the "law of the lens"[4] and have adjusted some of their processes to account for it. The following brief account of actual events which took place in 1942 in the middle of the Pacific Ocean surfaces one of these processes.

The U.S. Chief of Combat Intelligence, Commander Joseph Rochefort, knew within three to four hundred miles where most Japanese ships were located. Each day, he reported what he knew to Captain Edwin T. Layton, whose early warnings of the attack on Pearl Harbor had gone unheeded. Because of that experience, Layton consistently inflated Rochefort's estimates. He knew that the folks in Operations viewed the intelligence types as natural-born alarmists. The words of a luncheon partner the day before Pearl Harbor rang in his ears: "Here comes Layton with his usual Saturday crisis!"

So, if Rochefort estimated four Japanese carriers were on the prowl, Layton would increase the number to six. He bet on the hope that Naval Operations would assume that he had overestimated everything by at least a third. Then, because they so strongly believed in their assumption, they would discount by an equal amount his inflated estimates, and through this round-about route come back to the original Rochefort estimate.[5]

One could take the position that given the results of this particular episode (the Battle of Midway), this "trick-'em-into-using-the-right-facts" system actually worked. On the other hand, one could also take the position that asks, "Why have a system that relies on each party estimating how the other party is manipulating estimates when it is difficult enough to come up with accurate estimates in the first place?"

Unfortunately, though much has changed in our ability to gather critical information, our ability to integrate it into a decision process has not kept pace. In both the public and private sectors we see the results of this trick-'em-into-using-the-right-facts approach still affecting our decision process. Today, a good analogy to the relationship between Layton's use of, and the Operations Officers' belief in, combat intelligence for use in battle plans would be a divisional product planner's use of, and a corporate review staff's belief in, divisional market research results in the development of a forecast.

The law of the lens manifests itself in many ways. For example, new-product management teams tend to favor the introduction of new products with a frequency that is unwarranted by subsequent commercial performance. Analysis of many new-product failures highlights the tendency to design research and interpret research results in a way that does not allow evidence that runs counter to a new-product launch decision to arise.

The need to avoid the trick 'em approach is made clear when we contrast two analytical conditions that lead to conflicts over approving programs or selecting among alternatives:

> In the first analytical condition, those involved in the decision have different interpretations of an agreed-on set of facts. Conflicts of this type are *constructive* to decision making because they sharpen the analytical skills and encourage use of the intuitive and experiential strengths of the participants.
>
> In the second condition, those involved have failed to establish a common set of facts to interpret. Usually power, not merit, dictates the final decision—if a timely decision is made at all. This is a *destructive* type of conflict, which is both time-consuming and potentially costly.

Since both conditions operate throughout the public and private sectors, how do we go about ensuring that at least the market research function operates almost exclusively in the first analytical mode. A suggested first step

Exhibit 2-3
The Modified Information Pyramid

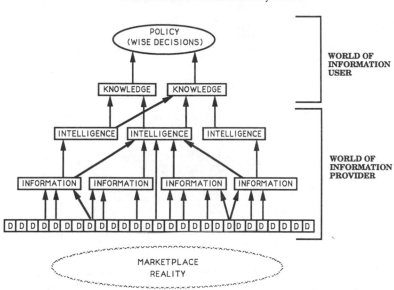

is to improve our understanding of the knowledge concept by modifying the traditional information pyramid to make it clear that the decision-making domain is different from the information-producing domain, and that although these domains are different, they should be integrated.

Exhibit 2-3 illustrates the relationship between data (D), information, and intelligence, and the knowledge and policy (or decision) world of management. The exhibit attempts to reflect how the reality of the marketplace is assessed through the collection and classification of data in as representative a form as is feasible. Then, portions of those data are analyzed to provide information (greater insight), which is then incorporated into intelligence reports which are relevant and of interest to potential users. Although all of this is of value, as C. West Churchman has noted, "Knowledge resides in the user and not in the collection. It's how the user reacts to the collection of information that matters."[6] Churchman's observation reminds us that as we move from intelligence to knowledge, we move from the domain of the providers to the domain of the users. That is why understanding the world of information users is so critical.

Exhibit 2-4 illustrates the imposition of the law of the lens on the information hierarchy, where the two domains interact. It recognizes the fact that decision makers' perception of reality has a direct impact on the manner in which they see and accept or reject intelligence reports. Their perceptions do not usually reflect the reality of the marketplace as perceived by those more

Exhibit 2-4
The Law of the Lens in the Information Pyramid

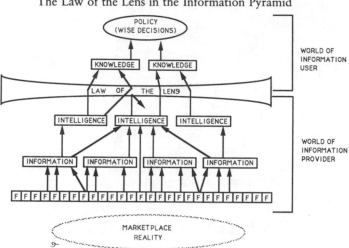

directly involved in assessing that marketplace. The point is that it is likely that the two groups will differ, not that either may be right or wrong. Indeed, for today's complex issues, for which there are multiple "right" answers, an understanding of why they differ (underlying assumptions and beliefs) is as important as the "right" answer.

Although our example illustrates the imposition of the law of the lens between the domains of the information provider and the information user, the manifestations of the law of the lens exist between each of the other elements of the information pyramid as well.

These observations regarding the difficulty of seeing reality are not new. Very similar thinking took place many centuries ago. In Plato's *Republic*, a magnificent discourse takes place between Socrates and others in an attempt to envision the perfect political state. It turns into a discussion of what people are able to know with certainty. There is also an allegory about a cave, where the acquisition of human knowledge is likened to the shadows (reflections) seen on cave walls. People and objects passing by the entrance to the cave appear different at different times of the day because of the way light shines into the cave. It would be naive for people inside the cave to interpret the shadows as the real world. As Socrates said, "The forms which these people draw or make . . . are converted by them into images. But they are really seeking to behold the things themselves, which can only be seen with the eye of the mind."[7]

For today's decision makers, the point is still relevant: While we strive to move closer to reality, our knowledge is based on our understanding of the images or reflections we see. Thus, systems that support decision making (the cave images) can provide no more than a reflection of marketplace reality.

Exhibit 2-5
Haeckel's Hierarchy Modified

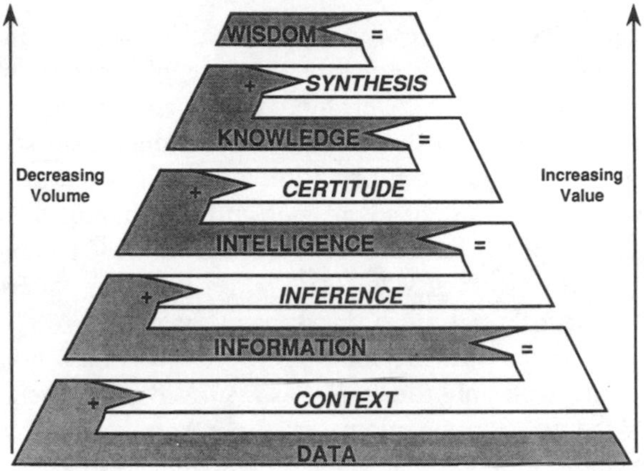

What we are searching for is a process that allows us to make—if not perfect business decisions—at least the best possible decisions. The goal is defined in terms of reducing the complexity of the overwhelming amount of data and other input that managers have at their disposal.

Haeckel's Hierarchy (Modified)

Past strategies used to achieve the goal—namely, increasing the amount and analysis of information—actually compound the problem. In effect, more is not better. In Exhibit 2-5 we have modified Haeckel's conception of an information hierarchy.[8] The basic objective is to achieve more with less. We start with many codified observations which we describe as DATA; by putting data in CONTEXT—a decision framework—we develop INFORMATION; by applying INFERENCE (judgment) to contextual information we generate INTELLIGENCE; as we gain CERTITUDE (greater certainty and acceptability) it leads to KNOWLEDGE; and by applying SYNTHESIS—holistically bringing together knowledge parts—we create WISDOM. In this way we can simultaneously decrease the volume of the data while increasing their value to the user.

Haeckel added significant insight to the concept of the information hierarchy. He also noted:

> The serious business issue behind this is that there is no value theory for the increasingly important asset called information. It seems clear that the value of information is enhanced by structure, organization

and context, but how much is it worth to provide the structure and how should one price the result?[9]

Answering Haeckel's question is not easy. Yet it is obvious how valuable it would be to reduce the amount of corporate and societal waste generated every day in the councils of government and corporate boardrooms because sincere and dedicated individuals do not fully understand significant issues. We feel that relevant market information is at least as important as the value associated with the promise of advertising and merchandising techniques, and that although we spend considerable resources on those techniques, our measured understanding of their value is no better than our understanding of the value of relevant information to the decision process.

As we indicated earlier, in today's complex world it is no longer of value for a manager to seek only the "right" decision. Rather, the greatest value is in managing the decision-making process in a way that increases the chances of choosing the best decision among the available alternatives—given all the circumstances at that time—and in having that decision effectively implemented. This type of decision-making process will require appropriate tools, expertise, and innovative momentum to achieve quality decisions in the complex world of today and tomorrow. If the inquiry center is to help in this new decision-making process, it must be integrated into that process. That is, the inquiry center must be adaptable to the environment in which it will operate and be considered an appropriate inquiring tool of the decision maker.

THE THREE DIMENSIONS

A successful inquiry center must be capable of integrating multiple perspectives. It must not only integrate the logic of decision making, but also draw on the energy, developed through collaboration, and the imagination of those who will affect, or be affected by, the outcomes. Much as Plato's cave had an implied structure of walls, a floor, and a ceiling, which can be perceived as a three-dimensional space, we can, in our blueprint, design the inquiry center's three dimensions to form a similar structure—that is, our own "knowledge loom"—the inquiry center.

Logic

Management is very comfortable with the logical perspective that is dominated by familiar theories, tools, and techniques. It is accustomed to decision making as an extension of an analytical process. At the heart of this approach is the separating or breaking up of a whole into its elements so as to find out their nature, proportions, functions, relationships, and so on. In using this dimension, however, we have been taught that to better understand a problem, we need more information. To deal with more information, we need more people, more sophisticated techniques, more state-of-the-art technology. But, as we have said, more is not necessarily better unless it is put into context, is used with appropriate judgment, and is accepted and synthesized with other knowledge.

Indeed, the issue of understanding the problem being addressed was recently highlighted by the National Academy of Sciences in its recent report to the White House on Decision Making and Problem Solving:

> Central to the body of prescriptive knowledge about decision making has been the theory of subjective expected utility (SEU), a sophisticated mathematical model of choice that lies at the foundation of most contemporary economics, theoretical statistics, and operations research. SEU theory defines the conditions of perfect utility-maximizing rationality in a world of certainty or in a world in which the probability distributions of all relevant variables can be provided by the decision makers (in spirit, it might be compared with a theory of ideal gases or of frictionless bodies sliding down inclined planes in a vacuum). SEU theory, as traditionally applied, deals only with decision making; *it has nothing to say about how to frame problems, set goals, or develop new alternatives.*[10] (our emphasis)

Energy/Collaboration

The second perspective within the inquiry center is the energy/organizational perspective (collaboration). Decision making and implementation in virtually any organization is a collective process. The two are shaped by the factors and dynamics that underlie human behavior in social settings. Sharing information from various perspectives is a start. However, the highest level that can be achieved in this dimension is when the interaction occurs in such a manner that not only do better ideas come forward, but they are developed in such a way that their implementation is accomplished promptly and consistently.

Imagination/Creativity

The third perspective within the inquiry center might be called imagination or creativity. People with access to diverse experiences and viewpoints can generate the best possible range of alternatives to solve an important complex problem. As a concept, "imagination," or "creativity," encompasses the full range of what is truly creative within the human psyche—whether it is called intuition, fantasy, inner imagery, or even inspiration.

The complexity of the relationship between the other two dimensions and the one of imagination is described by David Ogilvy.

The creative process requires more than reason. Most original think-ing isn't even verbal. It requires "a groping experimentation with ideas, governed by intuitive hunches and inspired by the uncon-scious." The majority of businessmen are incapable of original think-ing, because they are unable to escape from the tyranny of reason. Their imaginations are blocked.

I am almost incapable of logical thought, but I have developed techniques for keeping open the telephone line to my unconscious, in case that disorderly repository has anything to tell me. I hear a great deal of music. I am on friendly terms with John Barleycorn. I take long hot baths. I garden. I go into retreat among the Amish. I watch birds. I go for long walks in the country. And I take frequent vaca-tions, so that my brain can lie fallow—no golf, no cocktail parties, no tennis, no bridge, no concentration; only a bicycle.

While thus employed in doing nothing, I receive a constant stream of telegrams from my unconscious, and these become the raw material for my advertisements. But more is required: hard work, an open mind, and ungovernable curiosity.[11]

It should not be surprising that many individuals involved in creative functions such as design, product development, marketing communication, and so forth, identify with the notions in these comments, because they reinforce their perception of the type of environment most congenial to the creative process. Also, it is not hard to understand why someone who wants "total freedom" would interpret Ogilvy's comments to mean that the rather structured and logical procedures required to measure customer attributes and behavior are significant barriers to creative solutions to the problems they are asked to address. But one must be careful in using selected comments from David Ogilvy. For example, in an interview in the September–October 1986 edition of Ogilvy and Mather's *Viewpoint*, Ogilvy, in partial response to the question, "David, to what do you owe your success?" is quoted as saying:

Also—this is related to being objective—I came into advertising from [market] research and that gave me great advantage. I always ap-proached the creative role, I'd see the creative thing, through a researcher's eyes. I'm almost unique in that. Very few creative people do. A lot of creative people fight research and don't want much to do with it. I was the exact opposite. I came at it from research and suddenly I was doing very good campaigns. And that gave me great advantage I think. It was unique. Still is.[12]

To help decision makers use information in ways that allow them to move beyond the realm of facts and analytical thinking to improved decision quality and wiser decisions is the significant challenge of the inquiry center.

THE CHALLENGE

In our modified version of Haeckel's information hierarchy (see Exhibit 2-5) it is suggested that knowledge plus synthesis creates wisdom. Robert Waller offers a keen insight into the role of the inquiry center in this synthesis:

Complexity is composed of elements and intricate relationships among these elements. When humans confront complexity, they must discover these relationships and (in organizational life) communicate them to one another in an intelligible form. Conscious manipulation of elements and relations, however, is a function of the short-term memory. As was noted earlier, this part of the human cognitive apparatus suffers from some severe limitations.

This comes down to a design problem. On the one hand is complexity in all of its richness. On the other hand we see the human, restricted in terms of short-term memory, but with marvelous capabilities for long-term information retention, for judgment, for utilizing experience, for intuition, and, yes, for passion. Somehow, then, a way must be found that recognizes the central features of complexity and yet takes into account both the strengths and weaknesses of human cognition.

Human cognitive abilities cannot be modified to fit the demands of complexity. But neither can complexity be changed. If a problem situation is simplified to bring it within range of human capacities, then we are no longer dealing with the original problem (in fact, this sort of "undermodeling" probably occurs all the time, since we are unable to grasp the relational abundance of complex situations with our cognitive abilities).

Since neither the human capacity nor complexity can be changed, a way must be found to link the two without changing either. *In engineering terminology, an interface device must be sought that will link humans and complexity, while preserving the original properties of each.*[13] (our emphasis)

The inquiry center can provide some of the interface device requirements. It should first be noted that an inquiry center is much different from a typical meeting, conference, or even a "war room." The fundamental difference is that a war room is set up to display information on the walls—and to inform decision makers when anything changes from the status quo or plan. In other words, it is used to gather information about a specific problem, and then assist the decision maker relative to a required action. The inquiry center approaches problems from a different perspective. In some instances it might actually define and identify a potential problem before it becomes one!

The center will have within it the various data bases, meeting facilitating tools, processing equipment, and human resources that enable information users to function best within the three dimensions of logic, energy/collaboration, and imagination. "Within it," however, does not necessarily imply a central physical facility. Because information can be networked through decentralized, easy-to-use microcomputers or terminals, the "core" of the inquiry center need be no larger than a small room containing a central storage and switching facility. Important communications often happen on an informal level in an organization. The inquiry center must be designated to facilitate informal communications among those wishing to ask questions, test assumptions, or share information. The networking of information could even extend into a person's home. Decentralizing the center means that users have the option of accessing information without the assistance of experts. If users are always required to get information from experts, the inquiry center may be poorly designed. Although a user may not need to use an expert, experts should still be always available. Indeed, for especially complicated inquiries, or because a user does not have the time, experts can be both effective and efficient.

What the inquiry center needs most of all, however, is a supportive environment: explicit sponsorship by senior management, recognition and reward for use of new tools, skillful facilitation, and making sure good ideas are implemented. Although this environment can be quite costly, in terms of both dollars and the dramatic change in operating style which may occur, revising the allocation of existing resources can minimize many of the new costs. However, the incremental costs are justifiable if they ensure that the decision-making team has opportunity for making creative breakthrough decisions.

In essence, then, the inquiry center is the home for the tools (physical and human) operating within a three-dimensional space. It is an area where all the functions of a support system can be bundled during the decision process. Further, the inquiry center should offer a relaxed atmosphere in a variety of geographical settings. It will be a place where it's okay for people at all levels of an organization to experiment—and to risk being wrong. It is an open space for ideas, innovation, and learning. Indeed, it could be called an idea center, a creativity center, a decision center, or even a learning center. It is a "place" where individuals can learn efficient and effective approaches to decision making. Here is where they can learn about the needed level of support information, about the risk of alternative decisions, about the aspects of successful implementation, and how alternatives are compatible with, or affect, current strategy.

Perhaps most important, the inquiry center should not be "owned" by an organization such as the market research group or the information systems group. Rather, it should be owned by the people in the organization who must develop innovative ideas and solve problems. It should be their inquiry center—and it will likely take a different shape each time people participate in a collective effort to solve a particularly complex problem.

We have thus far portrayed the inquiry center as an abstract concept for solving organizational problems. But it is also a practical approach to integrating the three dimensions of logic, energy, and imagination into the decision-making process. The more fully these dimensions are explored, the more it appears that the line between what's possible and what is not lies mostly in the way we think about the center's potential.

AN IMPLEMENTATION OF THE INQUIRY CENTER CONCEPT

At the 1989 General Motors Market Research Conference, Lloyd E. Reuss, now GM president, commented:

> And if you bring together, the voice of the customer, the voice of the dealers, the voice of the public, you might look at that as the voice of the market . . . . Another important area [is that] when we listen to the voice of the market, [we need to remember] the customers are not going to give us all the solutions to their needs and wants. That means we also have to listen to the voice of GM . . . . You have to work at the balance between the market pull and the technology push.

Reuss's comments and direction led to agreement within the market and product planning community at GM to use the following definitions and illustrations in developing action strategies and educational programs for the use of market research in the company's product and market development processes.

> VOICE OF THE MARKET is "What the market indicates it needs and wants and is willing to pay for." By market we mean where exchange takes place. In this context, Voice of the Market includes all types of customers as well as entities that can affect our product; Voice of the . . . customers (external), regulators, competitive manufacturers, and so forth. (Market Pull)
>
> VOICE OF GENERAL MOTORS is "What GM is capable of and willing to provide to the Market." In this context we mean GM in the broadest business sense to include all the different functional areas within GM that are responsible for providing the product or service; Voice of the . . . Design Staff, Engineering, Manufacturing, Marketing, Finance, and so forth. (Company Push)
>
> MARKET-BASED GM is a GM where decision making is based on effectively and efficiently reconciling any differences between the VOICE OF THE MARKET and the VOICE OF GM. [GM has

Exhibit 2-6
Reconciling the Voice of the Market and the Voice of General Motors

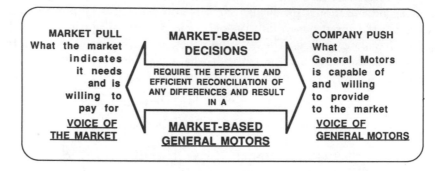

chosen the term "based" rather than "driven" to emphasize the point that decision making is a reconciliation between the two voices and is not being driven solely by either one.] Balance of market pull and company push.

Exhibit 2-6 reflects the relationships of the three concepts.

To reconcile the differences between the voice of the market and the voice of GM effectively and efficiently, a process was needed that caused the appropriate interaction between the providers of information and the users of information for any given decision. Exhibit 2-7 is the process model for representing the continuous interaction between providers and users, with shifting levels of responsibility as the two groups move from data management, "What do we know?" to analysis, "What does it mean?" to implications, "What should we do?" The exhibit implicitly assumes that no one group in GM owns or has sole use of the voice of the market. It is important that all affected parties understand that all users, not just the marketing department, own the voice of the market. The market research function, as the provider, is empowered to be a representative of the voice of the market—with the added responsibility of ensuring that the voice is relevant to the general as well as specific issues facing all functions of the company.

The relevance to the inquiry center concept is highlighted in the shaded part of the exhibit, which represents the "area" where information users and providers work together in an environment conducive to the effective interplay of logical analysis, consensus building, and creativity and innovation. This notion of a conducive environment is required if one is to accept the belief that the effective development and use of information depends on cross-functional teams crossing the functional line between user and provider

Exhibit 2-7
Relative Distribution of Information Provider and User Responsibility

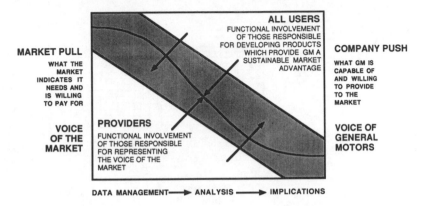

DATA MANAGEMENT──▶ ANALYSIS ──▶ IMPLICATIONS

to ensure that there is clear understanding of the issues being addressed as well as clear communication of the findings.

Although an inquiry center, by design, does not exist as an organization or entity at General Motors, the concept has been implemented on several projects.

QFD as an Inquiry Center

One of the projects at GM in which the inquiry center concept has been implemented deals with quality function deployment (QFD). The QFD process, developed in Japan, is being adopted by a number of American companies. GM's Market Research Department and the Systems Engineering Center are applying the inquiry center concept to QFD for use by the advanced engineering and manufacturing organizations and their product program managers. In essence, the process provides a framework for effective direct interaction among market researchers, program managers, and engineers, thereby minimizing the ambiguity or discrepancy that often exists between market information and product specifications. QFD structures the delivery of market information to program teams so that it is clear, readily usable, more complete, and less filtered than it has been.

Exhibit 2-8 illustrates the basic structure of the QFD process. The initial input into the process is the voice of the market, which cascades down the four matrices to the production process on the plant floor.

As an illustrative example (see Exhibit 2-9), consider "years of durability," a consumer requirement expressed through the voice of the market, which can be translated into a product requirement of "no visible rust in three years." A part characteristic required to meet this requirement could be paint

Exhibit 2-8
Basic Structure of the QFD Process

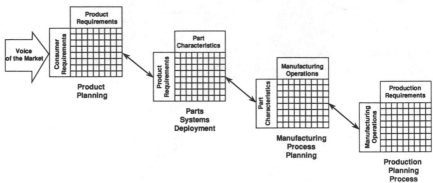

Exhibit 2-9
A Further Structuring of the QFD Process

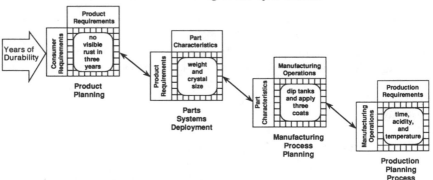

of a certain weight and crystal size. The manufacturing operations requirement may be the use of dip tanks and the application of three coats of paint.
Finally, the production requirement would specify the required time, acidity,
and temperature of the painting process.

How QFD and the inquiry center work together is illustrated by the
product planning matrix, the initial matrix for the QFD process (see Exhibit
2-10). The matrix serves as a single structure within which the program team
can consolidate the information for reconciling the differences between the
voice of the market and what GM is capable of and willing to provide, thus
moving GM in the direction of a market-based firm. Market Research, as the
providers of the information, collects the voice of the market, customer
requirements, the relative importance of those requirements, and the customer competitive evaluations. Although the market research function is to
collect the information, the research is conducted with extensive product
team participation. The product team uses this information, enhanced by its
experience and product knowledge, to translate the voice of the market into

Exhibit 2-10
A Basic Product Planning Matrix

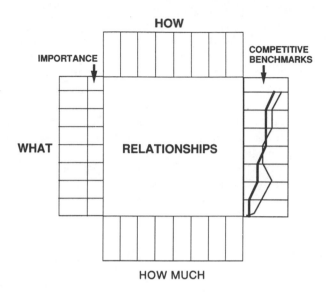

the characteristics of the product. Market Research assists the product team to ensure the most accurate translation. In this way the process of developing the product planning matrix forces cross-functional communication links between Market Research and the product team. These links are critical for the continuous improvement of Market Research's ability to provide the voice of the market and for the product team's ability to understand that voice and use it effectively for market-based decisions.

The development of the product planning matrix provides a practical demonstration of how providers and users of information should interact throughout the three stages we identified in Exhibit 2-7.

In the data management activity—the process of collecting, storing, and retrieving information, presenting it, and so forth—Market Research has the lead role; but the product team is involved to ensure not only that GM would be "doing things right," but perhaps more important, "doing the right things."

In the analysis activity, that is, determining what the data mean, there is extensive involvement of the Market Research staff to assist in understanding the substance of the data and their strengths and limitations as well. The product team, with its own voice, is also directly involved in this stage, since it participated in the data collection and can clearly add value to the analysis stage.

And finally, in the implications activity, determining what should be done, the product team is primarily responsible. But this activity also benefits from some level of involvement by Market Research—at a minimum as a source of credibility that the voice of the market has been accurately reflected in the plans eventually developed and presented to management. Indeed, when handled properly, the Market Research personnel should be seen and treated as members of the product program team.

An example will help illustrate what is meant by reconciling a difference between what the market is saying and what GM wants to do.[14] Consider that the market indicates that customers prefer a V8 engine in a particular vehicle. GM may prefer or even find it necessary, due to styling considerations, government regulation on gas mileage, and so forth, to provide a V6 engine. Indeed, GM may have a V6 engine that, when packaged with other features made possible by its use, would better meet overall customer requirements. But before GM can make the decision, it is necessary to understand why the customer prefers a V8: Can GM convince the customer the V6 will meet his or her requirements? What is more important to the customer—the V8 or other attributes GM can provide with a V6? What will the competition provide?

For Market Research, then, the product planning matrix is one of many very effective tools for providing market information to users. In this case, the users are product program managers and teams who seek extremely specific, timely, and actionable information. To be successful, however, the information must be a coherent, complete set of the requirements that ultimate customers have expressed for the product. While the ultimate customer (and beneficiary) of this effort is the car buyer in this example, it is necessary to first satisfy the internal customer—the product program team—if that ultimate customer is to be totally satisfied.

Designing an Inquiry Center for the GM Design Staff

Another application under development is the design of an inquiry center for GM's design staff. For the purpose of this chapter it is an important application to discuss because it is a real test of the ability of the inquiry center concept to bridge the gap between the many different worlds of market information users. This particular inquiry center operates in the world of the studio designer whose mission is to come up with vehicle concepts that transcend those that already exist. Therefore, the designer's need for and use of market information are different from those of the users of the QFD process, in at least two aspects:

1. Though market information is of value to the design function, that value is not perceived in the same way as it is perceived by marketing or engineering.
2. There is a wide range of opinion in the design community not only about the value of market information, but also about the type of information and the format in which it is most efficient and effective. Therefore, the

inquiry center must be designed to provide a broad array of information and multiple approaches to its access.

The design staff inquiry center is being developed to serve the market information needs of vehicle designers, design staff strategic planners, and the librarians at the design staff library.

Within the spirit of a process model that emphasizes people, teamwork, and continuous improvement, it is very important to be appreciative and sensitive to the beliefs and values of the design community. Therefore, we suggest that the inquiry center be developed in several steps.

Step 1. Develop a planning presentation system to be used by the design staff strategic planning department to ensure that market information will be presented in a form familiar to designers. As a beginning, this initial effort will allow the strategic planning department to become familiar with the approach and the processing equipment being developed. In addition, it will provide both the design staff and the market research community with an opportunity to begin developing guidelines and acceptable standardized methods for storing and presenting information for the design staff's inquiry center.

Step 2. Fully develop a design staff library inquiry center for designers having to use support personnel to access market information. Within the library, the inquiry center will be used to store and present market information, vehicle clinic results, focus group videotapes, and competitive data.

Step 3. Assuming acceptance by studio designers of the inquiry center library application, provide each of design staff's several studios with a direct link to a centralized inquiry data base.

This three-step process will begin in the Advance Studio where GM is currently applying advanced computer technology to the design process. This experience will be used as the basis for the decision whether to expand direct links to all studios. By starting in the Advance Studio, GM is attempting to take advantage of an environment that is especially suited to deal with electronic innovations to the design process with particular emphasis on the impact of these innovations on the studio designer. This application offers the opportunity to bring several benefits to the design staff by combining computer screen graphics with still or motion video to present data in a high-impact visual form.

CONCLUSION

As stated at the beginning of this chapter, the concept of an inquiry center refers to a set of attitudes that can improve thinking and action. These attitudes can create a stronger foundation for operational decisions as well as a better way of addressing strategic issues. While a formal market research function provides a sound basis for establishing an inquiry center, it is neither necessary nor sufficient. As with many important changes, establishing new attitudes and behaviors is best done by top management. That is, top management must demonstrate, during its reviews of proposals to allocate company resources, that it expects the kinds of market-based thinking that require the presence of an inquiry center.

Notes

1. Edna St. Vincent Millay, "Huntsman, What Quarry?," *Collected Sonnets* (New York: Harper & Brothers, 1941), p. 140.
2. R.E. Rice and E.M. Rogers, "Re-invention in the Innovation Process," *Knowledge: Creation, Diffusion, Utilization*, vol. 1, no. 4 (June 1980), p. 499.
3. T.S. Eliot, "The Rock," *The Complete Poems and Plays 1890–1950* (New York: Harcourt, Brace & World, 1983).
4. Gerald Zaltman, "Presidential Address," The American Association for Consumer Research 1982 Annual Conference, San Francisco, October 1982. See also the Brunswik Lens Model summarized by I. Postman and E.C. Tolman, "Brunswik's Probabilistic Functionalism," in S. Koch, ed., *Psychology: A Study of a Science*, vol. 1 (New York: McGraw-Hill, 1959); Robin M. Hogarth, *Judgement and Choice*, 2d ed. (New York: John Wiley, 1987), p. 10.
5. G.W. Prange, D.M. Goldstein, and K.V. Dillon, *Miracle at Midway* (New York: McGraw-Hill, 1982). This description is drawn from pp. 18, 19.
6. C.W. Churchman, *The Design of Inquiring Systems: Basic Concepts of Systems and Organization* (New York: Basic Books, 1971).
7. R.W. Sterling and W.C. Scott, *The Republic/Plato: A New Translation* (New York: Norton, 1985). The authors are grateful to Dr. Karl Joseph Does, of Eastman Kodak, who brought the allegory to our attention when we were first considering the concept of an inquiry center.
8. S.H. Haeckel, presentation to the Information Planning Steering Group, Marketing Science Institute, October 1987, Cambridge, MA.
9. Ibid.
10. "Report of the Research Briefing Panel on Decision Making and Problem Solving," *Research Briefings 1986* (Washington, DC: National Academy Press, 1986), p. 17.
11. David Ogilvy, *Confessions of an Advertising Man* (New York: Atheneum, 1963).
12. "David Ogilvy at 75," *Viewpoint* (September–October 1986), p. 9.
13. Robert J. Waller, "Knowledge for Producing Useful Knowledge and the Importance of Synthesis," in R.H. Killmann et al., eds., *Producing Useful Knowledge for Organizations* (New York: Praeger, 1983), p. 284.
14. For further examples of more detailed applications of the QFD approach, see J.R. Hauser and D. Clausing, "The House of Quality," *Harvard Business Review* (May–June 1988), p. 63; and Norman E. Morrell, "Quality Function Deployment: Disciplined Quality Control," *Automotive Engineering* (February 1988), p. 124.

CHAPTER 3

The True Customers of Market Research

Modern management recognizes that customers exist both inside and outside the firm. People involved with an inquiry center must view all functional areas and staff groups within the organization as their clients or customers. This is a departure from the more limiting and common arrangement where the market research department treats the marketing function as its only significant client. This broader perspective is difficult to achieve when a firm has no in-house research expertise and buys all such expertise from outside. For that matter, it is not particularly easy even when there is an internal research staff. Many market researchers are closely tied to the marketing organization and have little incentive to develop other clients. Additionally, the demands made of research staffs leave them little time to cultivate other clients. This problem is often compounded by the marketing function's resistance to sharing market data.

The central ideas in this chapter are summarized in Exhibit 3-1. It describes a chain of important ideas which begins with the notion that all groups within a firm do marketing and ends with the notion that earning the commitment of external customers will be a major goal of the 1990s. By helping groups throughout a company make better decisions through better use of information, the inquiry center increases the likelihood that firms will earn that commitment.

WHAT DO WE MEAN BY MARKETING?

It will be helpful to address the entire issue of marketing as it relates to the market research function. This will make clearer why an inquiry center should define its internal customers very broadly.

Exhibit 3-1
The Importance of Customer Commitment

GIVEN:

1. Marketing, particularly as experienced and understood by the marketplace, is a companywide activity.

THEREFORE:

2. The internal "customers" for market research are located throughout a company.

THE INQUIRY CENTER MUST:

3. Help all internal customers hear the voice of the market by providing information and the support necessary to use it effectively in the decision-making process.

AS A RESULT:

4. The quality of companywide marketing is enhanced.

THIS IS IMPORTANT BECAUSE:

5. The quality of companywide marketing affects customer perceptions of a firm's long-term commitment to providing high value in its product/service offerings.

AND:

6. Customers' commitments arise from their perception of the company's commitment to providing high value in product/service offerings.

What Is Marketing?

Marketing is the process of planning and executing the conception, pricing, promotion, and distribution of ideas, goods, and services to create exchanges that satisfy individual and organizational objectives. This generally accepted definition has many variations, all of which capture the idea that firms exist because of opportunities to create mutually beneficial exchanges or transactions with others. This is as true for single-person firms as it is for complex multinationals and is consistent with the view of marketing as "the discipline responsible for understanding and coordinating the relations between the organization and its environment."[1] Units within a company exist because they play a role, directly and/or indirectly, in helping the company respond to marketplace opportunities. Thus, they need to have market information corresponding to their direct and indirect effects on the marketplace.

The fundamental marketing objectives for any firm are threefold:

1. To make sure that customers understand the basic concept behind a product or service.
2. To show customers the relevance of the firm's product or service to their needs.
3. To remove or significantly reduce barriers to transactions or exchanges so that customers can engage in a transaction with minimum effort.[2] (Specific barriers are discussed in Chapter 10.)

Product concepts are the equivalent at the product level of the firm's corporate mission and, in fact, should be derived from and consistent with it. A firm's mission (a statement of why the firm exists) reflects the firm's competency in meeting particular market needs in ways that differ from those of competitors. Fulfilling a mission requires that a firm understand (a) its strengths and weaknesses, (b) changes in the environment, and (c) the broad class of market needs or opportunities that are consistent with its distinctive competency and with current and anticipated environmental conditions.

It is often through the firm's marketing activities that customers and other important groups understand the firm's mission. Similarly, the clarity of a firm's mission and how well it is communicated throughout the organization facilitate the accomplishment of more narrow marketing objectives.

What Are Market and Marketing Research?

Market research is the process of listening to the voice of the market and conveying information about it to appropriate management. Its intent is to learn about important stakeholders (customers, suppliers, regulators, and competitors) so that more knowledgeable decisions can be made. Market research is the process of collecting accurate, timely, and relevant information, but it is also the process by which managers and researchers interact in making good decisions. Market research is thus broadly construed to include understanding the characteristics of aspects of the environment that are relevant to the thinking of groups in the firm that need to develop a sensitivity to the market. Market research, in this context, is clearly an inquiry center activity.

A subset of market research is traditional market*ing* research, which is focused on market*ing* issues. Market research therefore includes marketing research. The distinction between the two is an important one. Marketing research focuses on advertising effectiveness, sales force deployment, site selection, customer reactions to potential product changes, customer perceptions of quality control, customer attitudes toward credit and billing procedures, and other activities in the domain of marketing managers. One reason for distinguishing between market and marketing research is to make clear that research about the marketplace does not belong solely to the marketing function. It belongs to all.

Who Does Market Research and Where Is It Done?

Market research involves people at all levels and at all steps in the moving of a product or service from conception to sale. Some people must provide information; others must use it. To use it effectively, the providers must know what information users need. Similarly, information users must understand the usefulness and limitations of the information collected. To borrow a statement often used in statistics, "Far better an approximate answer to the right question, which is often vague, than an exact answer to the wrong question, which can always be made precise."[3]

The market research function is, in fact, a business within a business— one that must produce, sell, and deliver its own product. The product is accurate and usable market information, produced and delivered early enough in the firm's product development cycle to aid all decision makers within the firm.

As a business within a business, the market research function needs to think and act with an entrepreneurial spirit. It must recognize the need to sell its products and services to management continually. By thinking and acting as a function that is integral to the decision-making process, the market research function is more likely to contribute to profitability. This requires strengthening broader relationships with the other functions in the firm and increasing the role of the market research function as a provider of useful and timely data describing the voice of the market.

THE NEW MARKETING MYOPIA

Because of the linkage between a firm's mission and its marketing activities, the activities of all functional areas and support staffs affect the achievement of both corporate- and product-level goals. It is misleading, therefore, to think that only the marketing function affects marketing outcomes and that only marketing managers are the customers of market research. This narrow viewpoint, as we mentioned earlier, has been called the new marketing myopia. A senior executive from a leading research firm described it this way:

> We used to think of marketing myopia as being the overly narrow definition of what market a company was in. The new marketing myopia is the overly narrow definition of who does marketing, of where marketing responsibility lies. While you get [lip service] that everyone contributes to product performance, especially in good times, all you need is a poor showing for a couple of periods and

suddenly no one outside the marketing group does marketing . . . The marketing group often doesn't have the clout to make [finance, engineering, manufacturing] stand up and be counted when problems arise. This is where a strong CEO is important. He can't have the new myopia. He's got to keep everyone's toes to the fire when there is poor product or market performance.

Readers should try to answer the following question with respect to their own or client companies: Of all the decisions made relative to basic marketing activities, what percentage are made solely by the marketing department? In exploring this question with CEOs and executives in several functional areas, not a single one suggested that even *most* of the key marketing decisions, that is, those affecting the three basic marketing objectives listed earlier, are made by the marketing organization. Moreover, each person gave examples of how the implementation of important marketing decisions had been affected—for better or for worse—by nonmarketing managers. At the same time, many of these people acknowledged that the new marketing myopia was a real problem—in fact, a long-standing one. One executive told the following story:

A world-renowned child psychologist had just finished pouring a new cement driveway at his home. Several minutes later a group of neighborhood children came running around the corner of his house and directly into the cement. Having seen this, the psychologist rushed from his home shouting obscenities and threatening physical harm to the children who ran off in tears. Several neighbors interceded and one said, with some puzzlement, "Doctor, I thought you liked children." And the famous child psychologist replied, "In the abstract, yes. But not in the concrete!"

For these executives, it is one thing to understand in the abstract the notion that everyone is involved in marketing but a very different matter to act on or practice it well. The inquiry center can be very helpful in moving this idea from the abstract to the concrete. The discussion below illustrates the importance of the impact all groups have on perceived value and quality, and hence the need for all groups within a firm to be market-based.

AN ELABORATION ON PERCEIVED VALUE

There is probably no more important determinant of marketplace success than perceived product or service value. As Frank Purdue has observed, "People will go out of their way to buy a better quality product, and you can charge them a toll for the trip." It will be helpful, then, to discuss this notion of perceived value as a way of showing how all groups throughout the firm can influence customers. Customers' judgments or perceptions of product or service value represent their summary evaluations of it, taking into account the benefits they perceive as offered and the price they perceive as required to obtain these benefits.[4]

Thus:

PERCEIVED VALUE equals PERCEIVED WORTH minus PERCEIVED PRICE.

This equation is illustrated in Exhibit 3-2. Perceived worth is what customers feel they should pay for the benefits they receive. Perceived price is the price customers believe they will be charged. In general, whenever perceived price is lower than perceived worth, perceived value is positive; customers feel they got more than what was paid for and thus "got a good deal." When perceived price exceeds perceived worth, customers conclude that the product is not of good value, "too expensive," "a rip-off," or a "poor buy for the money." When perceived price and perceived worth are equal, the value is neutral; a customer feels "I got what I paid for." (See Exhibit 3-3.)

One way of understanding these customer perceptions is to consider the effects of frequent price incentives or other promotions. If customers have come to expect rebates on a class of products such as automobiles or appliances and are accustomed to waiting for rebates to get a "good buy for the money," or a "bargain," they will also come to view the normal price as a poor buy for the money or at best a "fair" price. The size of the expected rebate, coupon discount, or other value-added incentive becomes a measure of the amount that customers perceive the manufacturer or vendor to be overcharging with the normal or suggested retail price.

The producer may think it unfair of the customer to conclude that if the product or service is not on sale it is a poor buy. Fair or unfair, however, the producer cannot walk away from the Thomas theorem, "If men define situations as real, they are real in the consequences."[5] This theorem, brought forward by W.I. Thomas years ago, is fundamental to the determination of value. In the first part, "If men define situations as real . . . " means that customers not only react to the facts of the situation, but also, quite frequently, to the meaning the situation has for them. They are more likely to have their consequent behavior driven by the meaning rather than by the "objective" facts surrounding the situation.[6]

As there are often good reasons to offer incentives and effective ways of doing so, we are not arguing against their use. Exhibits 3-2 and 3-3 illustrate, however, how expected or perceived price can alter perceived value. An important task for the firm is to create a strong sense of benefits or value, so that for a given price the perceived worth of a product or service is high. The objective, as shown in Exhibit 3-3, is to create an understanding among customers that, relative to competing products or services, perceived worth is high while perceived price (again, relative to competitors' prices) is moderate

Exhibit 3-2
Perceived Value Equals Perceived Worth Minus Perceived Price

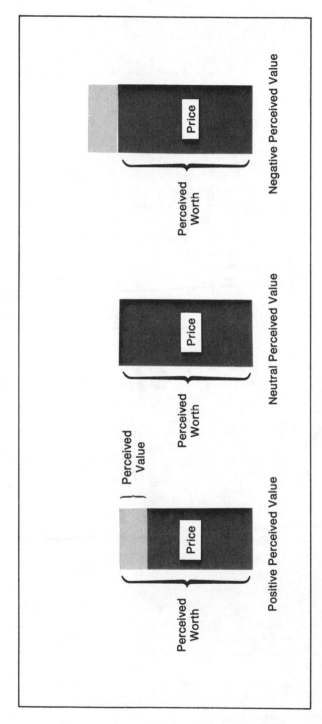

Source: C.W. Park and Gerald Zaltman, *Marketing Management* (Hinsdale, IL: Dryden Press, 1987), p. 514.

Exhibit 3-3
Value-Judgment Matrix

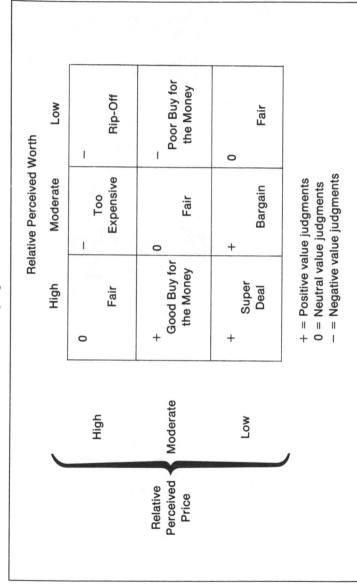

Source: C.W. Park and Gerald Zaltman, *Marketing Management* (Hinsdale, IL: Dryden Press, 1987), p. 515.

or low, or that perceived worth is moderate while perceived price is low.

QUALITY

There is probably no more important determinant of perceived value than perceived product or service quality.[7] Within a given product market, quality is usually the major determinant of perceived value. This is true even though the overall quality of competing alternatives (e.g., the low end or economy version, generics, and so forth) may be low relative to a prestige product in the same general product class. Customers may not expect or demand much quality at the low end, yet the perceived relative quality among products competing within that end will be a major determinant of success in that market. Customers will most likely choose the product they perceive as having the highest quality among the set of products having comparable prices. It is important, then, no matter how a firm positions its offerings, to examine the impact that various groups in a company have on customer perceptions of quality. While the marketing function's decisions have an important impact on such perceptions, other functions do as well. Collectively, the other functions usually have a greater impact on quality perceptions, and hence on marketplace performance, than does the marketing function.

A major problem of modern firms is that separate groups within a company do not perceive their joint impact on customers. In general, managers from different areas of the firm have different "thought worlds," which produce narrow definitions of an issue and hence make it difficult for the managers to see that they are all connected to the same issue.[8] For example, Deborah Dougherty's research on new-product development teams indicates that participants from different functional groups each

- have a qualitatively different understanding of the product development effort,
- have an understanding of this effort they consider "whole" or "complete," and
- have an alternative reality which contains vital insights but makes very different sense of the whole reality.[9]

Sources of Quality

Since perceived quality is so important in marketing, it is helpful to illustrate how nonmarketing groups affect this variable. For brevity, we focus here on just three nonmarketing areas. Of course, the exact way functional areas and staff groups affect quality varies considerably, depending on the industry, the customers served, how a company has organized itself, its culture and philosophy, and so on.

Human resource management. The most important cues for customers in making quality judgments are the personnel and other "factors of production" used in developing and delivering a product or service. For this reason, considerable efforts are often made to let customers know that a firm uses the best technologies available, the best workers, and the best materials.

Many manufacturers stress in their advertising the special attention they give to recruiting, training, and motivating production personnel. Service sector firms sometimes stress in advertising for new employees the kind of personal qualities they are looking for along with the normal experience and technical requirements; potential customers who are reading the want ads are as much a target for these messages as are potential employees.

The human resource function has a major impact on quality through recruitment, training, commitment development, compensation, and other motivation programs. In service-oriented industries the impact of human resource management policies is especially obvious. For example, at Disney theme parks, every employee is thought of and trained as part of the "cast." It is this fantasy world of places and cast members the public is buying. In fact, human resource management is now viewed more broadly to include the management of customers as well as workers. That is, policies and practices that help customers understand their role in acquiring a service benefit, how they can improve the value of the service, and how they are rewarded or motivated are the responsibilities of human resource management. This recognizes that the distinction between service provider and service receiver is increasingly blurred, especially when services are received on-site and where the production and consumption processes are blurred. The customer becomes another "employee" of concern to human resource managers.[10]

R&D personnel. Engineers, biologists, chemists, and others involved in research and development and the translation of product concepts into actual products have a major impact on how customers experience quality. For example, a major manufacturer of a fabric softener for home use had selected a fragrance that had great appeal to consumers when they were shown single sheets of the softener. However, during focus groups intended for another purpose it was discovered that the fragrance caused discomfort and even nausea. The chemists forgot to tell the product manager that increases in the intensity of a fragrance can produce very different sensory experiences. In this case, a large number of rolled sheets in an open box in a small room (coincidentally, the focus group met in a room not much larger than a normal home laundry room) produced a very unpleasant fragrance. Fortunately, the problem was caught before production had begun and the product launched.

The field of engineering psychology is explicitly concerned with perceptions of quality resulting from engineering decisions. Similarly, architects and interior designers have a major influence on the image and sense of climate customers experience in a bank, medical facility, shopping mall, restaurant, and so forth. Important judgments are made, reinforced, or contradicted by the physical setting and appearance of a product or the context in which it is purchased. For a good many products and services the setting or appearance is the object being consumed. Often it is not the technical quality of the gem or the food being served as much as it is the style and design of the jewelry or the atmosphere of the restaurant and the presentation of the food. These are not factors directly affected by the marketing organization. Similarly, the performance and appearance of an automobile are not determined by marketing management, although its judgment may be solicited. Quality control processes and the actual quality of the manufacturing process also help determine the level of quality customers perceive. Shipping department decisions affect customer satisfaction with the availability of a product. In many industries where purchasing agents try to maintain small inventories of raw materials or component parts, the reliability of a vendor's shipping department may be the single most important factor considered in selecting a vendor. Clearly, the avoidance of damage in shipment is another responsibility of shipping and may be a major part of the service customers seek.

Accounting department. Cost accounting procedures have a major impact on new product decisions and pricing strategy. In many cases accounting systems have not always kept pace with changes in production technology. For example, in calculating overhead, a major emphasis on labor hours may not be appropriate for modern high-tech production. Doing so may produce calculations that result in prices that are too high. This effect on pricing strategy can, in turn, affect perceptions of product worth. The procedures for handling R&D expenditures, especially where these costs are high and a firm is relatively new, can affect ROI policies and profit reports. These, in turn, may affect the decision to launch a new product, how readily price incentives can be given, and so forth.

Accounting systems also influence how easily products can be ordered and returned, rebates obtained, credit obtained for damaged merchandise, and so forth. Both finance and accounting functions affect the availability and terms of credit, which may represent an important transaction barrier. Billing procedures are another way the accounting function creates an important image of the firm and directly affects customer satisfaction with the purchase and use of a product. How accounting treats certain promotional expenses affects the use of promotional strategies. For example, treating frequent flyer mileage as a liability alters the balance sheet and hence discourages the use of that promotional tool. Internal control systems that are effective in rewarding a service department for doing a good job can positively influence the likelihood of the customer returning for another purchase.

Accounting control systems also affect how customer representatives deal with customers, for example, whether or in what ways customer representatives can shave prices, provide free samples, and so forth. Thus, how service, sales, and other personnel are evaluated from an accounting stand-point can influence the performance of staff who deal directly with customers. The accounting function can have a major influence on whether top manage-ment thinks in terms of profitability or market share. This, in turn, affects the relative importance of different functional areas as well as the use of particular marketing strategies.

External groups. Outside organizations and individuals hired by a company often influence customer perceptions of quality. Independent dealers may enhance or lessen the sense of quality a manufacturer provides. The quality of thinking about advertising strategy and about its creative execution provided by an outside agency may have a major influence on how a firm's offerings are perceived. Similarly, product rating services, the trade press, and government regulatory agencies can shape customer understanding of the value a company provides. Competitors, too, may have a significant impact on customer per-ceptions of a company's offerings. The large number of groups outside the firm and the number of internal functions other than marketing collectively affecting market performance are one reason why market share measures may not be a sound indicator of the marketing function's performance. It is being argued more often that market share is only useful as an overall measure of corporate performance, if that.

THE "CUSTOMERS" FOR MARKET RESEARCH

David Packard, of Hewlett-Packard, has been quoted as saying, "Market-ing is too important to be left solely to the marketing department." An important corollary to this idea is that market information is of importance to all major areas of a firm. Thus, the inquiry center can help a company become a market-based firm and establish customer commitment by helping all groups understand the value of market research and facilitating their use of it.

External Customers

The customers for the market research function or inquiry center fall into two categories, external customers and internal customers. External cus-tomers include:

1. *The suppliers.* Suppliers to the firm are in need of market information so that they can fulfill their responsibilities to the firm efficiently and effec-tively. For example, a major retail chain commissioned a study on changes in customer preferences for Christmas-related items such as gift wrap, cards, artificial trees, and ornaments to help its suppliers of production

materials understand the importance of making specific product changes and to provide guidance in making those changes.

2. *The end users.* These people eventually benefit from the conduct of market research by having their views, preferences, and level of satisfaction taken into account. The inquiry center represents the customers in the firm's decision-making process.

There is an important trend, especially in technology-intensive industries, in which information-based strategic alliances are formed between firms and their suppliers, distributors, and customers. Organizations that might normally be described as having conflicting interests are increasingly tied by common information systems which enhance cooperation among them. Examples include:

- Federal Express has the COSMOS customer service system, which tracks every movement of every package in the network (through hand-held computers carried by all employees who handle packages). This system is now providing customers with terminals and software so that they can tie into the system directly, in effect making Federal Express their shipping department.
- American Airlines' Sabre reservation system, originally designed for retail travel agencies, has been extended to in-house corporate travel departments.
- McKesson, whose pioneering ECONOMIST system (placing terminals in drugstores tied in to McKesson's central computer) rejuvenated the wholesale drug distribution industry, is now effectively managing the store for most of its clients.
- Kodak, which began by placing terminals with photographic retailers to help poorly trained store personnel do a better technical job of photo finishing, now sells a retail management system for photo finishers (and even retailers in other industries).
- Inland Steel maintains a computer network which began as an attempt to keep customers informed of the status of their orders. It now provides a wide range of value-added services, from billing and funds transfer to consulting on technical product specifications. This example shows how a firm in a traditionally noninformation-intensive industry can use information for competitive advantage.[11]

The entire channel from suppliers through customers becomes what Glazer calls an "information processing organism," as shown in Exhibit 3-4.[12] It is also an information-generating organism because it provides considerable knowledge about the marketplace. Further, it increases supplier, distributor, and customer commitment. As the trend toward information-based strategic alliances gathers momentum, there will be more opportunity

Exhibit 3-4
The Value-Added Chain as an Information Processor

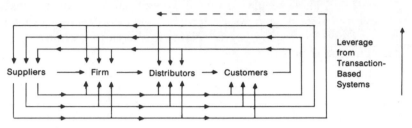

Source: Rashi Glazer, "Marketing and the Changing Information Environment: Implications for Strategy, Structure, and the Marketing Mix" (Cambridge, MA: Marketing Science Institute, 1989), p. 16.

for researchers to serve external clients, thereby creating still greater commitment within strategic alliances. These opportunities include the important task of helping suppliers and distributors understand how they influence customer perceptions, as well as convey to these stakeholders customer needs and other data.

Internal Customers

There are also important internal customers for market research. Traditional internal customers are the marketing staff (including sales and service staffs), analysts, economists, forecasters, senior management, and planners. Other important internal customers, although not served as often, include product engineers, designers, manufacturing, human resources, lawyers, purchasing agents, research labs, accounting, and finance.

Despite the importance of groups such as engineering, finance, human resource management, manufacturing, and public relations, all of which ultimately affect marketing activities, little attention has been paid to their specific market information needs. It is not surprising, therefore, that they have had correspondingly little interest in market research information. By focusing market research solely on issues of importance to the marketing organization, firms run the serious risk of not obtaining relevant, quality information in a timely way for all of their key market-based decisions. We found that the researchers most successful in representing the voice of the market throughout the firm are those who (a) view themselves as product managers with respect to their function and (b) are committed to the total satisfaction of their customers within the company.

MARKET RESEARCHERS AS PROGRAM MANAGERS FOR THE MARKET RESEARCH FUNCTION

It is necessary to be sensitive to differences among internal clients in how they perceive the value of information and what kind of information they want. There are three important questions market researchers should ask concerning the "product development" of their services. These questions correspond to the objectives of the marketing function discussed earlier.

1. How well do our internal customers understand the service we offer? Have we ever spelled it out for them?
2. Do our customers perceive what we offer as relevant to their information needs?
3. How effective are we in reducing the barriers between us and manufacturing, engineering, marketing, human resources, and other internal customers?

We have discussed these questions with internal customers of market research in many firms. Few give their research groups high marks on addressing any of these questions. In fact, few marketing management groups, the customers we expect to be most satisfied with research services, gave their research function high ratings on any of the three questions. For the most part, internal customers

• do not understand what the researchers' essential service is,
• do not understand how it relates to their needs, and
• use research services infrequently despite their having frequent, significant market information needs.

For example, most internal customers see market researchers as simply providing "raw" data. There are impressive exceptions, of course. This narrow view of the purpose of market research is at least as prevalent among firms that rely exclusively on outside providers as it is among those that have internal research staffs. While the collection of basic data is important, it is still only one service among many a research staff may provide.

Clearly, research staffs need to do a much better job as product or service managers in marketing their services, especially among nonmarketing customers. Improving the use of market research among all internal customers represents an important opportunity for the research function to help the company be competitive and healthy. Thus, the central purpose of the research staff should be to satisfy internal customer information needs by providing appropriate market information and helping managers use it.

EXTERNAL CUSTOMER COMMITMENT

Perhaps the major requirement for corporate success in the 1990s is the creation of customer commitment. Customer commitment involves the development of a sense of partnership between a firm and its customers based on mutual trust. It involves a sharing of information and an involvement in one another's important activities so that a common mindset is established.[13] In this way, the voice of the market and the voice of the firm are in harmony.

Customer commitment is earned through diverse, often subtle, and sustained activities by groups throughout the firm. It is marked by long-term loyalty based on the understanding that the firm keeps the customer's best interests in mind at all times, subject, of course, to the reasonable constraints necessary to maintain the firm's long-term health. A mistake by the firm is understood by customers as an honest error and not a reason to desert the company. Indeed, customers committed to the partnership help the firm correct and recover from an error.

Achieving a sense of commitment among customers requires that all major decisions of a company be made with a full understanding of the market, and especially of customers. This does not mean that a firm should do everything customers would like. Moreover, what is in the best interests of one customer group may not be in the best interests of another. However, knowledge of what customers say they want and are willing to pay for increases the likelihood that their interests are well served. More important, perhaps, it enables the firm to present its decisions in ways that increase customer acceptance of those decisions as proper ones.

CONCLUSION

The true customers of market research are all groups within a firm—and those outside with whom a firm has strategic alliances—that affect the firm's market performance. While this is a very broad definition, it is an accurate reflection of the many groups that need market information to help guide their decisions. The marketing function is only one of the many groups within a firm that actually do marketing, and hence is only one of many in need of market information. The market research staff also plays a major role in creating customer commitment, by helping the firm become more market-based.

Most market research staffs, as "product/service managers for their functions," face a major challenge in overcoming barriers that often lessen the use and appreciation of their services. These barriers are often sizable with respect to the marketing functions of a company, and get larger when the research staff deals with other functions and outside groups.

Notes

1. Rashi Glazer, "Marketing and the Changing Information Environment: Implications for Strategy, Structure, and the Marketing Mix" (Cambridge, MA: Marketing Science Institute, October 1989), p. 1.
2. C.W. Park and Gerald Zaltman, *Marketing Management* (Hinsdale, IL: Dryden Press, 1987).
3. John W. Tukey, "The Future of Data Analysis," *Annals of Mathematical Statistics*, vol. 33 (1962), pp. 13-14.
4. Park and Zaltman, *Marketing Management*, p. 512.
5. W.I. Thomas, cited in Robert K. Merton, *Social Theory and Social Structure*, rev. ed. (New York: Free Press, 1963), p. 173.
6. Karin D. Knorr-Cetina, *The Manufacture of Knowledge: An Essay on the Constructivist and Contextual Nature of Science* (New York: Pergamon Press, 1981).
7. Park and Zaltman, *Marketing Management*.
8. D.C. Dearborn and H.A. Simon, "Selective Perception: A Note on the Department Identifications of Executives," *Sociometry* 10 (1958), pp. 140-145; and J.P. Walsh, "Selectivity and Selective Perception: An Investigation of Managers' Belief Structures and Information Processing," *Academy of Management Journal*, vol. 31, no. 4 (1988), pp. 873-896.
9. Deborah Dougherty, Presentation to the Meeting of Trustees, Marketing Science Institute, October 1989, Cambridge, MA.
10. David Bowen, *Human Resource Management,* vol. 25, no. 3 (Fall 1986), pp. 371-383.
11. Glazer, "Marketing and the Changing Information Environment," p. 15.
12. Ibid., p. 16.
13. A.W. Brockband, Y. Yeung, and D. Ulrich, "Understanding Corporate Culture and Human Resource Practices: An Avenue to Strategic Business Partners," Working Paper, School of Business, University of Michigan, 1988.

PART II

DOING USEFUL RESEARCH

Many readers may have little direct or recent experience with formal methods of market research. Portions of Chapter 4, therefore, are presented as a primer for those who may want an overview or a "refresher course" on market research methods. Chapter 4 also presents a special framework for viewing the market research process. This should be of interest to all readers. The framework has four key components. When properly integrated, these components satisfy five information functions. A special technique we have developed to enhance each of these functions is presented in Chapter 5. This technique provides both "formative" and "summative" evaluations. That is, it is helpful in improving the value of a specific research project while it is unfolding (formative evaluations), and it also helps assess the value of a project after it has been completed (summative evaluations). The technique addresses a number of factors mentioned in Chapter 1 which are discussed more fully in later chapters. Thus, Chapter 5 also introduces the reader to a number of important processes affecting the use, nonuse, and misuse of data and provides guidelines for handling these processes.

CHAPTER **4**

The Market Research Process

The market research function supports the company's decision process by

- uncovering the need for evidence about the right problem;
- collecting and evaluating the evidence;
- presenting the evidence to the right people in the correct form and at the right time; and
- providing additional support to the manager who must make effective decisions.

This chapter presents a framework for viewing the process of reconciling what the market needs and is willing to pay for with what the company is capable of and willing to provide. The framework has undergone several stages of development and has been implemented formally or informally very successfully in several organizations. Here we use it to review some of the basic mechanics of market research. This discussion, and the exhibits, will be especially helpful to readers who would like to become familiar with the basic tools and concepts of market research and their use.

We will focus on formal market research. It represents one, but only one, important way of knowing about the market. We cannot stress enough the importance of direct managerial involvement in listening to relevant stakeholders. Other valid ways of knowing the market are also used in making decisions and are discussed elsewhere. In fact, formal market research is sometimes overruled when it is contradicted by insights derived in other ways. In Chapter 6 we discuss the importance of multiple ways of knowing, as well as constructive ways of handling contradictions in the knowledge they produce. We simply note here that one reason for using the term "inquiry center" is that it encompasses more easily a broader array of important ways of knowing, and facilitates the development, testing, and enrichment of these additional modes of inquiry.

A MARKET RESEARCH FRAMEWORK

To understand how market research aids decision making, we need to look at how the decision process in a market-based firm should work. The structure of the model has two environmental dimensions (see Exhibit 4-1). The first dimension reflects the well-established market back-company forward market mechanism. In the upper left corner is marketplace reality (A), exemplified by the voice of the market, which is a statement of what the market indicates it needs and is willing to pay for. In the lower right corner

Exhibit 4-1
The Decision Process in the Market-Based Firm

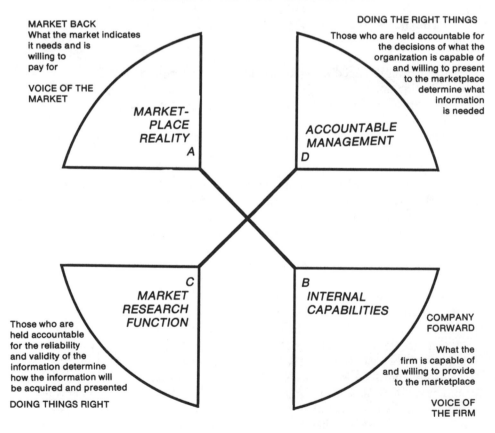

MARKET BACK
What the market indicates it needs and is willing to pay for

VOICE OF THE MARKET

MARKET-PLACE REALITY
A

DOING THE RIGHT THINGS
Those who are held accountable for the decisions of what the organization is capable of and willing to present to the marketplace determine what information is needed

ACCOUNTABLE MANAGEMENT
D

C
MARKET RESEARCH FUNCTION

Those who are held accountable for the reliability and validity of the information determine how the information will be acquired and presented

DOING THINGS RIGHT

B
INTERNAL CAPABILITIES

COMPANY FORWARD

What the firm is capable of and willing to provide to the marketplace

VOICE OF THE FIRM

is internal capabilities (B) whereby the voice of the firm decides what the firm is capable of and willing to present to the marketplace.

The second dimension of the model addresses the issue of how the firm best reconciles the differences between the voice of the market and the voice of the firm. In the upper right corner is accountable management (D), the research users responsible for decisions about what the organization will present to the marketplace. They determine what information is needed, that is, they make sure the right data are collected. At the other end of this dimension is the market research function (C). It is responsible for the reliability and validity of marketplace information. Thus, it is market research that determines how information will be acquired and presented; they make sure the data are right.

HOW IS MARKET RESEARCH DONE?

The many and varied steps of the market research process can be categorized into five distinct areas and related to the two environmental dimensions of the firm's decision process as shown in Exhibit 4-1. We illustrate this process in Exhibit 4-2 and then describe the five categories to help readers organize their thinking about the basic tools and concepts of market research. Various tools and concepts are specifically detailed for readers who are unfamiliar with formal market research methods or who would like to review them. The important issues of assessing market information and evaluating efforts to enhance the value of market information are also discussed.

Table 4-1 at the end of this chapter summarizes many of the central ideas discussed in the following pages.[1] Readers should find it a helpful general reference document. In addition, there are a number of excellent texts on market research technology.[2]

Assess Market Information Needs

Needs assessment is the process of determining what the ultimate users of research, such as human resource managers, R&D, and product managers, need to know about the marketplace. What is the problem? How should it be structured? What pieces of information essential to making a good decision are missing? A proper understanding of the kinds and amounts of information users need is necessary if researchers are to be effective. Needs may or may not be clearly articulated by users. Market researchers must become more active in establishing strong communication links with their clients to effectively assess their needs, determine issues, and turn these needs and issues into practical and effective market research designs. One way is through formal and regular contact with the user community. It may take the form of monthly

Exhibit 4-2
The Market Research Process

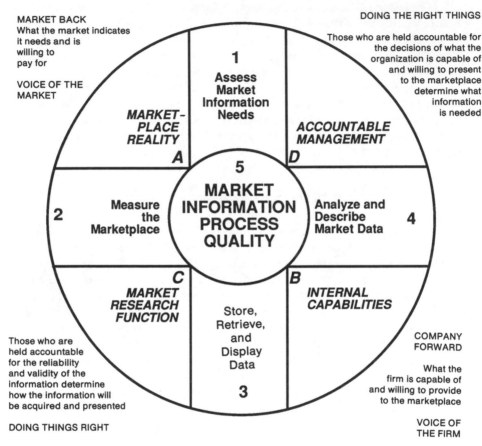

MARKET BACK
What the market indicates
it needs and is
willing to
pay for

VOICE OF THE
MARKET

DOING THE RIGHT THINGS

Those who are held accountable for
the decisions of what the
organization is capable of
and willing to present
to the marketplace
determine what
information
is needed

1 Assess Market Information Needs

MARKET-PLACE REALITY

A

D ACCOUNTABLE MANAGEMENT

5 MARKET INFORMATION PROCESS QUALITY

2 Measure the Marketplace

Analyze and Describe Market Data **4**

C MARKET RESEARCH FUNCTION

Store, Retrieve, and Display Data **3**

B INTERNAL CAPABILITIES

Those who are
held accountable
for the reliability
and validity of the
information determine
how the information will
be acquired and presented

DOING THINGS RIGHT

COMPANY
FORWARD

What the
firm is capable of
and willing to provide
to the marketplace

VOICE OF
THE FIRM

FROM THE VIEW OF THE
INFORMATION PROVIDER

meetings where market researchers and users come together to discuss new developments and new information needs and to identify the issues surrounding these needs. For example, a firm in the apparel industry has outside market research personnel meet bimonthly with various managers to discuss general research needs exclusive of any ongoing research project. These interactions help managers articulate their needs more precisely.

The information needs assessment task has at least five major components. They are:

1. Decision analysis
2. Continuous assessment of user needs
3. Review of existing information about the marketplace
4. Assessment of the significance of marketplace signals
5. Translation of user information needs into researchable questions

Decision analysis. Decision analysis attempts to achieve decision quality by combining aspects of systems analysis and statistical decision theory to deal with the logic of making choices in complex, dynamic, and uncertain situations.[3] Decision analysis specifies the alternatives, information, and preferences of the decision maker and then finds the logically implied decision.[4] The process of decision analysis has four key elements:

1. Structuring what the decision is about
2. Identifying the most important uncertainties
3. Securing the best judgments about the uncertainties
4. Putting together the decision structure and information to reach a logical conclusion

Continuous assessment of user information needs. This concerns always being aware of the information needs of the various users in the firm. These users include the strategic planning group, the product or service planning group, the analysts, the decision makers, and many others. The market research staff can determine what their information needs are in a variety of ways. Regular formal reports can be transmitted, and periodic meetings can be held to transmit data requirements. Equally important, however, are informal methods, such as impromptu meetings, telephone calls, and other kinds of interactions. In some firms, specific product or service plans indicating specific information needs drive the information needs assessment process. In many companies effective communication is established by the participation on a regular basis of the market researchers as active members on the product development team. This alternative requires a greater time commitment and therefore is dependent upon the availability of researchers within the company. Researcher communication with users on a regular basis through formally structured meetings and informal contacts is at the heart of the company's user needs assessment. This direct contact is supplemented by assessments of secondary sources of information within the company, evaluations of the marketplace, competitive assessments, and so forth.

Reviewing existing information about the marketplace. This involves reviewing information about both the present activities and the future needs of customers, competition, suppliers, dealers, and others. The needs of the rest of the corporation are important but not always visible. Regulations or legislation may affect the types of products that can be offered for sale. The competition is always doing something new, and it is best to know as much about that as possible. Finding out about these factors will indicate new information needs. Information about customers can be obtained through a variety of sources, including surveys already conducted by the company and several secondary sources (these are discussed below). It is in the best interest of those responsible for assessing information needs to review and understand the results of existing surveys. The results may provide insight into what customers are doing now, how they feel about the products they buy and do not buy, and their future plans. While this practice may appear obvious, many firms spend substantial sums on data services that are rarely reviewed.

Assessing the significance of marketplace signals. This requires knowing what those signals are. Reviewing the signals and understanding them is the responsibility of accountable management and market research personnel. Both groups must also judge the importance of the information collected.

Translate information needs into researchable questions. Once user information needs are identified, they must be converted into questions that are "researchable." It is of little value to know what your needs are when you don't know how to obtain the information to meet those needs. The only way to obtain the information in a useful format is to do the necessary research. To do the research, you must have clear and precise research questions set forth. This is discussed further in Chapter 7.

Measure the Marketplace

The measurement of market forces is the most fundamental of research activities. The inquiry center must obtain measures of market needs that are scientifically reliable and valid and thus likely to be believed by users.

Measuring the marketplace is what market researchers have traditionally done and is the function they are best noted for. The major tasks are

- collaborative design of the survey instrument;
- primary data collection, including probabilistic sample surveys and non-probabilistic sample surveys; and
- secondary data collection.

Collaborative design of the survey instrument. This refers to the preparation of the survey instrument, not only by those responsible for conducting the survey, but also with input from those responsible for storing and retrieving the survey information, and especially from those who will have to analyze it once it is collected. The time to involve all those who will have to deal with the information is right at the beginning of the process.

Probabilistic sample surveys. Many business decisions require information that is not available "off the shelf." It does not exist in any reference library or data bank, but must be collected for the first time. This is frequently done by surveys of a representative sample of the market, from which the researcher can generalize with some "probability" of accuracy. These surveys may be done by mail, telephone, in person, or by mixed mode. Each type of survey has its particular characteristics, limitations, benefits, costs, and so forth (see Table 4-1 at the end of this chapter). A general characteristic of probabilistic sample surveys is that their results are intended to be generalized to a larger target population.

One example of the use of a survey is the continuous tracking of certain aspects of the marketplace by General Motors. GM has a need to continuously monitor customer satisfaction with its own and competitive vehicles. Information is required by each car line, by plant of manufacture, and on a regular schedule. The data collected in this tracking study are classified by model, engine, transmission, and other variables of interest.

Since this data collection effort was to be a major undertaking, a decision had to be made on what type of survey to use. GM decided to use a mail survey, primarily because of the higher cost of the other available options. The mail survey in this case cost about $8 per completed response. A telephone survey, by comparison, would cost over $10 per response.

Several problems relating to mail surveys had to be addressed. One was that mail surveys typically have a very low response rate. To deal with the expected rate of 35 percent, a study of nonrespondents was done to show that the low rate did not introduce bias into the information collected. Another measure taken was to telephone recipients if completed questionnaires had not been received within thirty days. Another problem was that the mail survey is completely structured, and thus does not allow for descriptive responses to questions. Respondents can share their information only in the limited way the researchers have made available to them. To obtain more robust information on problems identified in the surveys, follow-up telephone interviews are sometimes conducted.

To increase response rates, General Motors attempted to make the mailed survey as personal and as high quality as possible. This included using a first-class stamped envelope, high-quality paper, a cover letter, and a return envelope. After five days, a follow-up postcard was mailed.

There are several problems in drawing a representative sample. Disproportionate sampling is needed to obtain adequate samples of all vehicles and plants. The sample is weighted to represent the entire population of retail sales. Commercial sales (fleet vehicles) are excluded because mail is an inappropriate method to use in obtaining commercial responses: One person might receive all the questionnaires for all 1,000 vehicles his or her firm purchases. Data from certain states are not available, and data on leased vehicles are not available (because they are registered to the leasing company, rather than to the individuals who drive them). These characteristics of the sample are explicitly addressed in the analyses of the information collected.

The diversity of user group needs within the firm adds to the length and complexity of the survey. In part to address this issue, and also to integrate market research into the decision process of the firm, there is a steering committee representing a multiple-user community that includes management, engineering, quality and reliability staff, and the assembly plants. Its responsibilities include eliminating redundancy and conflict in the market research efforts, ensuring that the research that is done is used, and ensuring that all research objectives are met. These objectives cover a wide range of interests and represent many different users. They include high-quality information, timeliness, low cost, and detailed information. There is a constant tension between the desire to have the survey remain constant over time and the need to include updated questions. This tension is continuously addressed in decisions pertaining to the revisions of the survey over time.

Information from the survey is prepared in graphic summary form for management. In addition, tabulation books and small summary cards are prepared. The information is installed into a user-friendly data base. The information is also customized for individual user groups.

Nonprobabilistic data. These data are obtained from surveys for which a probability sample has not been constructed. These efforts include, for example, convenience surveys and focus groups. A convenience sample is one in which respondents are recruited on-site or from within an existing group, such as a club or a classroom. Its basic characteristics are that it is inexpensive to draw together the participants (although it may be expensive to conduct the entire study) and convenient to identify the respondents. This type of survey might be done at a shopping mall or an airport, where passers-by would be asked questions by an interviewer. Focus groups are group discussions led by a facilitator. In this type of data collection effort, the activity includes brainstorming and idea generation about new products or other issues, with respondents discussing the issues in their own words.

Product clinics are data collection efforts (which may be based on probabilistic samples or nonprobabilistic samples) in which products are presented to respondents in a controlled environment. The respondents then observe and evaluate the product. Great care must be taken in developing generalizations about the results of these types of data collection efforts. They do, however, serve to provide additional insight into issues or questions that are important to the firm.

Secondary data. These refer to data that already exist, either within one's own firm or elsewhere. It may be in one of many forms, including computer-based data bases (such as census data and their analyses, for example, geodemographic cluster classifications, economic analyses or descriptors, or measures of media usage), trade journals, or information presented at professional meetings. These are data not collected for the specific problem at hand. Frequently they are collected by someone else so their quality may be questionable. They are often readily available, but may not be in the right format or have the exact content needed. It is wise to check the content, format, and quality of secondary data before acquiring them.

General Motors, like firms of all sizes and kinds, frequently needs to collect relevant and valid data on specific issues that are not likely to recur and consequently are not appropriate for inclusion in long-term tracking studies. These one-time, special issues challenge the researcher's creativity to design and implement studies that reduce the uncertainty around these issues in a timely and cost-efficient manner.

Consider, as an example, a significant improvement being planned for a product feature, such as the product's warranty. Decision makers might have questions about the potential impact of the improvement on sales, the likely increase in customer satisfaction, the potential for bolstering the company's quality image, or the components of the warranty that are most important to customers and why. The answers to these questions, and others, can be addressed through special-issue research.

Perhaps the first step in addressing this particular warranty issue would be to conduct a secondary data search. Some of the information may be available within the firm, and obtainable at little or no cost. Some specific areas to search within the company would include current-owner studies to determine if warranties have been mentioned as a reason for purchase, and if so, to what extent. Owner studies may also reveal the impact of the current warranty on overall owner satisfaction, and perhaps even probe into the satisfaction with the warranty itself. Studies of the target population of intenders for the product may also have relevant information, especially with regard to the awareness of the current warranty and its connection, if any, with the product image or the company's reputation.

It is very likely that after the secondary search, the specificity of this issue will require some primary research effort to more completely understand the mind of the customer. What do customers think of when they think about warranties? What are the important issues? Is the interest level for product warranties high enough for customers to even answer the research questions? Unless the research user and/or the research provider are confident that they know the answers to these questions, some nonprobabilistic, exploratory customer research will be necessary to provide the issues framework and customer language for probabilistic research to follow. A focus group technique could be used to gather together a sample of product owners and/or target consumers in select geographic areas. Insight can be gained through careful moderation of group discussion.

With this background in place, the researcher would be able to design and implement probabilistic sample surveys (by mail or telephone in this case).

The sample could be constructed to represent the target population for the product, rather than only current owners. This would ensure that all consumer viewpoints—for both current owners and potential owners—would be gathered. As examples of what might be done, ratings of warranty features could be taken directly along with ratings of competitive offerings. Tasks could be designed for the respondents to evaluate the various features of the warranty such as the length of term, the breadth of coverage and the caveats of abuse, deductibles, and limitations on service locations. Respondents could also be asked to choose among proposed warranty features, or evaluate a proposed warranty package.

An actual survey of vehicle buyers occurred when the vehicle warranty offered by the company changed in the middle of a model year. To be fair to the individuals who purchased their new cars before the warranty change, the company decided to offer the new warranty to those buyers as well as to the future buyers of the vehicle. To estimate the number of people who would choose the new warranty, a survey was conducted in three cities of a sample of people who had purchased cars within the last few months. Preferences for warranty options were made by respondents. When the new warranty was offered to those people who had purchased their vehicles prior to its availability, of those who responded, approximately the same percentage of people opted for the new warranty as the survey had predicted.

Store, Retrieve, and Display Data

Valid and reliable information about marketplace needs must be retained and distributed by the inquiry center in a way that informs decision makers throughout the firm.

The major tasks in this area are:

- Store the data
- Retrieve the data
- Reformat the data
- Prepare early mockup tables
- Display information
- Prepare documentation
- Training

The information collected by the market research function must be put into a form that others in the firm can effectively use. This involves a range of tasks having to do with reformatting the data; preparing the data for efficient storage; documenting everything that has been done, including the collection of data, and method of retrieving them so that they can be understood and accessed by the users; training all those who will be accessing the information so that they understand how to obtain the data and how to interpret them; and preparing early mockup tables so that the users will be able to see what the output will look like when it is in final form (this allows for early adjustment of certain formats, if necessary).

Analyze and Describe Market Data

Descriptive analyses are pictures of ongoing events that enable account-able management to evaluate policies, strategies, and tactics. Thus, this func-tion serves as the interface between accountable management and the firm's internal decision process. For example, descriptive analyses explaining why changes in market share or dealer satisfaction have occurred help accountable management determine whether past decisions were correct and what others may be necessary.

The major tasks of descriptive analyses include the following:

- Descriptive statistics
- Data reduction
- Inference
- Prediction
- Decision making

These are technical tasks for which researchers have had to prepare them-selves by formal study. Still, accountable managers can make use of their results if they understand a bit about their underlying purpose.

Descriptive statistics. Techniques that simply describe the data that have been collected include calculating the mean and variance of the sample, preparing box plots of the data, and calculating correlations of variables in the data set. The mean is simply the average of the collected data, equal to the sum of the values of the variable of interest divided by the number of observations of that variable. The variance is a measure indicating the extent to which a variable is dispersed about its mean. Box plots are graphic techniques that provide information about central tendency, variability, and shape of distribution. Correlations are measurements of the degree of association between two variables.

Data reduction. These techniques include factor analysis, principal compo-nents analysis, multidimensional scaling, cluster analysis, and product posi-tion maps. Factor analysis is a technique that searches a large number of variables to determine if they have a small number of factors in common that account for their intercorrelation. Principal components analysis is one of several approaches to factor analysis. Multidimensional scaling is a technique that uncovers how individuals perceive the relationships among products by identifying the relevant dimensions along which products or brands are compared. Cluster analysis is a set of techniques for sorting objects into mutually exclusive groups so that the groups are relatively homogeneous. Product position maps are spaces that represent the perceived relationships among brands, with shorter distances between brands indicating greater similarity in perception of relevant attributes.

Inference. Inference refers to the process of gaining information about a population based on samples of observations on that population. One method of drawing inferences is hypothesis testing, which is a general term referring to the procedures for the statistical determination of the validity of an hypothesis. Regression is a technique used to establish a quantified relationship between a dependent variable and one or more independent variables.

Prediction. This refers to generating information about the future based on data collected about the past. Available prediction techniques include conjoint analysis, regression, Box-Jenkins, and smoothing. Conjoint analysis is a set of techniques used to derive the relative preference respondents assign to each attribute when selecting from among several alternatives. It also allows an estimate of the best combination of attributes. Regression can be used not only to establish a relationship among historical variables, but also to predict future values of variables based on those historical relationships. The Box-Jenkins technique is a forecasting method based on time series models. It relies on being able to capture the trend, cyclic, and other systematic characteristics of the time series statistically. It is very accurate in the short term. Smoothing techniques use a series of historical data to predict the value of some future event of the series. Smoothing assumes there is some pattern in the series that will repeat in the future.

An example. The collection of market research data frequently yields a great quantity of consumer responses across many questions. For these data to be useful to the accountable manager in the decision process, some of the techniques discussed above must be employed to analyze and describe the data. The issue of brand image provides an example.

Clearly, a brand's image is an important part of a product's bundle of attributes. In fact, for some product categories where there is considerable emotional involvement with the product (perfumes, jewelry, designer clothing, automobiles, and so forth), brand image can be paramount. A strong brand image can sometimes overshadow physical product shortcomings and temporarily support market share, while a weak brand image may keep an otherwise competitive product from ever getting its foot in the door with customers.

The research issues surrounding the collection and interpretation of data on brand image can often be complex. How does the researcher capture the concept of image from consumers? One method for assessing image is to gather ratings of a brand across a broad spectrum of attributes, with each of these attributes potentially accounting for a part of what a brand's total image might be. For the purpose of our example, consider the following list of brand image attributes as such a broad spectrum.

Practical	High-quality	Safe
Affordable	Reliable	Complex
Expensive	Durable	Simple
Expressive	Popular	Fun
Distinctive	A good value	Well-engineered
Common	Prestigious	Conservative
Exciting	Stylish	Technically advanced

Assume that three brands—A, B, and C— had been rated by 500 respondents on each of these attributes using a 1 to 10 scale, where the higher the number, the more that attribute applies to the brand. The task, then, becomes how to describe and analyze these data, which include 31,500 separate data points (3 brands × 21 attributes × 500 respondents), each having a magnitude of 1 to 10.

The first step in working with the data might be to describe them by calculating mean (weighted average) scores for each brand on each attribute. For example:

	Brand A	Brand B	Brand C
High-quality	8.5	8.2	5.0
Reliable	8.8	8.6	6.2

and so on . . .

This simple summarization of the data would allow the user to compare brands across individual attributes and to track a single attribute score over time in subsequent studies. The variance for each of these mean scores should also be calculated to better understand the extent to which individual respondent scores are distributed across the 1 to 10 scale. To further explain this point, consider the 5.0 mean score on High-quality for Brand C. Obviously, many possible combinations of respondent scores could have been averaged to obtain this particular score. The extremes would be: all respondents rating Brand C as a 5 on High-quality, and conversely, half rating it a 1 and half rating it as a 10. As is easily seen, the variance would have a significant impact on how the mean score would be interpreted in each case.

Even with the data simplified as described above, the total number of attributes may still be too cumbersome and too inconvenient to work with in a meaningful way. Consider the possibility of reducing the list of twenty-one

attributes down to two or three factors that would describe the major components of brand image. A factor analysis technique applied to the total data
set in our hypothetical example might yield three distinct factors, which we
could call:

Factor 1	Factor 2	Factor 3
Quality	Upscale	High-tech
High-quality	Expensive	Technically advanced
Reliable	Prestigious	Well-engineered
Durable	Expressive	Complex
Safe	Popular	
A good value	Exciting	
	Distinctive	

Each of the factors would result from the intercorrelation between various attributes. The attributes that have the greatest impact on the creation of
each of the factors are listed in order of importance.

While the factor analysis helps to make the data more manageable for
assessing a brand's competitive positioning, the question still remains, What
is the total image of Brand A relative to Brands B and C? To answer this
question, a product position map could be used to produce a two-dimensional
picture showing where each brand would be in a perceptual space created by
the data. A product position map is shown in Exhibit 4-3. Whether the
underlying technique used to produce a map is factor analysis, principal
components analysis, multidimensional scaling, or one of many others, the
idea is to spot a specific location on the map which will best represent a
brand's aggregate image position relative to other brands.

One further analysis technique which may expand the understanding of
the brand image data is the process of inference. The accountable manager
might legitimately ask, "What impact does brand image have on product
sales?" To address this question, a regression analysis could help to reveal the
relationship between the image attributes (or the image factors) and sales.
Assuming that product preference had been gathered from respondents when
image attribute ratings were completed, the preference (a surrogate for sales)
could serve as the dependent variable against which the independent variables, the image attributes, could be regressed. The outcome would identify
the relative strength, or importance, of each attribute in its potential to impact
consumer preference.

Descriptive analyses also permit a reexamination of key assumptions
about what the firm is capable of and willing to offer the marketplace. For
instance, accountable managers in one firm assumed that foreign competition
in the domestic market would not become a significant factor for at least five
years and that price adjustments were unnecessary until then. Further, these
managers chose not to allocate the resources necessary to create a distinctive

Exhibit 4-3
A Product Position Map

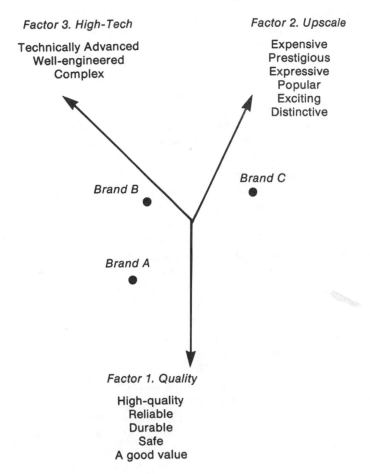

Factor 3. High-Tech

Technically Advanced
Well-engineered
Complex

Factor 2. Upscale

Expensive
Prestigious
Expressive
Popular
Exciting
Distinctive

Brand B

Brand C

Brand A

Factor 1. Quality

High-quality
Reliable
Durable
Safe
A good value

image among its customers. However, the research staff, using available data and a special model of the consumer brand-switching process, concluded that foreign competition could make substantial inroads into the domestic market very quickly and easily. This led accountable management to develop a program to buttress itself against foreign competition. The managers assumed that potential competitors could learn as readily as they did just how easily and successfully the domestic market could be entered.

Researchers and users should consult with each other during the interpretation phase of the research, regardless of who has the responsibility for the interpretation task (see Chapter 5). It should be decided at the onset of the research who has responsibility for this task. All too often, researchers assume that users will interpret the data, while users expect researchers to provide interpretations. Regardless of how responsibility is assigned, researchers and users should discuss jointly whatever interpretations are developed. Researchers can provide guidance about potential restrictions that the research methodology imposes on the interpretation of data. Users can provide additional insights about actual contexts that may affect the interpretation.

A highly effective technique, discussed in the next chapter, involves simulated interpretation of data prior to the actual collection of information. This exercise enhances immensely the usability of the final data.

Researchers should be consulted by users when translating research results into specific action. Findings or qualifications that the researcher did not consider important and hence did not report may be highly relevant to a planned action. Consulting the researcher enables this information to be retrieved. As an example, a research project led users at the Bomax Corporation to create a new business unit for the development of a luxury line of prefabricated vacation cottages designed to appeal to high-income customers. Among the alternative ways of implementing this action were (a) acquiring an existing line of luxury prefab designs from a firm that was dropping such a line and (b) designing a new line. Consulted by users at the implementation stage, one of the staff researchers was able to add information from secondary data sources that had not been placed in the research report because the data were not considered relevant. The added information made it clear which way of implementing the action was most likely to succeed.

When the researcher is asked to make a judgment. Managers are regularly confronted by strategic questions for which there is only highly fragmented and/or tangentially related data. The question to researchers is usually posed something like this: "Okay, I see what the data say about Plan A, but we are also considering Plan B. What do you think would happen if . . . ?"

Here the questioner is asking an experienced individual, familiar with a broad range of data, to heuristically combine that mental store of information, to analyze it, and then to offer an opinion. One caveat: Market researchers should be very clear when they answer such questions that their answer is a "personal judgment" and is not directly supported by a market research project.

Market Information Process Quality

Market information process quality is concerned with a critical question, one that exists at the heart of the research process: Is the right information about the right problems reaching the right people in the right form, and are these people applying the information in the right way? If the answer is negative, the firm is wasting time and money; even worse, it is failing to hear what the market is saying. It must go back and reassess its execution of the other four functions of the marketing process. If the answer to this critical question is positive, the firm knows that it can chart its course with greater confidence. The evaluation of research applications is as difficult as it is important. Chapter 12 discusses the importance of learning about our fundamental ways of using information. The techniques discussed here are more oriented to the evaluation of a specific project.

Several techniques are available to assess and enhance market information usefulness:

- Action audits
- Simulation of final results
- Discrepancy analysis
- Insurance premium calculation
- Information as arbitration
- Assess market research project

Some of these techniques are addressed in more detail in Chapter 5.

Action audits. During the initial steps of the market research, managers need to brainstorm the array of conceivable actions they might take with regard to the issue being researched. For each action there should be a corresponding set of research questions developed to ensure that adequate information is obtained about that action. This has two added advantages. First, it helps ensure that relevant, useful, and actionable information is obtained. Second, it helps get managers to think sooner about the use of information in developing actions. For each action managers are asked to indicate what type of information would suggest that the action is sound or unsound.

Hypothetical data. It is often useful to prepare a mockup of the final presentation with simulated findings presented in the way actual findings will be. The data would represent both good news and bad news. This stimulates thinking about additional research questions and different kinds of analyses and presentations. It has the benefit of reducing "post-survey regret" in which managers and researchers say, "I wish we had asked . . . " It also provides a basis for rethinking fundamental assumptions about the issues being addressed. Additionally, it affords the researcher some insight into the different agendas managers may have concerning the issue.

Discrepancy analysis. Here, managers are asked to predict particular research findings; for example, the average importance rating customers will assign to a product attribute. Later this is compared with the actual result. Each manager receives information about his or her prediction, about the group's prediction if several people are involved in the decision, and the actual result.

The greater the discrepancy between what was predicted by managers (individually and as a group) and the actual result, the more valuable that item of information is. This can be weighted by the importance of that item of information. These weighted discrepancies would be summed for all items. The larger the score, the more useful the entire research effort is.

Insurance premium. Much research is intended as an insurance premium; that is, to confirm that a particular idea or action is or is not sound. The research serves as insurance against a wrong decision. In this sense market research need not contribute new ideas or alter the choice of the right thing to do or how to do it right. The primary purpose of the research here is to increase the sense of certainty about a planned action and to detect possible problems however unlikely their occurrence. A firm can evaluate the utility of this research in the same way it would an insurance policy: Is the cost (financial and otherwise) of the wrong decision, weighted by its likelihood of occurrence, greater than the cost of the research? This use of research focuses on the decision to act rather than on the development of the idea to be acted on or how to best implement an idea. The greater the expected cost of a wrong decision (probability × magnitude) relative to the cost of research, the greater the value of doing the research.

Arbitration. One function of market research is arbitration, or reconciling differences in viewpoints among functional areas. The market research function is the "representative" of the marketplace, a kind of impersonal ombudsman. It can be used to reconcile differences in viewpoints between, say, engineering and manufacturing or marketing. That is, the perspective adopted in reaching a decision should be the one that is closest to what customers, dealers, and so forth are suggesting (within the limits of what the firms can provide). The more that information helps to (a) reconcile these differences and (b) produce a perspective that is a creative blending of the different perspectives (including those of relevant groups in the marketplace), the more useful that information is.

Project assessments. At the end of a project, managers should take the opportunity to assess it. For example, Exhibit 4-4 shows a simple but very helpful assessment document used at the Cleveland Clinic Foundation. The instrument is sent to all clients of projects requiring twenty hours or more of effort approximately two to three months after the project's completion. Over 90 percent of the participants provide feedback. Projects are evaluated to determine if they were technically flawed; were misleading because important data were not collected or, if collected, not reported; were irrelevant to decisions; were not presented in manners in which their actual relevance or utility is clear; increased uncertainty more than they increased certainty; were inadequately or incorrectly interpreted; were poorly translated into appro-

Exhibit 4-4
Strategic Planning and Market Research Client Satisfaction Questionnaire

---

DATE:

TO:

FROM: Bill Gombeski
        Director, Department of Strategic Planning and Market Research

Last fall, Analyst X completed the ABC study for you. The purpose of the study
was to:_____.

One of our goals is to provide the best possible service we can within the cost and
time parameters outlined by a client. Your comments and suggestions are valuable
in helping us evaluate our efforts on your behalf. Would you take a few moments
and share your thoughts and feelings?

1. How satisfied were you with the outcome of the above project?
    ___ Very satisfied
    ___ Somewhat satisfied
    ___ Somewhat dissatisfied
    ___ Very dissatisfied

    Please explain what contributed to your selection of the specific satisfied or dis-
    satisfied category.
2. What suggestions can you make which would help SPMR be more effective in
    working with other departments or committees like yours on similar projects in
    the future?
3. How have you used the information generated? (Check all that apply)

	Currently	Future
To improve patient care	___	___
To improve patient service	___	___
To increase revenue	___	___
To reduce costs	___	___
To increase productivity	___	___
To generate action	___	___
To change behavior	___	___
To implement a program	___	___
Other_____	___	___

4. Please share any additional thoughts in the space below.
Thank you for your time and please return in the attached envelope.

Source: William R. Gombeski, Jr., "Client Satisfaction Questionnaires: Why Research Managers
Should Use Them," *Marketing Research, vol. 1, no 4* (December 1989), p. 46.

priate actions; or answered the wrong question. Information can be abused and market research can have a negative utility if it is used solely as a report card rather than as instruction; used to support particular agendas and is not pursued with an "equal opportunity" methodology in which opposite conclusions have, in principle, equal chances of showing up; and is deliberately misconstrued to advance a prior position.

An example. An example of some of the techniques is provided by a manufacturer of gift wrap supplies. The firm was planning a new line of gift wrap products but had not intended to do any consumer market research. While key managers were in agreement that the line would be successful, considerable disagreement developed as to just how successful it would be in the first eighteen months. This was an important issue since crucial capacity-related manufacturing decisions had to be made which could not be altered easily later and which influenced production plans for the firm's other product lines. A research firm the manufacturer had worked with before was hired to help acquire relevant information. Key personnel in both organizations knew each other well, and the research staff had some familiarity with the product line.

Preliminary discussions about basic research issues took place, and a questionnaire was developed and reviewed by the manager team and research staff. When it was felt that the questionnaire was ready for pretesting, the project research director took several steps prior to pretesting. These steps were included as part of the project contract. In fact, they were also followed in prior work performed for the manufacturer by the research organization and hence were familiar to some of the managers. The first step was to have the six managers record what they felt the final results would be with respect to the most important questions being asked of consumers. Thus, for some questions, managers recorded what they thought the average rating would be among consumers. On other questions, they indicated what percentage of consumers would check particular options, what the "average intention to buy" score would be, and so forth. Later, when the final research results were presented, the average predictions of these managers as a group were also presented. In many instances, the managers as a group were fairly accurate in their predictions. In two very critical instances, however, all six decision makers were off significantly in what they had expected. Later, the firm's CEO claimed that having the information on just these two items was worth several times the cost of the research. In a few other instances when managers had very different expectations from one another, the actual results were quite clear in their implications and helped resolve the respective issues in a straight-forward way. These items along with the two "surprises" had the greatest relevance to the critical production capacity decisions. It was quite evident that a decision made without the research would have been quite different from the actual decision made with the benefit of the research.

Early in the research process, the project's research director engaged in another activity. Prior to any questionnaire pretesting, but after managers had provided their predictions about specific research results, the researcher conducted a simulated presentation of results. (Note that this is similar to the technique discussed above under Store, Retrieve, and Display Data, in which hypothetical data are presented in expected output format to achieve early buy-in from the users of the information.) This had been done before with other projects, and the CEO had specifically requested the activity for this one. In making this presentation, the researcher asked questions such as the following: "What if we got this result?" What else would you need to know to understand it? To believe it? To make use of it?" "How would you use this information?" "What decisions or actions are suggested?" Questions of this sort helped the managers think more carefully about their actual use of the research while it was still early enough to change the questionnaire. In fact, several questions were either altered significantly or dropped, while others were added. About 30 percent of the questionnaire underwent some change. This 30 percent would have later been the source of considerable post-survey regret, reflected by statements such as, "I wish we had asked . . . " or "It's too bad we didn't use a different scale." The simulated presentation also facilitated the use of the actual information when it was presented. Managers had a strong sense of alternative uses of the information and could proceed more quickly.

Every research project should have a research-use evaluation component. Responsibility for this evaluation may lie with the research team or with the users or may be contracted to a third party. Such an effort would yield substantial insight into the entire research-use process and should result in ideas for strengthening future research-utilization efforts. Considerations as to how the research process will be evaluated should begin at the planning stage of the project rather than appear at the end. Chapter 5 discusses a procedure that helps in the evaluation of a research project as it is unfolding so as to improve its value and to aid in the determination of its contribution to management thinking after it has been completed.

Table 4-1, below, identifies some of the complete range of techniques available to the researcher in each of the five areas of our basic framework. Across the top of the table are noted the specific techniques, and down the side are listed particular characteristics, requirements, or criteria related to the techniques.

In Table 4-1 you will notice differences in the contents from task area to task area. This is due to the very different natures of the tasks. For example, some descriptions will be quite precise, others much less so. There is a range among the entries in the matrices from qualitative to quantitative, from easy to hard, from inexpensive to costly, from the very practical to the more theoretical, and from slow to fast. However, there are some major similarities

Table 4-1
The Market Research Encyclopedia

References

Vincent P. Barabba and Gerald Zaltman, *Hearing the Voice of the Market* (Boston: Harvard Business School Press, 1991).

George E.P. Box and Gwilym M. Jenkins, *Time Series Analysis: Forecasting and Control*, revised edition (San Francisco: Holden Day, 1976).

Harper Boyd, Ralph Westfall, and Stanley Stasch, *Marketing Research: Text and Cases*, 5th ed. (Homewood, Ill.: Richard D. Irwin, 1981).

Norman M. Bradburn and Seymour Sudman, *Polls and Surveys* (San Francisco: Jossey-Bass, 1988).

Gilbert Churchill, Jr., *Marketing Research Methodological Foundations*, 4th ed. (Chicago: Dryden Press, 1984).

William Cleveland, *The Elements of Graphing Data* (Monterey, Calif.: Wadsworth Publishing, 1985).

Don A. Dillman, *Mail and Telephone Surveys* (New York: Wiley Interscience Publications, 1978).

W.R. Dillon, J. Madden, and N.H. Firtle, *Market Research in a Marketing Environment* (St. Louis, Mo.: Times-Mirror/Mosby College Publishing, 1987).

S. French, ed., *Readings in Decision Analysis* (New York: Chapman and Hall, 1989).

C.W. J. Granger and Paul Newbold, *Forecasting Economic Time Series* (San Diego: Academic Press, 1977).

R.M. Groves and James M. Lepkowski, "Dual Frame Mixed Mode Survey Design," *Journal of Official Statistics*, 1985.

R.M. Groves et al., *Telephone Survey Methodology* (New York: John Wiley & Sons, 1988).

Joseph F. Hair, Jr., Rolph E. Anderson, and Ronald L. Tatham, *Multivariate Data Analysis with Readings*, 2d ed. (New York: Macmillan, 1987).

Samuel Holtzman, *Intelligent Decision System* (Reading, Mass.: Addison-Wesley, 1989).

Ronald A. Howard, "Decision Analysis: Practice and Promise," *Management Science*, vol. 34, no. 6, June 1988.

Thomas C. Kinnear and James R. Taylor, *Marketing Research*, 3d ed. (New York: McGraw-Hill, 1987).

Leslie Kish, *Survey Sampling* (New York: John Wiley & Sons, 1965).

J. T. McClave and P. G. Benson, *Statistics for Business and Economics*, 4th ed. (San Francisco: Dellery Publishers, 1988).

Robert S. Pindyck and Daniel L. Rubinfeld, *Econometric Models and Economic Forecasts* (New York: McGraw-Hill, 1981).

Calvin F. Schmid, *Statistical Graphics: Design Principles and Practices* (New York: John Wiley & Sons, 1983).

J.Q. Smith, *Decision Analysis: A Bayesian Approach* (New York: Chapman and Hall, 1987).

George W. Snedecor and William G. Cochran, *Statistical Methods*, 6th ed. (Ames: Iowa State University Press, 1967).

Gerald Zaltman, "The Management and Use of Market Research," presented at the Conference on Making More Effective Use of Market Information, April 12-13, 1989, Phoenix, Arizona, (Cambridge, Mass.: Marketing Science Institute).

Gerald Zaltman and Rohit Deshpande, "Increasing the Utilization of Scientific and Technical Information" in William R. King and Gerald Zaltman, eds., *Marketing Scientific and Technical Information* (Boulder, Colo.: Westview Press, 1979).

William G. Zikmund, *Business Research Methods* (Chicago: Dryden Press, 1984).

① Assess Market Information Needs

	Decision Analysis	Assess User Needs Continuously
	Strategic Planning Group	
Description	Frame the decision to be made	User/provider meeting to identify issues/uncertainties and lead to research questions, timing decisions, assessments, and needed quality/value of information
	Determine most important uncertainties	Needs define type of research
		Process should lead to full analysis plan
	Obtain best judgments about the range of uncertainties	Before approving research, management should review issues, methods, anticipated results, analysis plan, and costs
	Determine the need for and range of research	
When to Undertake Activity	Throughout information-needs assessment process	Regularly, before update of strategic plan
Time Required	Depends on the complexity of the decisions at hand	Varies from 1 to many meetings and 1 day to several months, depending on number of users, timing needs, and complexity
Collaboration Required	All knowledge producers and users with those assigned to decision analysis support	Involvement of user groups plus liaison with market research function and with management review
Data Required	Information relevant to the decision at hand, determined during the analysis	Clearly defined plan or objectives with identified uncertainties that can be reduced
		Clear relation between reducing uncertainty and resulting change
		Timing until decision or action
		Value of differences between alternative decisions
Incremental Cost	Cost of staff time	←
Importance	Ensures that parties jointly determine information needs	←
References	Holtzman; Howard	Churchill; Kinnear and Taylor; Zikmund

(Continued)

① Assess Market Information Needs (Continued)

Review Information About Marketplace: Customers, Corporation, Legislature, Competitors		Interpret Marketplace Signals	Translate Users' Information Needs into Research Questions
Current Influences	**Future Influences**		
Image studies by mail or telephone, involving financial leaders, legislators, and other politicians	Discussions with thought leaders, groups, think tanks, and innovators	Using qualitative research, determine meaning of signals and reasons for them	Interviews Careful probing
		Possibly use expert surveys/studies	Determine issues, needs, timing, decisions affected by information produced, and impact
Competitive assessment studies	Development of regressions, and trend analyses scenarios	Use consumer studies	
		Do studies on factors related to signals	
At least every quarter or with major changes in the environment	Continuously, or at least prior to start of new product/service program	Continuously, or with a significant change in the environment	At start of research project and frequently thereafter
			In meetings over the course of the project
1-3 months	3-6 months	Depends on complexity of project; could be lengthy	A few hours to several months, depending on when output is required
Product engineering	Strategic planners	Product engineering	Users and researchers must understand each other's requirements
Technical staff	Marketing planners	Technical staff	
Product design	Economists	Product design	
Quality/reliability staff	Designers	Quality/reliability staff	
Sales management	Engineers	Sales management	
Product/service planning		Product/service planning	
Other staffs, including public relations, government relations, financial, and environmental activities		Outside experts	
Image ratings from financial leaders, and politicians	Trends in demographic, psycho-graphic, economic, environmental, regulatory, and legislative factors	Data containing signals plus qualitative data to interpret them	Data containing signals plus qualitative data to interpret them
Competitors' plans		Extensive market/sales data	Extensive market/sales data
	Company capabilities assessment		
$10,000-$100,000 (for initial data collection)	Depends on level of effort and breadth of product line	Depends on complexity ($10,000-$100,000 for intial data collection)	Cost of staff time
Develops and adjusts company policies and programs	Required for product/service development	Determines direction of products and programs	Crucial in ensuring communication among parties
Boyd, Westfall, and Stasch			Churchill; Zikmund

Product Planning Group	Market Analysts	Decision Makers	Other Users
User/provider meeting to identify issues/uncertainties and lead to research questions, timing decisions, assessments, and needed quality/value of information			
Before approving research, management should review issues, methods, anticipated results, analysis plan, and costs			
At stages in market planning process, including before concept initiation	As needed to respond to market events and anticipated internal actions	Use regular channels for requests Plan periodic research	
Varies from 1 to many meetings and 1 day to several months, depending on number of users, timing needs, and complexity			
Involvement of user groups plus liaison with market research function and with management review			
Clearly defined plan or objectives with identified uncertainties that can be reduced			
Clear relation between reducing uncertainty and resulting change			
Timing until decision or action			
Value of differences between alternative decisions			
──────── Nominal ──▶			
────────── Most critical part of research ──────────────────────────▶			

(Continued)

② Measure the Marketplace

Primary Data

Probabilistic Sample Surveys

	Mail	Telephone	In-Person	Mixed Mode
Description	Self-administered survey mailed to respondents	Administered over the telephone	Administered by an interviewer in respondent's home or in a central location	Combination of mail, telephone, or in-person survey
Implementation Technique	Self-administered Paper and pencil	CATI (computer-aided telephone interview) Respondents called from a phone-interview facility Audio taping	CAPI (computer-aided personal interview) Paper and pencil Use visual aids for more complex respondent tasks Audiovisual taping Private setting preferable	Self-administered Paper and pencil CATI CAPI
Benefits	Least expensive probabilistic method Wide geographic coverage Large sample sizes	Fastest method Permits moderately lengthy questionnaires Flexible Lower item nonresponse rates Control over who responds Low chance of misinterpretation of questions	Highest response rates Permits longer, more complex interviews Lower item nonresponse rates Low chance of misinterpretation of questions Enables interviews on personal issues Can use available computers and products themselves	Combines advantages of different methods Creates flexibility in amount and detail of information collected
Limitations	List quality can vary Low response rates Introduces potential for bias Long field time Limited length and complexity of questionnaires Limited control over who completes survey High potential for item nonresponse No chance for interviewer to probe	Limited time Potential bias if topic is correlated with characteristics of no-phone households or unlisted numbers Unlisted and outdated phone numbers may reduce list quality Little time for respondents to ponder questions	Large field staff or long data-collection period required Potential for interviewer bias Outdated names, addresses, and phone numbers may reduce list quality Expensive to control quality of interview	Difficulty of getting high-quality list Potential for losing respondents between waves Potential for differential impact of mode on responses Combines expenses of two modes
Response Rates Without Incentives	10%-85%	20%-85%	70%-90%	65%-90%
Cost per Completed Interview	$5-$10	$20-$90	$150-$400	Depends on modes of data collection and percent collected by each
Source of Sample	Complete, accurate list of the target population	Complete list of target population Use of random digit dialing is possible if list is unavailable	Complete list of target population If this is an area probability sample, detailed geographic data are required	Complete list of target population If this is an area probability sample, detailed geographic data are required
References	Dillman	Groves et al.	Kish	Groves and Lepkowski

			Secondary Data
Nonprobabilistic Data			
Convenience Samples	**Focus Group**	**Central Location Interviewing (Product Clinics)**	
Administered to respondents recruited on-site in high-traffic areas or from existing groups	Small discussion led by a facilitator	Respondents come to a central location to evaluate products	Existing data sources developed internally or externally
Computerized	Discussion	Self-administered	Obtain data from existing sources like warranty claims or point-of-sale terminal
Paper and pencil	Audiovisual	Personal interviews	
Self-administered	Tape recorder	Computer administered	
In trailer, van, rented store, or street location	Focus group room/facility with one-way glass preferred	Paper and pencil	
		CAPI	
Probably less expensive than other methods	Group synergy generated	Gives product feedback from static or dynamic evaluation under controlled conditions	Small time delay in obtaining data
Fast	Encourages brainstorming	Allows respondent exposure to actual product	Possibly low cost (depending on source)
	Respondents discuss issues in their own words	Under certain conditions, a representative sample can be obtained and statistics generalized to the entire population	Many sources are censuses of information
High proportion of unrepresentative responses	Information collected is more directive and suggestive than projective	Very expensive	Generally does *not* include the exact questions and samples of interest
Information collected is more directive and suggestive than projective	Facilitator, vocal participants can dominate the results	Responses in this artificial environment may not reflect responses in the market	May be of variable and unknown quality
Ability to generalize results is limited	Ability to generalize results is limited	Complicated logistics	
Survey must be short and simple		Development of test product can be time consuming and expensive	
Not applicable	Varies widely by topic and market	Tends to be low, though varies widely by product and market	Not applicable
Varies widely	Varies widely	Generally quite expensive but varies widely	Not applicable
High-incidence location for target population	List of target population	List of target population	Not applicable
	Sometimes organization lists of members can be used		
Dillon, Madden, and Firtle —— Bradburn and Sudman ——	Churchill	Churchill	Churchill ——————→

(Continued)

③ Store, Retrieve, and Display the Data

	Store Information	Retrieve Information	Reformat Data
Description	Preparation of data-delivery specifications Creation of new variables for permanent storage Storage of new and cleaned data	Run computer programs or packages to retrieve data	Reformat from data's raw source to meet organizational objectives or requirements Includes cleaning, coding, and checking the data
When to Undertake Activity	Data-delivery specifications prepared before data collection Creation of variables and data storage begin after data collection	Routinely and as needed	As soon as data are received
Time Required	Extensive; influenced by quantity of collected information	Time needed to run program	Much time needed to clean, code, and check the data
Collaboration Required	System users with data providers	System users to define needs	With system users and data providers
Requirements	User friendly Effective Consistent across data sets Mergeable Trackable User transparent	Standardized retrieval package Transparent file linkages Menu approach Electronic selection assistance Meaningful and functional file prefixes User can write own programs Fast retrieval capability Cost effective User friendly Can download to a PC environment	Standardized applications Meets user needs for specific as well as general applications Common format, menu driven to allow retrieval for observation and analysis User friendly Flexible to allow for users with a range of skills Self-explanatory names of variables Easily understood output Database/system compatibility
Expected Output	User-friendly database	Data, charts, comparisons, tables, maps	Reformatted, clean data Manipulatable data to obtain required information
Cost	Variable, depending on the quality and quantity of data, system they are resident on, communication links and requirements, method of data transmission (disks vs. hard copy) For some repetitive efforts, initial costs may be higher than later costs Cost considerations should include the value added of the data considered		
References	←————————————————————————— Company's own market information system documentation		

Prepare Early Mock-Up Tables	Display Information	Prepare Documentation	Train Users
Early in the process, prepare expected output tables to obtain user groups' reactions	For some applications, readily understood software packages such as MacDraw, Tell-A-Graf, Atlas, or Page Maker are useful Computer use ranges from PCs to mainframes	For: Data collection System File contents Analysis Display of information	Users must know how to manipulate data, prepare graphics, understand statistical and analytical techniques used, and present data effectively so that they can benefit fully
As early as possible and ongoing	After analysis to enhance written report During analysis of data	From database development onward	Initially and as needed
Several days spread over several months Variable and depending on the requirements	Short if staff has training in display packages (depends on necessary detail)	Long; enough to budget for Depends on complexity and quantity of data	Not as much time as other efforts Time is front-loaded
Before complete analysis, present to expected users to determine usefulness	With system users so that they understand system capabilities With researchers to ensure correct presentation With suppliers	With data suppliers	User feedback is necessary
Collaboration with users Clear presentation of hypothetical output in expected format	Ensure clarity to user of output device and analysis and graphics techniques Graphic display capability Menu driven; standardized report materials	Electronic access to documentation Easily understood documentation	Equipment Instructional materials relevant to users' needs
Information display mechanism	Data, charts, illustrations, presentations, decision trees, tables, maps	Documentation on file contents, on method of use of equipment and analysis techniques, and on analysis interpretation	A confident and skilled user community that can use data effectively and efficiently
	Cleveland; Schmid	Review existing documentation for similar applications	

(Continued)

④ Describe and Analyze Market Information

	Descriptive Analysis	Data Reduction
Examples of Analysis Techniques	Mean	Factor analysis
	Variance	Principal components analysis
	Box plot	Multidimensional scaling
	Correlations	Cluster analysis
	Graphic analysis	Product position maps
When to Undertake Activity	←	
	←	
	Before data reduction	Before inference activity
	As part of exploratory activity	As part of exploratory analysis
Time required	Minimal; depends on the quantity of data and analysis package	1-2 weeks (more than descriptive analysis)
Collaboration Required	None	With builders of database and users of information
Data and/or Sample Size Required	Values of the observed variables	Fairly large sample size
Expected Output	Summary of data	Maps
		Knowledge of structure of underlying relationships in the data
Importance	Simple overview of data	Gives insight into structure of data
References	Snedecor and Cochran	Hair, Anderson, and Tatham

Inference	Prediction	Decision Making
Hypothesis testing	Conjoint analysis	Bayesian statistics
Regression	Regression	Decision analysis
	Box-Jenkins	
	Smoothing	

In response to requests ——————————————————————————▶

As part of ongoing market research analysis ——————————————▶

Before prediction and decision-making activities	Before decision making	Before commitment of major resources
In special studies	In special studies	
1 week to several months, depending on messiness of the data, complexity of the problem, depth of analysis required, and time horizon of the problem	Can be quite extensive but also very fast on completion of previous activities	Varies; may range from minutes to months
With data providers and information users; can be extensive	With users of analyses and company stakeholders	With decision makers, company stakeholders, and data providers
	Possibly with builders of database	
Data collected that are relevant to analysis	May require output from descriptive analysis, data reduction, or inference	Output of inference and prediction activities
Input to prediction and decision making	Data on feasible alternatives and their likely outcomes	Commitment of resources
Knowledge about structural relationships among variables	Output may cause revision of thinking	Crucial to survival of organization
	May affect allocation of capital resources	
	Box and Jenkins; Granger and Newbold; Pindyck and Rubinfeld;	French; Holtzman; McClave and Benson; Smith

(Continued)

⑤ Evaluate the Research and Assess Its Usefulness

	Action Audits	Simulation of Final Results	Discrepancy Analysis
Description	For each contemplated action, develop a set of research questions to determine its soundness	Prepare mock-up of final presentation using simulated findings presented as actual findings will be	Predict research findings, compare them later with actual findings High levels of discrepancy between the two indicate usefulness of findings
When to Undertake Activity	Start of the research project	Before data collection	Before final data are distributed to managers
Time Required	1-2 hours	8 hours for researchers; 2 hours for managers	½ hour of manager time; 1 hour of researcher time
Collaboration Required	Managers with researchers	Managers with researchers	Among managers
Data Required	None	Simulated	None
Expected Output	Inventory of possible actions	Mock-up of alternative results Rehearsal of research-use process	Comparison of managers' expectations with actual results
Clarity of Expected Output	High; explicit statements of plans	High	High
Cost	No out-of-pocket cost	Managers: no out-of-pocket cost Researchers: 1 day of research time if outside supplier is used	No out-of-pocket cost
Frequency of Use	Moderate	Low	Low
Principal Benefits	More relevant and more actionable research Faster use of research	Clearer sense of issues More relevant research instruments and final data More useful research reporting	Gives a measure of the value of information Reduces "I told you so" behavior
Principal Limitations and Obstacles	None Managers may be unwilling to disclose possible actions to researchers	None Time required may be perceived as extensive	None Managers' reluctance to admit uncertainty
References	←		

Insurance Premium Calculation	Information as Arbitration	Assess Market Research Project
Research determines if the cost of a wrong decision, weighted by its likelihood, is greater than the cost of the research Serves as insurance against wrong decision	Market research information is used to reconcile differences among functional areas	Information is dysfunctional if technically flawed, misleading, irrelevant, poorly presented, incorrectly interpreted, or deliberately misconstrued
As part of decision whether to do research	After research is completed	After research is completed
Less than ½ hour	½ hour per decision maker	½ hour per participant Corresponding time of an auditor
Among managers	Managers with auditor	Managers with qualified auditor
Cost of research and approximate cost of an unsuccessful action	None	None
Ratio indicating desirability of doing research	Qualitative assessment	Qualitative assessments by auditor
Mixed; ratio is specific, its interpretation less so	Moderate to high	Moderate
No out-of-pocket cost	No out-of-pocket cost If outside auditor is used, 1 day	No out-of-pocket cost If outside auditor is used, 1 day
Moderate	Low	Low
Guideline concerning potential value of doing research	Better understanding and appreciation of the role of research	Guidelines for improving research-use process
None Difficulty in calculating cost of an error	Difficult to get managers to reflect on changes in their perspectives Managers may not want research in an arbitration role	Securing candid assessments from managers Managers' reluctance to disclose abuse of research

Barabba and Zaltman; Zaltman and Deshpande; Zaltman ⟶

in the descriptions. These include the description of the technique listed, its cost and timing, relevant citations, and necessary interactions. The most important of these is the necessity for interaction between the information provider and the information user from the start of the decision process.

CONCLUSION

This chapter has presented a basic framework for doing market research. The framework consists of the assessment of market information needs, measurement of the marketplace, the storage, retrieval, and display of data, the analysis and description of market data, and market information process quality enhancement. This last element in the framework is the primary focus of the next chapter. The basic framework, while oriented toward formal market research, is equally appropriate for other ways of learning about the market. Thus, the full framework as shown in Exhibit 4-2 is generic to all kinds of market inquiry processes.

Notes

1. Vincent P. Barabba, "The Market Research Encyclopedia," *Harvard Business Review* (January–February 1990).
2. The reader may find the following books helpful: Alan R. Andreasen, *Cheap But Good Marketing Research* (Homewood, IL: Dow Jones–Irwin, 1988); Harper Boyd, Ralph Westfall, and Stanley Stasch, *Marketing Research: Text and Cases*, 5th ed. (Homewood, IL: Richard D. Irwin, 1981); Gilbert Churchill, Jr., *Marketing Research Methodological Foundations*, 4th ed. (Chicago: Dryden Press, 1984); and W.R. Dillon, J. Madden, and N.H. Firtle, *Market Research in a Marketing Environment* (St. Louis, MO: Times-Mirror/Mosby College Publishing, 1987).
3. Samuel Holtzman, *Intelligent Decision Systems* (Reading, MA: Addison-Wesley, 1989).
4. Ronald A. Howard, "The Evolution of Decision Analysis," in Ronald A. Howard and James E. Matheson, eds., *Readings on the Principles and Applications of Decision Analysis* (Menlo Park, CA: Strategic Decisions Group, 1983).

CHAPTER 5

Research-Use Technology

A central component of the framework discussed in Chapter 4 is knowledge-use evaluation. When the use of research in decision making is evaluated, if at all, it is usually in a "how-well-did-it-work" way after a decision has been implemented. While this is important and helpful, it is more constructive to do evaluations as the research is being developed, while there is time to increase its value for a given decision. The result is a more effective and efficient functioning of the framework and the research process we discussed in Chapter 4.

This chapter focuses on a procedure that increases the value of research to managers. **We base our ideas on the premise that the quality of thinking about an issue prior to data collection is the major determinant of the quality of thinking after the data have been collected.** The procedure recommended here serves the best interests of both managers and researchers. It increases the chances of doing the right thing and doing it right.

A major theme of this book is that management today faces a significant task in making more effective use of market information in decisions throughout the organization. In fact, failure to acquire appropriate information or use it effectively is one of the major impediments to increasing productivity, improving competitiveness, going to market more quickly with new ideas, and so on. While there is considerable variation among companies with respect to how useful, and how well used, their research findings are, even the most exemplary companies can improve their use of market research. Firms such as AMOCO, Citicorp, Eastman Kodak, and General Motors, whose research-use practices are very effective, are aware of the need for further improvements and are the most committed to making them. These firms realize just how large the payoff can be when relevant, accurate, and timely data are presented to managers in meaningful ways. The CEO of a major European firm commented on this when speaking about the firm's decision to establish a corporate-level market research function:

113

Once I saw that a 10 percent improvement in the quality of information could improve the quality of our decisions by at least 10 percent and that those improvements [enhanced] our corporate performance by even more than that, I became [convinced]. The financial leverage provided by having and using the right information makes [the research function] one of the most productive units in this corporation.

One researcher, Martin Weinberger, executive vice president of Oxtoby-Smith, wrote an article concerning an oil company which was persuaded to reallocate $100,000 from its $2-million annual media budget to find out whether the $2 million was being spent well.[1] It was discovered that the advertising which had already run for two years was actually exaggerating the problem the company was trying to correct. The company may have found the $100,000 to be one of its better investments. This is a common example of improved research use.

Doing versus Using Technologies

The technology for acquiring information, performing quantitative analyses, and storing data is quite sophisticated. It is making an increasingly broad array of information available to managers. In contrast, the technology for using data is underdeveloped. There are few established procedures for increasing the relevance of data and their ultimate translation into sound decisions. This is a significant issue since competitive advantage will reside increasingly in how information is used rather than in who has it.

There is an important fundamental difference between the technologies for doing research and those for improving its use. Technologies for data acquisition and processing are oriented toward "people proofing." That is, they strive to eliminate or at least isolate human bias by establishing "objective" guidelines for experimental design, sampling procedures, the construction and administration of questionnaires, reliance on formal analytic procedures, and so on. In contrast, the process of using information is a judgmental matter. Moreover, it is not desirable to depersonalize information use even if we could, since the effective use of information relies on the nonresearch frames of reference decision makers bring to a problem. As we move from data collection, processing, and storage to information use we move from science to art or craft. Thus, technologies for improving research use must be "people involving."[2] The conversion of data into knowledge is necessarily a human (behavioral) process; no computer can do it alone. We intend to help address certain of these behavioral processes. We begin with an overview of three information-use situations. We then discuss several behavioral processes that need to be addressed in specific research projects. We go on to introduce a set of tools for improving the use of specific research results.

INFORMATION-USE SITUATIONS

There are at least two basic kinds of information managers need to make decisions: instrumental and conceptual. Both are commonly discussed in the research literature.[3]

Instrumental Information Needs

Information is often collected in response to specific needs. It has a direct application to, and thus an explicit role in, decision making. For this reason it is often called "instrumental" information. For example, managers may need to know what product features customers consider most important. This information can be instrumental in guiding specific engineering decisions during product development or in deciding what features to stress in promotional material. This kind of exploratory research is often done in the early stages of product and promotional planning. Confirmatory research, that is, research that verifies whether a particular decision is a sound one, also has a crucial role in decision making, and is usually done in the later stages of the planning process (e.g., whether customers like the way a particular product feature is designed). Such research can be instrumental in fine-tuning the packaging, coloring, or shipping container of a product, deciding whether to include a particular feature, or even launching a new product.

Conceptual Information Needs

The second kind of information need is for background, or "conceptual," information. Background information is collected to enrich the general thinking about an issue rather than to provide a specific solution or to identify alternative actions. For example, managers within the prepared foods industry may want to know what trends are occurring with respect to customers' food preferences. Tracking studies are sometimes done to provide background information about market-changing corporate images and product awareness, and to indicate potential problems. Surveys of buyer spending intentions, analyses of demographic trends, and articles in the professional media about new techniques and practices are additional examples of background information. Background information is always important and at any given time represents most of the information managers have about an issue. In comparison, the information contributed by a new study, while possibly important, may represent only a small part of what a manager knows about a product market he or she has been working in for some time.

The difference between instrumental and conceptual information needs and uses is partly a matter of timing, circumstance, and a manager's perceptions. For example, suppose that a competitor is introducing a new product line that will not compete with yours. This may still be useful background information. It might suggest, for example, that during the time the line is being introduced, the competitor will have fewer resources to promote those lines that do compete with yours. This information will be helpful when you begin to think about your promotional opportunities and budget. Now suppose your firm is considering the addition of the same product line. The information now has a specific use as you select a market niche or time the introduction of your firm's new line. Similarly, one manager may perceive an instrumental use for a research finding, where another manager with different experiences or perspectives may see the information only as helpful background.

Both kinds of information are needed for describing what managers know and do not know. What data are readily available? What data must be obtained? The inquiry center can be helpful in assessing the information and expertise available either within the company or by purchase. It can also be helpful in assessing what managers need to know versus what would simply be nice to know in order to make an effective decision. Finally, inquiry center personnel are frequently asked to give a second opinion, against which to check the consensus opinions of management.

Particularly interesting are those situations where managers have clear ideas in mind but assume, erroneously, that they are shared by others. Hence, they fail to discuss them with others prior to making decisions. Normally this error is discovered only when it is too late to collect clarifying information, or after a survey is completed and disagreements over the interpretation and application of the data have surfaced. Thus, it is important to have information that can identify the absence of fundamental consensus among managers. Once this lack of agreement is understood and discussed, a decision can be made whether or not to collect additional market information to help reconcile the differences.

SEVEN DEADLY OBSTACLES TO THE EFFECTIVE USE OF RESEARCH

To get the most out of information in both situations, it is necessary to manage those behaviors among information users that can lessen the value of research. Typically, the researcher must take the lead. The seven important behaviors that are the most common and serious obstacles to the effective use of specific research findings are related to one another and may surface around the same event.

Post-Survey Regret

This obstacle refers to the regret, following the collection of information, that certain questions were not asked or were not asked differently. (See

Chapter 7 about solving the wrong problem by failing to ask the right question.) It is reflected in such statements as, "I wish we had asked . . . " "Why wasn't 'X' included as a question?" "It's too bad we didn't include . . . " "Why did we bother asking this?" "We should have included 'Y' as a possible response" "It's too bad we didn't use a 'Z' scale instead of . . . " Some post-survey regret is unavoidable. It can, in fact, be a positive sign that some learning has occurred as a result of the study. More often, however, it reflects a failure to think about the use of information early enough in the research process. That is, had we thought about what information we might use to answer one question, we might have realized that it was necessary to ask another one. Significant post-survey regret need only occur a few times, in some cases only once, before managers become discouraged about the potential value of market research.

One way to eliminate many sources of post-survey regret is to simulate the use of information before doing the field work. This prompts thinking about the actual use of information and leads to changes in research methods and instruments which will produce more usable results.

Data-Poor Thinking

There is a tendency to think differently and more richly about an issue when it is illustrated with relevant data (recall David Ogilvy's comments in Chapter 2). This is true even when the "relevant" data are hypothetical or simulated. Thinking without the added stimulus of formal data is poorer than thinking with it; it tends to be less creative and less comprehensive than data-rich thinking. The stimulus to thinking that simulated data provide helps identify important differences in perspectives among managers. By thinking about specific empirical outcomes well in advance of actual findings, managers and researchers are better prepared to interpret final results and can do so more quickly, perhaps shortening the decision time. They are also better prepared to translate research results into specific actions. Thus, the likelihood of doing the right thing and of doing it right is considerably higher when preresearch thinking is data-rich rather than data-poor.

Pseudo-Clairvoyance

This phenomenon is reflected in such statements as, "I could have told you that," "I already knew that," or "That's pretty obvious." The dynamics of pseudo-clairvoyance work something like this: (a) a particular result (e.g., the number of people expressing satisfaction with a product attribute) triggers thinking about what might have caused the result; (b) with the benefit of hindsight, causal factors become more obvious; (c) managers conclude that they would have given these factors much greater weight relative to factors producing other outcomes; and (d) from this they conclude that had they been asked to predict an outcome, they would have correctly given special attention to the factors causing the actual outcome and hence would have correctly predicted it.

Pseudo-clairvoyance, also called hindsight bias, may lead to the conclusion that the research was unnecessary or uninformative, since "It is only telling us what we already know and could have predicted." Controlled experiments with this process show that it is present even in cases with surprising outcomes. Thus, even unexpected results are sometimes dismissed as "hardly surprising at all."

One way of addressing pseudo-clairvoyance is by asking managers to predict important data outcomes. This serves two related purposes. The first is to document for the individual manager the difference between what he or she predicted and the actual outcome, thereby providing a better sense of the value of the research. The second purpose is to be able to calculate the value of individual questions and of the overall project to managers. This is illustrated later in this chapter. The higher the discrepancy among managers' expectations and predictions for a given questionnaire item and the more important that item is, the more valuable are the findings for that particular question to the individual and/or the group. Had the question not been asked of respondents, and had managers used only their "priors" of what the response would be, they would have proceeded on an incorrect assumption and hence possibly chosen the wrong thing to do or the wrong way to do it.

Misunderstanding Comfort Zones

Comfort zones are the expected and acceptable ranges for research findings. For example, a manager might expect that about 50 percent of all respondents will like a certain product feature. If many more than half the respondents dislike the feature, a manager might not feel comfortable with the research results. Such a finding does not ring true with his or her knowledge and experience. The manager's discomfort with these findings calls the research into question. The tendency in such cases is to find out what the source of the error is, for example, an improper wording of the question, a biased sampling plan, and so forth, and to dismiss the result because of the error. Being critical of findings that fall outside a comfort zone can be valuable in some instances and harmful in others. In either case, it is important to understand just how broad or narrow comfort zones are with respect to important research findings. Sometimes the more knowledge or expertise managers have the narrower their comfort zones become. Expertise tends to create a fairly specific expectation and considerable confidence that formal research will yield a result close to that expectation. Thus, an inexperienced manager may expect a "satisfactory" rating between 45 and 55 percent, whereas an experienced manager might expect a rating between 48 and 52 percent.

Knowing whether managers have broad or narrow comfort zones helps researchers decide how to present results. For instance, if a finding falls outside the comfort zone of a key decision maker, the researcher should verify and be prepared to discuss the technical validity of the result. The researcher might also present other evidence supporting the finding. Additionally, by presenting and discussing simulated surprises before the final results are in, the researcher may be able to widen comfort zones. For example, the researcher may determine that a narrow comfort zone exists among key research users and may suspect that an important finding may fall outside it. In this case, the researcher may want to put forth a hypothetical finding outside the comfort zone. This might entail asking users what other evidence they need in order to believe the result or what other questions they need answered in order to understand it. This approach can lead to the collection of additional data which yields more useful information. Exploring an unexpected finding prior to the field work facilitates the use of that information if it actually appears.

It is important for researchers to have a good sense of their clients' comfort zone for another reason. One of the many bases for establishing personal trust between researchers and managers is a manager's knowing that the researcher will not come up with an embarrassing surprise. That is, if there is an unexpected result, the manager knows he or she will be informed privately in advance of any open discussion among other managers. By knowing who might find what to be an uncomfortable surprise, the researcher is better prepared to extend the courtesy of forewarning.

Failure to Perform Action Audits

One of the most common sources of post-survey regret is when research results suggest a novel decision or action but do not provide sufficient data for its evaluation since it had not been anticipated. For example, interviews with hospital purchasing agents suggested a particular shipping container design that management had not contemplated, even though the stimulus for the study was dissatisfaction with delivery problems and the high incidence of damaged goods. Had more thought been given to what might be done with answers to the single question about the containers, more helpful information about improving them might have been obtained. Instead, a follow-up study was required. Thus, it is important to enumerate alternative actions or decisions prior to the design of a questionnaire.

A wide array of possible actions and better information about those possibilities are obtained when managers explicitly consider: (a) the importance of a question, (b) the question's utility in developing an action, and (c) what else is needed in choosing or implementing a decision for a given question to be useful. It is important to elicit, perhaps using simulated results, an array of actions that might be suggested by the research beyond those that have already been identified. The researcher should identify the questions that relate to various actions and the kinds of analyses that will be done with the final data. Managers should then indicate where the data may be insufficient and/or excessive for evaluating these actions.

Unequal-Opportunity Methodologies

An equal-opportunity research methodology is one that gives a bad news answer the same opportunity as a good news answer to show up. An unequal-opportunity methodology favors the good news answer. Unequal-opportunity methodologies are seldom the consequence of a deliberate effort to skew results. More often they are a consequence of not thinking carefully about potential answers, including unwelcomed ones. If an important potential response, welcomed or not, is not anticipated it is not likely to show up in a research project even it if exists in the marketplace. When managers and researchers fail to ask questions that focus on that important response, or fail to word questions in ways that could elicit it, they have to rely on luck to learn about it.

The sources of bias toward particular outcomes are many and varied. A sampling procedure may result in a cluster of people being over- or under-represented, thereby giving incorrect emphasis to their thoughts and practices. Subsequent analyses may not be correct because of this sampling bias. Bias is often found in the design of a questionnaire, and particularly in the wording of the individual questions. Rating scales may use unbalanced anchor labels. At one end may be "very likely," and at the other end, "rather unlikely," which does not allow for people, whose response would be a much stronger "very unlikely," to express the intensity of their feelings.

When unequal-opportunity methodologies surface, it is almost always unintentional. There may be an honest conviction that a particular answer is correct and that therefore all that is necessary is research that verifies the judgment. In this case the research is an insurance policy against the unlikely outcome that the judgment is wrong. The research may be designed adequately to allow the disproof of the judgment, but little or no allowance is made to find out what the alternative answer(s) might be.

For an unwelcomed finding to have a chance of surfacing it has to be anticipated. Sony's announcement in the early 1980s that it would produce an electronic still-image camera was considered bad news at Eastman Kodak. Kodak undertook a study to determine the value in customers' minds of all forms of electronic imaging. Because of the significance of the study, Kodak's CEO, Walt Fallon, became involved and expressed initial skepticism about the ability to make reliable determinations about the importance of electronic imaging to customers. To address this skepticism and to ensure the highest-quality research, about twenty senior technical and planning managers throughout Kodak were involved in a test of the study. One consequence of the test was the raising of an important question: "What impact would electronic video (motion) cameras have on the still photography business?" Because Kodak had gotten out of the amateur motion picture camera business and had seen a drop in the 8mm amateur film business, this question had not been raised initially. The possibility that electronic video could affect the demand for still photography film had not been anticipated. In fact, one of the CEO's concerns was that the study would have a silver halide bias, that is, a bias toward Kodak technology. The inclusion of this and other questions increased everyone's confidence in the study and its value in the decision-making process. The conclusion was reached and accepted that silver halide photography would have a long and healthy future throughout the decade.

A false sense of comfort can occur when research is not done until after important decisions are made. For instance, an advertising agency conducted research to find out which design features of an industrial product were most important to its client's customers, and therefore which features they should stress in promotional pieces. Unfortunately, the research was done long after design commitments had been made. In the survey sample customers were asked to rank the product's features in terms of their relative importance. Months after the new version of the product was introduced it became evident that, with just one exception, the most important features in the minds of R&D personnel were not particularly important to customers. Initially, the agency was blamed for not discovering this. However, senior management of the client firm correctly concluded that its own overconfidence about the importance of the redesigned features kept it from doing evaluative research early enough to make a difference in the actual product design. In fact, the agency had suggested finding out how important, relative to other features, the redesigned features were to customers, but the product management team had asked that the issue be deleted as unnecessary. Management was reminded of this when one of the engineers began to question why the overall importance of the redesigned features was not considered by the agency. In this case, management's certainty that the redesigned features were the most important ones to customers led them to actively preclude opportunities to discover that they were wrong. The agency research director commented: "They were penny wise and pound foolish. They just did not want to pay for the extra 'white space' on the questionnaire. In retrospect we should have paid for this ourselves. It would have changed our copy."

Missing Information and Uncertainty

Doing research is like piecing together a jigsaw puzzle. We never have the time or the funds to position all the pieces, only just enough of them to give us a sense of the true picture. The remaining pieces we fill in from our other knowledge—from facts not formally researched. Such facts are derived from experience as well as from related research. Most information used in the decision-making process is usually derived from these experiences. (In a very technical sense, it is the data that are missing from experience that are usually sought out through formal research.)

Research results are generally evaluated and translated into action based on assumptions about variables not directly addressed by the project. Frequently, these assumptions are not made explicit and they are sometimes the source of conflict about the accuracy, meaning, and use of specific research findings. When not made explicit they are difficult to examine for accuracy or relevance, even though they may be central to a decision. Failure to identify differences of opinion about the missing data early in a research project means that an opportunity to resolve these differences in the formal research effort is lost.

Just as important knowledge is available from other experiences, so, too, some important areas of uncertainty cannot be lessened by either experiential knowledge or knowledge derived from formal research. In these cases managers must act as if they were certain about these issues even when they are not. This uncertainty gets absorbed and is represented by a best guess.

Managers seem to appreciate those researchers who are willing to join them in absorbing uncertainty. It is important to identify early in the research process the areas where uncertainty will likely persist even after formal research and relevant experiences are brought forth. Decision and risk analyses can be made as to whether resources should be (re)allocated to reducing any of these persistent uncertainties, rather than to reducing those uncertainties already being addressed by the planned research. Also, a common understanding between managers and researchers about what uncertainties will remain reduces certain post-survey regrets and better prepares the researcher to deal with the uncertainties when asked to do so. For example, some issues can be pursued in exploratory research that might help interpret data later on, even though these issues could not be pursued in the more formal project.

A TECHNOLOGY FOR IMPROVING KNOWLEDGE USE

We now describe six steps, each of which enhances the utility of a market research project. (The Appendix at the end of this book discusses other current and near-term technologies for implementing the inquiry center concept.) These steps address the seven "deadly obstacles" to effective research use. Although a computer software package is available to facilitate these activities, they can often be carried out simply and with considerable value to the user with a basic calculator. We refer to the bundle of steps as KNOWLEDGE USE©.[4] First, we illustrate the steps by using a survey question posed to patients in a health care facility. We then present the summary results of another application. Each assumes a typical survey questionnaire (only one of several applications for our ideas), developed by researcher–manager discussions and informal reviews of the instrument, and that a team of managers is involved in the decision to be made.

Once a near-final draft of the questionnaire is developed, the researcher selects key items, or questions, and enters them into the KNOWLEDGE USE© package. The researcher then sends a portion of the package to the managers, either through a computer network or simply by giving each a disk. Alternatively, a hard copy of these key items can be sent to managers. The KNOWLEDGE USE© software presents the managers with a simple procedure to follow. Upon completion the managers return the information to the researcher. The researcher then uses a KNOWLEDGE USE© option to summarize the information and to prepare for a meeting with the managers. Again, a hand calculator can suffice. The researcher does not disclose who said what, although he or she will have access to that information.

The following sections discuss the six steps that are central to KNOWLEDGE USE©.

Step 1. Expectations about Results

Each manager receives an information packet from the researcher. It contains certain instructions and the questionnaire items the researcher believes to be most important. The instructions direct the manager to provide the following information with respect to each question.

A. Expected result. The average results managers expect. For example, for a question with a rating scale, each manager indicates what he or she thinks the average rating would be; or, where a "yes" or "no" response is required, the percentage of all respondents he or she expects to say "yes."

B. Comfort zone. The range of results that managers would not find surprising and/or difficult to believe. Each manager indicates the average ratings (by consumers) they think would have an 80 percent chance of turning up by indicating the numbers above or below their prediction that have only a 10 percent chance or less of being obtained. We assume that these points define the managers' comfort zones. With some experimentation more accurate estimates can be made. In fact, it is possible to determine them for each group of users on a project-by-project basis.

C. Significance. Managers are asked to rate the importance of each question. Importance is equated to the significance of their being wrong in their expectations of results. That is, how serious would it be if, in the absence of a research result, managers acted on the basis of their expectation of what the result would be and were wrong?

D. Comments. As they think about each question, managers can record the thoughts that occur to them on a note pad. These comments can be sent electronically to any other person involved in the project.

Step 1 is illustrated in Exhibit 5-1. It concerns one of a larger set of questions that would be asked of patients in a health care facility. Let's assume that the managers of the facility consider this question alone to be highly important. That is, if they prove wrong in their expectations of results, the consequences would be highly significant. In Exhibit 5-1 are the expectations of one of five managers from the corporate staff. This person expected that the average response to the question in the survey would be 2.5, or in the direction of "strongly disagree" on the 7-point scale (A). Moreover, this manager expected that an average response of 1.5 had a 10 percent chance (or less) of being obtained, as did an average response of 4.0. That is, there was an 80 percent chance that the actual average response would be between 1.5 and 4.0, although in expecting a 2.5 he was leaning more toward the 1.5 (B). The two points, 1.5 and 4.0, define this particular manager's comfort zone. He also felt that if he acted on the basis of the average answer he most expected (the 2.5 average), and was, in fact, in error, there would be serious consequences (C).

Exhibit 5-1
Knowledge Use
Step 1: Expectations about Results

It is difficult to find a hospital you can trust.	1 2 3 4 5 6 7 Strongly disagree .... Strongly agree	
A. Expected average response	2.5	
B. Lowest-likely average response	1.5	
Highest-likely average response	4.0	
C. Importance of question (significance of being wrong)	6.0	
D. Note pad		

Step 2. Aggregation of Data

All manager responses in hand, and through the statistics option in KNOWLEDGE USE©, the researcher calculates the amount of consensus (i.e., the variance) among managers with respect to the following information aggregated for all managers.

- The average predicted outcome.
- The expected average upper and lower boundaries (comfort zones).
- The average importance.

Step 3. "Good News," "Bad News," and "Surprise" Simulations of Key Results

The researcher then develops a set of analyses that simulate the final analyses. To the extent possible, these are presented in the format planned for the final report. The analyses are based on the predictions provided by managers and on the nature of the comfort zones. Researcher judgment is used to determine the exact data for the simulation. In presenting alternative results in the simulation, the researcher may be influenced by the knowledge of the individual managers (including their past experience in using research and their frames of reference as revealed in the first two steps) and by his or her own knowledge of the market (including intuition about likely research findings).

Three alternative kinds of results should be simulated: good news, bad news, and surprises. There may be overlap, of course. Sometimes a particularly favorable or unfavorable result is a surprise and other times it is not.

Step 4. Sharing Summary Data

Exhibit 5-2 is an example of the data aggregated for five managers. The first line indicates that the average expected outcome among the five managers was 3.0, in fact, a good deal of consensus. The expected outcomes for each individual manager are shown on the second line of the exhibit. The third line shows that every manager but one felt this to be a very important question. The final line of the exhibit indicates the average comfort zone for all managers. The upper and lower ranges are also provided. Here, one manager thought that a 1.5 average among patients had a 10 percent chance of happening while another manager felt that the outcome above her predicted result of 4.0 that had a 10 percent chance or less of happening was a 5.5.

The researcher meets with the management team and presents in summary form the information the team provided along with simulated alternative results. The researcher says something like the following in order to stimulate discussion:

Exhibit 5-2
Knowledge Use
Step 4: Sharing Summary Data

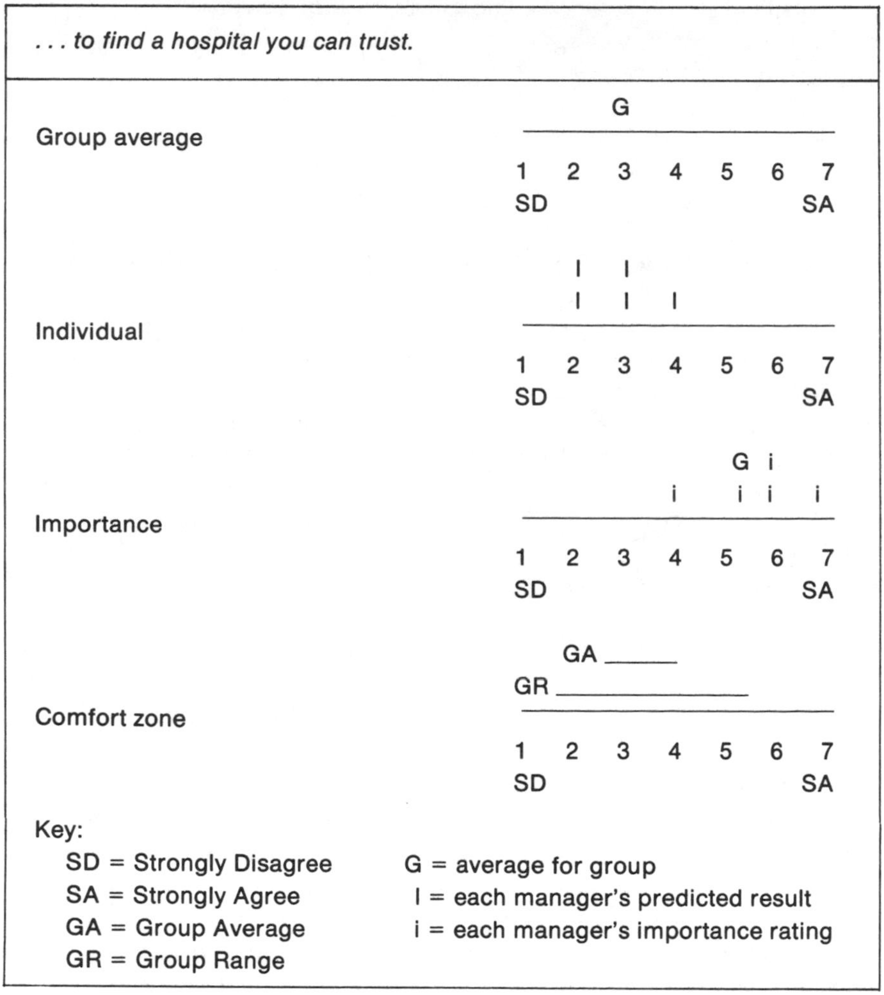

. . . to find a hospital you can trust.

Group average

G
_____

1   2   3   4   5   6   7
SD   SA

Individual

I   I
I   I   I
_____

1   2   3   4   5   6   7
SD   SA

Importance

G   i
i   i   i   i
_____

1   2   3   4   5   6   7
SD   SA

Comfort zone

GA _____
GR _____
_____

1   2   3   4   5   6   7
SD   SA

Key:
   SD = Strongly Disagree   G = average for group
   SA = Strongly Agree   I = each manager's predicted result
   GA = Group Average   i = each manager's importance rating
   GR = Group Range

"As you can see from this chart, there is a wide range of expected outcomes among you on this question. Let's look at the highest prediction. Why would you expect this? Will our information be adequate to explain such a high rating by patients? Can we use this information?"

Similar questions are raised with respect to the lowest-predicted outcome. If there is consensus, the researcher may say something like the following:

"There is strong agreement among you about what patients are going to tell us. Moreover, you are all quite confident that the actual result will very likely be close to your prediction. Why are you so sure? How do you know you know? Should we bother to go ahead and ask this question? How serious would it be if we don't ask this question and if we are way off on our expectations? Is the consequence of being wrong sufficiently serious that we should verify this assumption? Now, what if the average rating patients give us is actually way over here, well beyond what you expect? What else would you want to know before you'd believe it? How useful is this information? What action is suggested? Do you have enough information to evaluate this action?"

To discuss the importance of a question, the researcher may begin with:

"Some of you are saying this is an important question and others feel it isn't. Why might this be important to include? Should we delete it? Is it simply nice to know or is it something we need to know? How does it help us make a decision about what is the right thing to do or how to do it right? Is there some other information we need to collect to make this question more useful?"

Discussions such as these are likely to result in changes in the questionnaire that otherwise would not have been made, thus reducing sources of post-survey regret. A revised questionnaire may then be circulated to managers for a final review.

Step 5. Actual Results

After the data have been collected, analyzed, and shared, each manager receives a printout that shows the average of the actual survey results, the average predicted result for the group, and his or her own prediction. This helps address the issue of pseudo-clairvoyance. Managers also receive information about their own and the group's comfort level (see Exhibit 5-3). It is evident from Exhibit 5-3 that the actual average obtained from the patient survey was just about 4.0, a surprise for all but one of the five members of the management team.

Step 6. Assessing the Value of Information

Managers also receive a printout of the information shown in Exhibit 5-4. A brief interpretive narrative by the researcher should be provided as well. The interpretive narrative is guided by certain propositions:

1. The greater the discrepancy between actual and expected results, the greater the likelihood that an incorrect action might have occurred. In this case a discrepancy of 2.0 for the individual manager in Exhibit 5-4 is significant, given the importance of the question to this manager.

Exhibit 5-3
Knowledge Use
Step 5: Actual Results

```
┌─────────────────────────────────────────────────────────────────┐
│  . . . to find a hospital you can trust.                          │
├─────────────────────────────────────────────────────────────────┤
│                                                                   │
│                                    i  G       A                   │
│                                  ─────────────────────            │
│                                                                   │
│                                  1  2  3  4  5  6  7              │
│                                  SD                 SA            │
│                                                                   │
│                                                                   │
│                                     i _____                    │
│                                      GA _____                      │
│                                   GR _____                │
│   Comfort Zone                   ─────────────────────            │
│                                                                   │
│                                  1  2  3  4  5  6  7              │
│                                  SD                 SA            │
│                                                                   │
│  Key:                                                             │
│      SD = Strongly Disagree      G = average predicted result for group │
│      SA = Strongly Agree         i = each manager's prediction    │
│      GA = Group Average          A = actual survey result         │
│      GR = Group Range                                             │
│                                                                   │
└─────────────────────────────────────────────────────────────────┘
```

Exhibit 5-4
Knowledge Use
Step 6: Assessing the Value of Information

. . . to find a hospital you can trust.		
	Value of Information	
	Individual	Group
Discrepancy	2.0	1.5
Importance (significance of being wrong)	6.0	5.75
Uncertainty (comfort zones)	1.5–4.0	1.5–5.5

2. The greater the variation in expected results among managers, the greater the value of information. Data become useful in resolving differences in perspectives among managers. In this case, there was a reasonable consensus among managers about what the expected result would be, with one person posing an exception. The data were useful in resolving the difference between this person and the rest of the group.
3. The greater the importance of a question or finding (i.e., the greater the significance of acting on a wrong assumption) and/or the greater the variation among managers in assigned importance ratings, the greater the value of simulating final results and the value of auditing possible actions. In this case, the question was considered important by most managers. Hence, it was valuable to ask the question, if only as insurance against acting on an incorrect assumption. The cost of the insurance paid off: Most managers were surprised by the result and had to alter their thinking and the actions they were originally inclined to take.
4. The greater the uncertainty about particular results, the more informative the findings. In this case there was considerable uncertainty about likely outcomes concerning an important question.

What may be far more important than the reduction of the most common sources of post-survey regret is the surfacing and sharing of managerial assumptions about expected outcomes, information utilities, and comfort zones. This is especially important when there is a lack of consensus among managers and an unawareness of it. It is almost certain there will be at least one and probably several items of information (e.g., questionnaire items) where two managers each have a very narrow comfort zone on an important question, where each thinks the other shares essentially the same assumption, and where, in fact, they differ considerably.

In the absence of clarification of assumptions, managers may suggest that a specific question be deleted since it is pretty clear what the answer is going to be, ordinarily a good reason for deleting a question or set of questions. A problem arises when managers are unaware that they differ in their assumptions and hence are likely to differ in their interpretations of the actual data. The important process of absorbing uncertainty brings forth expected outcomes with respect to possible "missing" data. Differences in interpretations of data, or in how they should be translated into specific decisions, may stem from different results being assumed for "missing" data and/or differences in the importance attached to the data.

Another Application

Here we present the summary results of an application of KNOWL-EDGE USE© by Tender Care Learning Centers. This organization, part of Bradford Capital Partners, is a highly regarded child-care organization with

eleven centers in the Greater Pittsburgh area. The center directors and corporate staff are market-based in terms of the children and their parents and
the competitive environment and industrywide trends. They collect information on these topics on a continuous basis. Their most substantial effort to use
the voice of the market is an annual parent satisfaction survey. The survey
identifies changes in the strengths and weaknesses of each center, ways of
addressing these changes positively, and service improvement objectives for
each center.

Exhibit 5-5 contains the responses of a fairly new director to a few of the
nearly fifty issues covered in the survey for her center. Averages for all centers
are shown as well. The first illustration (a) concerns parent perception of each
center director as being trustworthy. The "A" on the second line is the average
for all eleven centers of the actual ratings on this dimension obtained from the
parent satisfaction survey and shows an exceptionally high level of perceived
trust. The "D" is the average ratings predicted by each director for his or her
own center. The "i" on the third line indicates that this director felt this to be
a very important question to have answered. The closer to a seven, the more
important the question. (It does not reflect how important they feel the issue
is to the parent.) The "d" shows the most likely average rating this director
expected parents would give. It is important to recall that this director was
new to the center. The bar line below the rating scale, that is, the comfort
zone, shows that the poorest average rating this particular director expected—
and which would still (if only just) be believed—was 3, whereas the highest
expected, believable rating would be 6. The actual average rating by par-
ents/guardians was 6, as shown by "a." This actual result fell just at the margin
of this person's comfort zone. There was also a considerable discrepancy
between the actual result, "a," and what this director felt was most likely, "d."

The second illustration (b) concerns transportation services. Here we see
that there tended to be a major discrepancy for all center directors on this
dimension, "D" versus "A." The exhibit further shows that this particular
director

• considered this to be important information to have;
• had most expected an average rating of 5;
• was considerably more certain about this prediction than she was about her
  predictions on other questions; and
• found the actual rating of just slightly above 2 to be a major negative
  surprise.

The third illustration concerns another center attribute: inside
space/roominess. This question was not considered as important as the others.
Although the calculation is not shown here, this particular director was considerably more certain of her prediction than was the case for the other
questions, and was, in fact, pretty accurate in making it (the small discrepancy
between the "d" and the "a").

Exhibit 5-5
Parent Satisfaction Survey

a

Using the following 7-point scale, how would you rate the director at this Tender Care Learning Center on

Trustworthiness

| 7 | 6 | 5 | 4 | 3 | 2 | 1 |
Excellent   Poor

Centers' average

    A   D

| — | — | — | — | — | — |
7   1

Center Director

   i

   a   d

| — | — | — | — | — | — |
7   1

Comfort zone   ████████████

b

Please evaluate the following specific characteristic about this Tender Care Learning Center for your oldest child.

Transportation Services

| 7 | 6 | 5 | 4 | 3 | 2 | 1 |
Excellent   Poor

Centers' average

     D   A

| — | — | — | — | — | — |
7   1

Center Director

    i   d   a

| — | — | — | — | — | — |
7   1

Comfort zone   ████████████

Exhibit 5-5 *(Continued)*

c

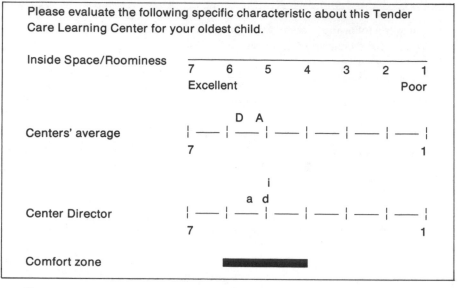

Please evaluate the following specific characteristic about this Tender Care Learning Center for your oldest child.

Inside Space/Roominess

| 7 | 6 | 5 | 4 | 3 | 2 | 1 |

Excellent   Poor

Centers' average

Center Director

Comfort zone

Key:

D = predicted average for all directors
A = actual average for all directors

a = center's actual average
d = center director's predicted average
i = center director's importance rating for the question

Each center director was also provided with three graphs. In one graph, importance and comfort zones were drawn as horizontal and vertical axes and the questions plotted according to where they fell on the graph. One director, for example, was able to see that there were six questions she considered to be especially important (considering the average importance she tended to assign questions in general) and about which she was very certain as to their outcome (relative to her normal level of certainty or uncertainty). She was also able to see that there were twelve questions she believed to be extremely important and whose outcomes she was very uncertain about. The second graph showed her the number of questions for which there were high (low) levels of uncertainty and considerable (minor) discrepancies between actual and expected results. Finally, another graph showed the total number of questions she considered to be of great (minor) importance to ask and for which there were considerable (relatively minor) discrepancies between actual and expected results.

CONCLUSION

The conversion of data into meaningful, believable, and actionable information is a human process, and thus any effort to improve the use of information must focus on human behavior. We described various information-use situations, several major obstacles encountered in making more effective use of information, and a special approach for dealing with these obstacles. An important message emerging from these discussions is that the quality of thinking about a decision after data have been collected is largely determined by quality of thinking before data are collected. Other important aspects of this process are discussed further in Part III.

Notes

1. Martin Weinberger, "Seven Perspectives on Consumer Research," *Marketing Research: A Magazine of Management and Application,* vol. 1, no. 4 (December 1989), pp. 9–17.
2. For a discussion of group decision support systems, see the special issue of *Decision Support Systems: The International Journal,* vol. 5, no. 2 (June 1989). For a discussion of decision support systems in marketing, see John D.C. Little and Michael N. Cassettari, *Decision Support Systems for Marketing Managers* (New York: American Management Association, 1984); and John M. McCann, *The Marketing Workbench: Using Computers for Better Performance* (Homewood, IL: Dow Jones–Irwin, 1986).
3. Robert Rich, *Social Science Information and Decision Making* (San Francisco: Jossey-Bass, 1981).
4. Gerald Zaltman, *Knowledge Use©,* The Joseph M. Katz Graduate School of Business, University of Pittsburgh, and the University Consulting Group in Marketing, 1990.

PART III

COMPETENT CURIOSITY AND PLAYFULNESS

Curiosity is prerequisite to human discovery. The history of science tells us that most fundamental discoveries about the laws of nature were the result of hard work and thought spurred on by human curiosity. Perhaps the best indicators of the current health of a firm's inquiry center are just how curious its managers are about what is happening or likely to be happening in the marketplace and how committed they are to satisfying their curiosity with timely, relevant, accurate, and cost-effective data.

Curiosity has two layers. The first is limited to knowing where the water buckets and exits are in the event of a fire. Most managers are curious in this way. The second layer has a more enduring impact on strategic thinking. It encompasses a need to understand where and why fires may develop; and it lessens the need to use knowledge acquired in the first layer of curiosity. The second layer is the most competent kind of curiosity. It is reminiscent of the old saying, "Give a man a fish and you feed him for a day. Teach him to fish and you feed him for a lifetime."

This second layer of curiosity requires an understanding of our own frames of reference, challenging our assumptions and decision rules, and understanding how we come to believe or reject information. We discuss these issues in Chapters 6, 7, and 8. Chapter 6 is concerned with frames of reference and with the question, "How do we know we know?" Chapter 7 addresses the need to ask the right question the right way. Chapter 8 concerns understanding what we know and what we still need to learn.

All three chapters encourage a certain playfulness, a toying with ideas, and "what-if" speculation. This playfulness is serious business. It is not to be done to look smart or to avoid looking dumb. Just as there are serious consequences for a firm if it is not playful, so, too, are there serious consequences if it is not playful in competent ways. For example, one of the most significant sources of insight in every field is serendipity, that is, fortuitous

135

accidents that reveal information crucial to solving an important problem.[1] Serendipity is a consequence of competent playfulness.

Two observations about serendipity in the diagnosis and solving of problems are especially relevant here. First, it is not the case that some managers, researchers, or scientists are luckier than others in having serendipitous events. Rather, they engage in activities that may bring about more serendipitous events. And, second, the more successful managers have mindsets that are better prepared to find value in serendipitous events than do their colleagues who are experiencing the very same events. What distinguishes the two groups in terms of their mindsets is that one is playful in competent ways, while the other is not.

Note

1. See, for example, Robert Scott Root-Bernstein, *Discovering, Inventing and Solving Problems at the Frontiers of Scientific Knowledge* (Cambridge, MA: Harvard University Press, 1989); Solomon H. Snyder, *Brainstorming: The Science and Politics of Opiate Research* (Cambridge, MA: Harvard University Press, 1989); and Gilbert Shapiro, *A Skeleton in the Darkroom: Stories of Serendipity in Science* (San Francisco: Harper & Row, 1986).

CHAPTER 6

Intelligence: How We Know We Know

Will Rogers once commented that, "It's not what we don't know that gives us trouble. It's what we know that ain't so." Winston Churchill had a related thought: "Men occasionally stumble over the truth, but most of them pick themselves up and hurry on as if nothing happened." Both men raised the intriguing and important question: How do we know we know? That is, how do we make judgments about what is and is not valid or true?

The problem of separating perception in illusion and reality was first articulated by Plato in his *Republic* and remains relevant today, particularly for people inside the halls of government and in boardrooms across the world. As we strive to move closer to reality, our knowledge is based on our understanding of the images or reflections we see. But the systems we rely on today—systems that support decision making, like Plato's cave images—provide no more than a reflection of reality. We begin our discussion of the world of the information provider by focusing on the distinction between *data, information*, and *intelligence*.

Data may take many forms: rumors, forecasts derived from complex mathematical models, intuitive feelings, personal observations, recommendations, opinions, and almost anything else that purports to describe or relate to a past, current, or future situation. Data are representations of reality that may or may not have meaning, accuracy, or believability. When the meanings of data are clear, they are called information. If we do not know what data mean, they are uninformative. Not every meaning or interpretation of data is believable. We may believe a given interpretation is "correct," given the specific data, but we may feel it is wrong for other reasons (past experience, other research, and so forth). For example, we might believe that were certain additional data available, we would make a different interpretation. When a given meaning or message is believed or accepted as true it is called intelligence.

Harold L. Wilensky, in his book *Organizational Intelligence,* refers to intelligence as information—questions, insights, hypotheses, evidence—relevant to policy.[1] He describes high-quality intelligence as information that is

- *clear* because it is understandable to those who must use it;
- *timely* because it gets to them when they need it;
- *reliable* because diverse observers using the same procedures see it in the same way;
- *valid* because it is cast in the form of concepts and measures that capture reality (the tests include logical consistency, successful prediction, and congruence with established knowledge or independent sources);
- *adequate* because the account is full (the context of the act, event, or life of the person or group is described); and
- *wide ranging* because the major policy alternatives promising a high probability of attaining organizational goals are posed or new goals suggested.

Thus, data that have meaning are called information and information that is believable is called intelligence. Intelligence, then, concerns how we form beliefs that something is or is not true. It goes far beyond data. It is concerned with the basic question: "How do we know we know?" For example, how do we know:

- We've asked the right question?
- The data are valid and reliable?
- The correct analysis has been performed?
- We have the appropriate alternative actions?
- What the right decision is and the right way to do it?
- What the important lessons are, given the results of our decisions?

The tests that managers and researchers apply when determining the believability of data are called truth tests, or sometimes reality tests. Truth tests are a part of what are called frames of reference. We discuss truth tests more fully later in this chapter.

FRAMES OF REFERENCE

Frames of reference have three basic components:

- A set of *general assumptions,* that is, what we are willing to take for granted and need not bother testing. One might be an assumption that no technological breakthrough which might alter current R&D planning will occur in the next five years.

- *Decision rules*, that is, our guidelines for responding to different situations. For example, if I know Company A is bidding for the same contract, I will add a penalty clause if we are late on a delivery of materials.
- *Expectations*, that is, the patterns and processes we believe are taking place. Customers are anticipating inflation to increase significantly and thus are willing to increase current consumption of certain durable goods.

Frames of reference reflect our perceptions of the world and serve three very important functions. They influence our orientation toward problems, the way we conceptualize problems, and the kinds of solutions to problems we prefer.

Orientation

Frames of reference cause us to focus on some factors or objects and not others. This is expressed by the law of the instrument: Teach a child to hammer and soon all the world begins to resemble a nail. Managers and researchers have specific research and decision-making approaches. Research issues and corresponding actions concerning customers or competitors are approached with essentially the same model of customer or competitor behavior, even when the uniqueness of an issue or action warrants a different orientation or model.

Once managers or researchers become skilled in using a particular research method, decision tool, action plan, and so forth, they tend to apply their skills as an "instrument" to a wide variety of tasks. A problem arises when the favored approach is inappropriate or when a far better approach is available but ignored. A senior planning executive commented to us:

> People here are in love with [a specific decision tool] and you know what they say: "Love is blind." We'll need to accumulate many more misapplications before [a senior management committee] will entertain some other approaches.

Conceptualizing Problems

Frames of reference help us determine how problems or issues are conceptualized and even whether something is perceived as a problem. For instance, different functional areas using the same data may view customer resistance to a new product differently. Some managers may see it as a marketing problem, others see it as an engineering problem, to others it is a manufacturing problem, and so on.

Frames of reference are self-reinforcing. They cause us to see the things we expect to see (see the law of the lens in Chapter 2).[2] They cause us to avoid cues that create dissonance about our decisions and the perceptions of reality we embrace.[3] Francis Bacon described well the avoidance of disconfirming, dissonance creating information:

> When any proposition has been laid down, the human understanding forces everything else to add fresh support and confirmation. It is the peculiar and perceptual error of the human understanding to be more moved and excited by affirmative than negative.[4]

It is useful to periodically examine our preferences for particular concepts and the assumptions that we bring to a situation. Failure to recognize these assumptions ultimately leads to the familiar "convenient-light" syndrome:

> Late one evening a policeman comes upon a young man who is down on his knees feverishly searching under a light post. The policeman asks what he is looking for. He replies that he has lost his wallet. The policeman inquires where he last had it. The young man replies that he purchased some flowers from a vendor about a half a block away. "Why not look there?" the policeman responds. Questioningly, the young man looks up and says, "The light is better here."

The convenient-light syndrome is a source of difficulty for managers and researchers alike. Still, there were a few instances reported in our interviews for this book where decision makers took the important first step of confronting their own orientations before addressing a significant issue.[5] Many more instances, but still not a lot, were reported in which this was done as a postmortem to a major issue that was not handled well. The inertia that inhibits reexamination of critical assumptions is widespread. One of the nation's leading consultants in this area described a recent experience in which she and her colleagues were helping a senior management group prepare to make a major decision. One of the executives commented, after a particularly difficult but successful exercise, that the consultant's staff must go through this "energy draining" effort a lot with regard to their own consulting approach.

> There was an embarrassing silence in which everyone realized that we didn't often practice what we preach. It was a classic case of the shoemaker's children going barefoot. Like our clients, we get so caught up in the operational issues of our business—helping them explore their frames of reference—that it is difficult to take the time to critically appraise our own approach. We have taken steps to correct that.

Determining Possible Solutions

Frames of reference may also determine the kinds of solutions we find acceptable and the methods we consider appropriate in seeking them. Two contrasting examples illustrate how frames of reference determine solutions. The first involves the "not-invented-here" syndrome in which ideas, recommendations, or decisions perceived as originating outside the company (or division or department) are systematically rejected.

The not-invented-here syndrome has many causes. It assumes that an outsider, often a consultant or research firm, cannot possibly know a firm's or manager's situation well enough to be able to develop a workable solution. Another cause is that those inside the organization may feel threatened by the fact that an outsider, who knows their situation less well, came up with a solution that eluded them.

There is also the need to feel ownership of an idea in order to feel comfortable with it. A sense of ownership is harder to develop when the idea originates elsewhere. Seasoned consultants and researchers do not seem to object to managers taking credit for their ideas. Many consultants commented on this issue, saying, in effect, "You must be prepared to forgo all rights of authorship or ownership with regard to your ideas if you want to be successful in this business." Research personnel in advertising agencies and research provider organizations often describe their job as one of "making the client's brand managers look good."

Furthermore, there is the occasional practice of withholding information from a research report so that it can be presented to superiors as one's own idea. When questioned about this, managers we interviewed indicated that they needed to show they are adding value; that is, they are coming up with special ideas which at least appear to be theirs and are not merely acting as conduits between their superiors and the research staff.[6]

The second example involves the "hard-to-be-a-prophet-in-your-own-land" phenomenon. Here ideas, recommendations, decisions, and other kinds of solutions are perceived as more credible because they originated elsewhere. People we interviewed in a wide variety of organizations gave many illustrations of this. For example, research reports provided by outsiders are sometimes given more serious attention than had they been developed by an internal group, which might be perceived as furthering its own special agenda. This is symptomatic of a lack of trust between researchers and managers. As we will discuss shortly, this absence of trust can have a significant impact on the research effort. Other examples were mentioned where outside consultants were brought in to introduce an idea that a manager knew would have trouble getting accepted because it would be perceived as his or her own idea. In other instances, an idea gets serious attention only after a competitor picks up on it.

The not-invented-here and hard-to-be-a-prophet-in-your-own-land syn-dromes reflect biases toward solutions based on the origin of the solutions. Sometimes, of course, these biases are warranted. For example, outsiders may lack the requisite knowledge for an effective decision, and insiders may pursue agendas that are self-serving. It is because these biases are sometimes war-ranted that they may persist.

Frames of reference influence the methods and approaches that lead to solutions for problems. Our frames of reference determine the criteria we use for assessing validity and reliability. Many readers will be familiar with certain statistical procedures or tests used to assess traditional market research data. While these are important, we cannot address them here. However, if the technical validity and reliability of a part of a study fails to pass these tests, the entire effort may be disregarded.

THE TWO-COMMUNITIES METAPHOR

The idea that researchers and managers represent different cultures or "knowledge" communities has been suggested to explain why research is often used poorly by managers. It suggests that managers and researchers have sufficiently different training, reward systems, experiences, languages, and so on, that their ability to work together is impaired. Social scientists use the term "social construction of reality" to explain this phenomenon.[7] While there is some truth to this, the reverse is also true: Differences can enhance the use of information in decision making. The two communities are most likely to enrich one another when they understand, respect, and to some extent can accommodate each other's frame of reference. However, insularity or even a kind of xenophobia, the fear of strangers, can arise between the two cul-tures—making cooperation difficult. To lessen these problems research pro-viders must

- understand the user's big picture, that is, their information needs and the underlying reasons for those needs;
- understand the uses and limitations of data and data analysis and be able to explain these strengths and weaknesses in terms the user can understand;
- involve users early and during every step of the knowledge acquisition and utilization process;
- ensure broad awareness by establishing a forum for users and potential users of information; and
- learn to communicate in the language of the user and develop an under-standing of the constraints under which the user operates.

On the other hand, users of information need to

- accept the fact that getting and properly using information requires hard work, up front and through every step of the process, and that there are no shortcuts;

- make the effort to learn about the difficulties and the general aspects of gathering useful and adequate information;
- encourage providers of information to become part of the user team without delegating policy-related aspects of the information gathering and analysis; and
- plan ahead for information needs. Last-minute requests usually get what they deserve—inaccurate, untimely, irrelevant, and difficult-to-use information.

The Interrelation of Aims, Facts, Methods, and Problems

Both managers and researchers have certain, and frequently different, assumptions, expectations, and decision rules about

- appropriate research methodologies;
- appropriate purposes (e.g., to forecast, explain, or manipulate an event) for undertaking research;
- what constitutes a "fact"; and
- what constitutes a problem (e.g., why it is necessary to explain, forecast, or manipulate an event) requiring research in the first place.[8]

These influence one another, as shown in Exhibit 6-1. Depending on whether we want to explain or simply predict an event, we may prefer one methodology over another and consider some facts as more important than others.

Exhibit 6-1
The Interaction of Aims, Methods, Problems, and Facts

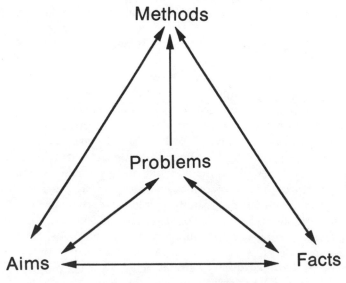

What we are even willing to consider as a fact may influence the methods we use. The elements, as illustrated in Exhibit 6-1, are thus linked via frames of reference. Managers and researchers may also differ in what they consider to be appropriate methods, aims, facts, and problems for a given event. The following experience was related by a product manager of a major food firm.

She was concerned about offering a cents-off coupon as a repurchase incentive. She was an experienced manager and so knew a great deal about customers and the situational factors affecting their use of coupons. Her basic question concerned the minimum incentive required to encourage repeat use. A journal article by an academic researcher on the subject was brought to her attention. The article emerged from research on the role of incentives in customer decision making, but that research did not involve the product class or use situation. The researcher had used a laboratory experiment involving student subjects. This was appropriate given the researcher's aim to understand the cognitive processes elicited by incentives. The manager, however, was concerned with the specific context in which an incentive might be appropriate. The motivations of the researcher and the product manager were different. One was intrigued by a basic process with general implications; the other was interested in a specific manifestation of the same process in a specific context. Moreover, the researcher was concerned with explaining behaviors while the manager was concerned with predicting and controlling them. They also differed in their methods. The manager would have preferred using a representative sample of actual customers. Each made different assumptions about the nature of facts relating to incentives. Additionally, the researcher had construed the problem as a closed system in which many things were held constant, while the manager operated in an open system where many things were happening at once. The researcher strongly believed his results; the manager questioned their validity as far as her purposes were concerned.

The range of possible researcher/manager interactions are illustrated in Exhibit 6-2. To reap the benefits of the different frames of reference and thinking used by managers and researchers, it is necessary to go from the adversarial situation implied in the example above (a) to the more amicable situation (b), and beyond that to synergy (c). A synergistic relationship suggests that with a sensitivity to their own and others' views of reality, researchers and managers may enrich the perspectives beyond those that each ordinarily brings to the table. When thinking and methodologies intersect, the separate structures are still visible, but there is a new overall structure. The new structure, the star, provides managers and researchers with a window through which to observe their prior frames of reference (a). Their respective assumptions and realities are no longer seen in isolation. This does not necessarily lead to or require the adoption of new methods, aims, or criteria for assessing evidence, but it does increase an appreciation of the similarities and differences between the two groups. This appreciation provides a common ground for making effective use of information.

Exhibit 6-2
Manager/Researcher Interactions

a. Adversarial Relationship between Manager and Researcher
Reflecting Xenophobic Cultures

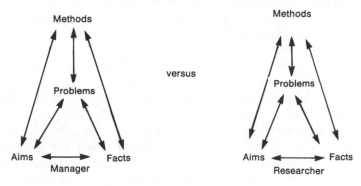

versus

Manager

Researcher

b. Cooperative Relationship between Manager and Researcher
Reflecting Amicable Cultural Contact

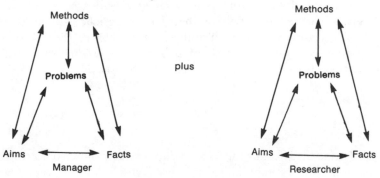

plus

Manager

Researcher

c. Synergistic Relationship between Manager and Researcher
Reflecting Consistent and Compatible Culture

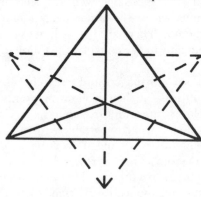

Solid Line = Manager
Dotted Line = Researcher

TRUTH TESTS: THE REASONS WE REACH THE
CONCLUSIONS WE DO

Frames of reference also determine how we react to new information. As young children we receive and process the information that comes our way in an unbiased, naive manner. Only as we become older, more experienced, and more complicated do we develop a particular frame of reference, and weigh information based upon its source and content. A humorous example of this is the way most adult Americans react to the statement: "I'm from the government, and I'm here to help you." We in business could easily substitute "central office" for government.

An important set of decision rules are called truth tests, or sometimes reality tests. Truth tests are guidelines used for assessing the accuracy of a particular experience or observation. They also influence the kinds of data that are collected, how they are collected, and how they are interpreted and acted upon. For example, some marketing managers distrust sales force opinions about customer needs, whereas others, even in the same firm, find such information accurate and rely on it heavily. The former group will seek information directly from customers to a far greater degree than will the latter. Many managers rely heavily on their own experience and make little use of formal, quantitatively oriented studies, while others do the reverse; still others rely extensively on both sources of insight. We now turn to a discussion of personal trust, before considering specific truth tests.

Personal Trust

Of all the factors affecting the relationship between knowledge providers and users, none is more important than trust. Trust is a condition between people, or even companies, that reflects the extent to which they can predict each other's behaviors; can depend on one another when it counts; and have faith that the other will act responsibly even in uncertain situations.[9] Trust develops out of situations where the other party could have acted in an unacceptable way but did not. There are many dimensions of trust and ways of developing and maintaining it. We consider the following to be paramount.

Being a team player. Effective managers and researchers know when to be "a team player" and when to dig in their heels over points they feel strongly about. Being a team player often requires that researchers go along with managerial actions they do not feel comfortable with but are not judged to be harmful to the firm. This does not mean winking at the misuse or misinterpretation of information. When a researcher believes data are being misused he or she needs to say so explicitly. However, when it is not clear that a particular interpretation or application is right or wrong, the researcher should say, "Okay, but let's understand that the validity of this use of data isn't clear." To make such judgments, the researcher needs to be familiar enough with the firm to know when a particular use of research will or will not have serious consequences. Being a team player may mean sacrificing some methodological or interpretive norms so a client can meet a product deadline. A researcher's flexibility in responding to special client needs is a quality appreciated by managers. Flexibility makes the researcher more credible in those situations in which he or she must draw the line, when it is necessary to dispute a use of information or when a task must be declined because sufficient time is not available to do it properly.

When researchers always demand that exactly the right thing be done regardless of cost and time, managers rightfully question their team spirit. On the other hand, managers distrust someone who is always willing to compromise his or her values, ideas, or training to meet client demands. More trust is established when a researcher takes a firm stand on the important issues. Researchers must be sincere in their attempts to help clients yet secure in their opinions about the use of a particular piece of research. Balancing these two postures is not always easy. As one researcher put it:

> The dilemma is that if you always dig in your heels and fight for your ideas you are considered arrogant and foolish. However, if you constantly back off when the client challenges one of your ideas you're considered a pushover. You need to know when to cry "Wolf!" and when not to.

One constructive way researchers address the issue is to provide users with what they see as the potential positive and negative consequences of alternative uses of information.

Being a truth teller. Honesty is a necessary ingredient in building trust. Researchers, in particular, feel the need to be honest with their clients by "showing all the cards" even if they are not all positive. As one researcher stated, "You've got to be a truth teller. You just can't play politics. Once you've got a reputation for being a truth teller you've got it made in terms of having your research accepted."

In our interviews, people from advertising agencies and from client companies acknowledged that they withhold information from one another. Not surprisingly, each party believes the other holds back more data more often—a reflection of a basic lack of trust in these relationships. One reason that agency people do not share all research with their clients is that clients often jump prematurely on a particular finding in exploratory research, thereby inhibiting the agency's thinking about an issue. Likewise, managers may not share how they used information provided by the researcher or obtained elsewhere if they have interpreted the research in a biased way. Moreover, when managers do not feel they can trust researchers to support their research agendas or interpretations, they may refrain from asking for research or from using it when available.

Two factors, among others, affect the ability of researchers to be truth tellers. First, as suggested earlier, when a user perceives the researcher to be acting in the company's best interests, even when presenting bad news, trust in the researcher increases. Second, when research departments have a discretionary research budget or are otherwise less dependent on a few internal clients for their funding, they can be more independent in making judgments. Independence increases the researchers' inclination to act more in line with overall corporate interests, to be more honest with clients, and to present bad news. This budgetary arrangement indirectly fosters independent, honest, and trusting relationships between researchers and managers.

Mutual understanding. A common understanding between researchers and users with respect to each other's needs, abilities, and goals is essential to a trusting relationship. It helps both parties set more realistic boundaries on what they expect of one another and therefore increases the likelihood that they will perceive one another as predictable and dependable. This understanding is achieved best when researchers are in physical proximity to users. Proximity allows researchers to develop better personal rapport with users and therefore to feel a larger stake in the user's performance. Proximity also increases researcher familiarity with the marketing problems, which, in turn, creates more focused and relevant research and a more realistic basis for interpreting data. Unfortunately, many organizations do not have internal research staffs, or those staffs are spread so thinly that they cannot develop close relationships with their internal clients.

Another factor that improves understanding between researchers and managers is having experience in one another's jobs. When researchers have had line experience and/or managers have had research experience their ability to empathize with the other increases.

Creating this situation is difficult, however. Some firms arrange for managers to have a limited assignment in the company's research department. But since some research activities require very specific technical skills, this is often not practical. In some instances, firms such as Polaroid and Gillette try to have the appropriate mix of experiences by assigning researcher and manager roles to people who have had both kinds of experiences. Researchers at Eastman Kodak, Procter & Gamble, and Westinghouse, for example, make a "canned" presentation whenever a new manager arrives. This is a private presentation about market research techniques and what market research can and cannot do. Depending on the manager's initial research knowledge, the presentation may vary from a single half-hour session to several sessions over a period of a few months.

Managing bad news. The ability to manage bad news is central to the development of trust between researchers and managers. Strangling the messenger of bad news is no longer fashionable, but the emotion behind that practice persists. Researchers need a special sense of etiquette for communicating findings that do not meet with managers' expectations or that could be embarrassing for them. Managers agree that if they cannot count on their research team's sensitivity when it has discovered bad news, the researchers are less trusted.

Bad news management has four requirements. First, and perhaps most important, is the researcher's ability to present constructive ways of responding to bad news. The impact of the news can be softened if researchers can suggest viable strategies for coping with the problem. Second, the worse the news, the greater the need for researchers to balance it with whatever good news is available. Most research projects of any scope have several findings, many of which support expectations, identify attractive decision options, and verify the appropriateness of past decisions. Care should be taken to bring these findings forward. Third, the more significant the bad news, the greater the need to develop valid explanations of the findings. People are as capable of learning from failure as from success. An explanation of why reported data reveal unexpected results helps managers feel they are being given greater insight, not just data.

Finally, it is necessary to be prepared to defend the validity and reliability of the bad news. Social psychologists have always known that people's first inclination is to reject information that does not conform to preconceived notions. In 1978, a comprehensive study of the "reprographics" market was conducted by the Xerox Corporation. This was the first time since the company's founding that an attempt had been made to measure the entire market. Because of the complexity of the study, the fact that it was the first one, and the anticipated impact of the results, considerable effort was made to ensure that the results would be carefully analyzed, and its challenges to existing market assumptions explained (see Exhibit 6-3). Notice how the five functions of market research were employed in the study:

- *Assessment of market information needs* was carried out through the development of critical market planning questions (CMPQs, item B2). Active involvement by relevant management was assured by the creation of the Research Utilization Group (RUG) and an understanding that senior management would review and approve the work of the group (items B1, B2, A1, and A2).
- *Measurement of the marketplace* was handled by the market research function. It involved itself early in the determination of critical questions (item C1).
- *Storage, retrieval, and display of data* were facilitated by having an understanding of the type of questions that would be asked as well as the types of individuals who would be doing the asking.
- *Analysis and description of market data* were facilitated by the ability to

Exhibit 6-3
Flowchart of Xerox Reprographics Market Study

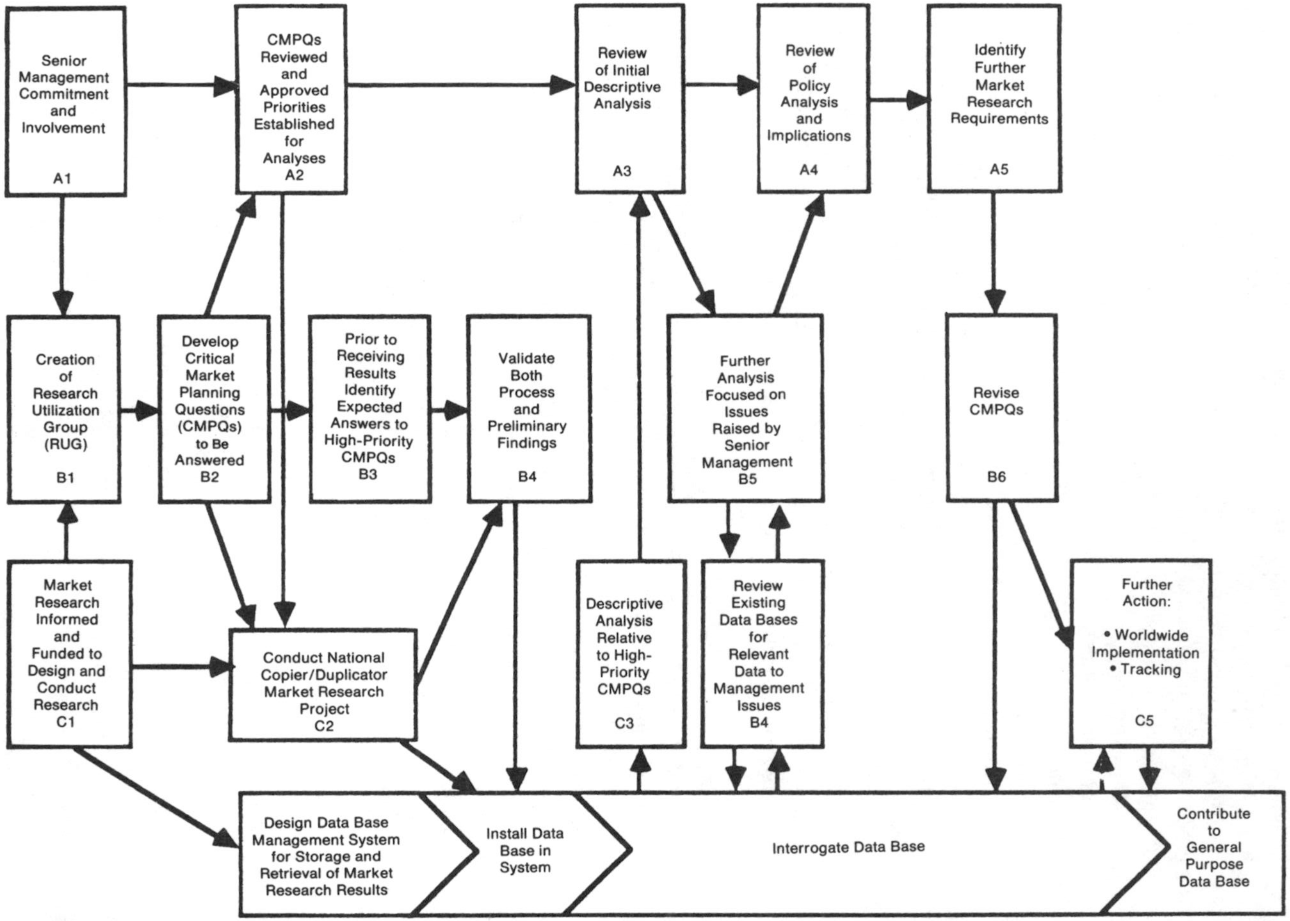

review preliminary findings in the context of expected results.
- *Enhancement and assessment of market information value* were facilitated by comparing what was found with what was accepted, and contrasting those findings with prior estimates (items B2 and B3). The findings were of high value because they were significantly different from existing estimates—and were accepted and acted on by management.

Before the results were available, the Research Utilization Group agreed on a set of critical market numbers that represented its best estimate of the level of reprographic activity in those areas that would need to be compared to actual study results.

The results of the study made it clear that many assumptions about the size of the market, and assumptions that were supporting new product and existing programs, had been overstated—in some segments by a factor of two.

As might be expected, there was concern that the dramatic differences between the study results and the existing planning assumptions would lead to at least two negative outcomes: The results would not be believed, and the careers of those involved could be hurt. Initially, the RUG toyed with the notion that to gain credibility, it should modify the study results to the level where they would still have an impact but not show the extent to which the current assumptions were erroneous. Given the impact of the findings on the future of the company, that notion—to get within the comfort zone of management—was quickly discarded.

Fortunately, at the time of the study, Xerox leased virtually all of its copiers; therefore, it knew the extent to which each copier was being used. Since this information was the basis of the Xerox billing system, management generally accepted the results of that data base. The Research Utilization Group did a comparative analysis of the two data sets and was able to demonstrate that both sets generated estimates of Xerox equipment and volumes that were substantially identical. Armed with this corroborative evidence, the research director, after background meetings with influential senior managers, presented the study results to Xerox's executive management committee, which had been prepared to hear some bad news. Management not only accepted the results, but directed product and market planning management to review the process that developed the existing estimates and to determine the source of the differences.

Managers and researchers agree on the importance of giving advance warning of bad news. One researcher told us: "You should show a draft of the research memo to decision makers first. This approach does run the risk of appearing to be a pushover, but you are also showing that you aren't going to surprise and embarrass decision makers." When this is done managers have an opportunity to work with researchers to present results in a less dramatic but still truthful way, and have time to think about constructive responses. The result is less effort by managers to discredit the validity of bad news.

Absorbing uncertainty. Another factor relates to trust in an indirect but important way: a researcher's ability to absorb uncertainty. It is rare when a formal research study provides all of the information needed for important decisions. A truly comprehensive research effort may not be feasible, because of budgetary reasons, time constraints, methodological limitations, and the inherent difficulty of researching particular questions. The research itself may uncover but not clarify important issues. Also, every research approach has limitations, particularly with respect to how the data can be analyzed and interpreted. For these reasons, pockets of uncertainty remain after research results are in hand. In fact, the more important an issue or decision, the more likely it is that important uncertainty will remain.

Trust is essential in these situations. Some researchers have a special ability to "fill in the blanks" where data are missing and to be quite accurate in their assumptions about what the missing data would have looked like had they been acquired. A researcher's ability to absorb uncertainty rather than pass it along to managers in the form of qualifications and reservations is a valuable one. Research findings often fall into a gray area, where, by themselves, they neither endorse nor reject unequivocally a particular proposition. They must be used along with other kinds of information in decision making. Thus, a researcher's ability to act with confidence in an atmosphere of ambiguity is a virtue. There is an intuitive process involved in going beyond specific research findings or analyses. For researchers this intuitive sense derives from other research experiences, particularly developmental and exploratory research projects. Managers, too, absorb uncertainty by augmenting research data with other information. Experienced managers draw heavily on their product market knowledge, which is based partly on other formal research studies. Most of it, however, is based on an array of learning experiences in similar situations.

One kind of intuition that some researchers seem to be adept at using merits special comment here. In the process of developing and pretesting research instruments, and in analyzing data, certain feelings and special insights emerge about the data and the issues they address and go beyond specific analyses or observations. These feelings and insights often suggest that new analyses with the data should be done. It is the same kind of feeling and insight that an expert on Aristotle would draw upon in describing how that philosopher would respond today to an issue that did not exist in ancient times—genetic engineering, for example. It is the same kind of insight used by a subordinate who knows her superior well enough to anticipate how that superior would respond to a problem that has never before surfaced.

Because managers must act as if data are clearer than they often are, they depend on researchers who are willing to go beyond the data. When managers find they must extrapolate from research or use their reflected experience to make decisions, they need both the guidance and the intellectual company of their researchers. Researcher guidance in these situations enhances the likelihood of making the right decision; and the companionship researchers provide leads to a sense of team effort and—occasionally—to a basis for a future sharing of blame. In either case, when researchers can help absorb some of the uncertainty about an important issue, managers feel they can depend on them.

Tradition

A traditional truth test is one that uses past experiences and beliefs to determine the validity of a current observation or experience. In reviewing the results of a market research study, a manager using a traditional reality test might ask:

1. Are the results consistent with what we've learned in the past?
2. Are the results compatible with existing policies and practices, or do they indicate that a major change in philosophy, organization, or marketing programs is needed?
3. Were research procedures used that meet established standards and requirements?

Traditional truth tests represent an effort to imitate what has gone before. This does not mean that new ideas are not accepted. Rather, they are accepted as long as they do not fly in the face of existing ideas and values. In fact, traditional truth tests can be applied in highly creative ways to show that a particular methodology or finding is, in fact, compatible with existing ideas and values.

Problems sometimes arise when researchers and managers have different opinions about research methods. This is often a source of conflict between advertising agencies and clients. Agencies, on the whole, are comfortable with a wide array of qualitative and quantitative techniques. Many client firms, on the other hand, rely on more conventional quantitative survey research methodologies. Different preferences for methodologies can create serious barriers to believing research results unless there is a high level of trust between the organizations.

Authority

The acceptance of information is often based on who has collected, analyzed, or endorsed it. When researchers and consultants are well known for a distinctive expertise, their findings are more believable. Many firms will pay a premium to have a particular research organization do a project because they trust that firm and its methods.

Some managers pay little attention to the actual data and almost no attention to how they were collected. They assume the data are accurate simply because of the researcher's authority and technical competence. In these instances, managers claim they can focus their attention on the interpretation of data and the development of actions.

Another authority test is involved when a firm blindly adopts the new strategy of a market leader without either waiting to see how well that strategy works or questioning its appropriateness for them. One manager remarked, "The best way to get an idea adopted here is to say, 'The Japanese are doing it!'"

Consensus

Consensual truth tests rely on group opinion to determine what is or is not true. Here what most people agree is true and/or accurate is taken as the final judgment.

Since consensual truth tests do not draw heavily on empirical or rational criteria, they are difficult for an individual to challenge. This is not to say that the consensus that develops may not be based on empirical data or is not the result of a rational decision process. Rather, it is the existence of consensus that forms the basis for belief. Prevailing opinion becomes accepted truth. A process known as "groupthink" sometimes emerges in which there is a rapid development of consensus which does not tolerate alternative perspectives. The group's frame of reference becomes inflexible and self-confirming. Usually one group member assumes the informal role of "mind guard" and may viciously put down alternative views to the point of discouraging them altogether.

Individual managers are understandably reluctant to oppose consensus decisions. If their contrary position is accepted and fails, the entire blame falls on them, perhaps with a vengeance, since they disagreed with the thinking of their peers. When a consensus decision fails, however, no individual is made the scapegoat. There is safety in numbers. If a manager or researcher successfully challenges the weak consensus and prevails with an alternative action, he or she will receive some credit if it is successful. Since the group endorsed the alternative action, it, too, receives some of the credit, if not the lion's share. If the alternative action is unsuccessful, the manager or researcher gets most of the blame. Therefore, individuals are reluctant to challenge a weak consensus, and there is the appearance of strong group support for an action since few if any alternatives are considered seriously.

Rationality

Rational truth tests typically assess data in terms of consistency. People who use rational truth tests believe that reason and logic alone are sources of knowledge superior to, and independent of, actual empirical observations. When presented with a research report, a person who stresses rational truth tests will focus on the internal consistency of its arguments. Do the conclusions logically follow from the initial assumptions? Are the concepts included comprehensive? Are they related in a consistent manner? Are findings from related yet different research projects consistent with one another? Do the findings of a given project tell a coherent story? Managers often evaluate surprising results in terms of their logical consistency with unsurprising results. The more logical a surprise finding is, and the more compatible it is with those data that are consistent with expectations, the more believable the surprise.

Aside from being organized and persuasive, it is important that research be presented in a manner consistent with how managers process and use information. This, too, is part of a manager's rationality. Some managers prefer extensive analyses; others do not. Some managers are more comfortable with "pictures" of data rather than numbers. If the presentation can be tailored to meet the individual needs and capabilities of the audience, its believability increases. As one advertising agency researcher suggested:

> Client trust is won through a two-step process. First, you need good interpersonal skills in preresearch consultation. Second, you need to do a good job presenting the results. A problem here is that clients are often not sophisticated enough to appreciate a good presentation.

Empirical Experience

Empirical truth tests rely directly on experience or observation to determine if something is true. Examples are found among the standardized set of methodologies used by the scientific community, such as tests of internal and external validity, procedures for random sampling, establishing control groups, and so forth. There is great concern for controlling for possible biases; the manner in which an "observation" is collected, analyzed, or interpreted becomes paramount. Debate usually centers on whether a method was used in the correct way or if it was the correct one to use in the first place. There is also greater reliance on quantitative rather than qualitative data. Criticisms of the results of a study are likely to focus on deficiencies in method rather than on deficiencies in logic.

Pragmatism

Pragmatic truth tests are based on the belief that the meaning of information is to be sought in its impact on actual practice. Their chief function is to guide action, and their validity is tested by their practical consequences. Internal logic and the application of the scientific method are secondary to the action implications of using a particular research result in everyday practice. For example, people employing pragmatic reality tests use the following questions as criteria in assessing the truth and usefulness of research results:

• Does the study analyze the effects of factors that decision makers can do something about?

- Is the study targeted; that is, does it focus on a narrow set of factors?
- Does the study contain explicit recommendations?
- Do these recommendations have direct implications for a course of action?
- Do the results add to a practical knowledge of the operation of current or future policies and programs?[10]

Interactions among Truth Tests

Truth tests are seldom used in isolation. Just as different research methods are used to get convergent validity, so, too, are multiple truth tests. The larger the number, and the more tests a judgment or idea satisfies, the more confident a manager is in that judgment. This does not mean that all truth tests have equal importance or weight. Usually one will have greater importance than others, and interpretations and actions that do not pass may be rejected even before other tests are applied.

It is helpful when making a research presentation or writing a report to take into account the most likely truth tests to be used by a client, especially when the "client" consists of several managers. This approach should never alter the content of a presentation, but if the researcher anticipates the truth test–related questions managers are likely to ask, he or she is more credible. This may seem obvious, but frequently researchers are more prepared to answer questions about methodology than truth test questions, and these may be the ones that truly matter. Managers, on the other hand, rarely ask methodology questions—assuming that researchers know what they are doing—but instead focus on truth test questions.

We can predict fairly well when certain truth tests are likely to be used. When the focus is on the source of information—who provided the information—traditional, authoritative, and rational truth tests will most likely be used. If the focus is on the consequences—what did or will happen—consensual, empirical, and pragmatic tests are favored. Certain truth tests are more likely to be used when clients are more concerned with learning why something has occurred (to create new skills, insights, and so forth) or with applying what they already know. Exhibit 6-4 identifies the truth tests most closely associated with different research purposes, together with those associated with source or consequence concerns.

Exhibit 6-4
Typology of Truth Tests

	Source	Consequences
Application	Traditional Authoritative	Consensual
Learning	Rational	Empirical Pragmatic

CONCLUSION

Frames of reference are viewing lenses for describing, explaining, predicting, and controlling events. They consist of assumptions, expectations, and decision rules and influence what we consider to be legitimate facts, appropriate methods, appropriate research aims, why we consider an event to be a problem, and how we structure that problem. Our frames of reference are heavily influenced by our position in an organization. For this reason different functional areas and staff positions may have different ways of viewing market events. Consequently, an important task for managers and researchers is to understand these differences, take advantage of the additional insights they provide, and use the voice of the market to resolve them.

Frames of reference contain the truth tests managers and researchers use when evaluating the accuracy of data, their interpretation, and application. Usually multiple truth tests are used, although one may have special prominence. As the number of people involved in a decision increases, so does the variety of truth tests used. Researchers should anticipate these truth tests so that they can provide meaningful answers or responses to managers.

Notes

1. Harold L. Wilensky, *Organizational Intelligence: Knowledge and Policy in Government and Industry* (New York: Basic Books, 1967), Chapter 2.
2. Gerald Zaltman, "Presidential Address," in Richard P. Bagozzi and Alice M. Tybout, eds., *Advances in Consumer Research*, vol. 10 (Ann Arbor, MI: The Association for Consumer Research, 1983), pp. 1–5.
3. Leon Festinger, *A Theory of Cognitive Dissonance* (New York: Row, Peterson, 1957), p. 3.
4. Francis Bacon, cited in Festinger, *A Theory of Cognitive Dissonance*, p. 31.
5. Ian I. Mitroff, Ralph Kilmann, and Vincent P. Barabba, "Management Information versus Misinformation Systems," in Gerald Zaltman, ed., *Management Principles for Nonprofit Agencies and Organizations* (New York: AMACON, 1979), pp. 401–432.
6. Rohit Deshpande and Gerald Zaltman, "Factors Affecting the Consumption of Market Research: A Path Analysis," *Journal of Marketing Research*, vol. 19 (February 1982), pp. 14–31.
7. Burkart Holzner and John Marx, *Knowledge Application: The Knowledge System in Society* (Boston: Allyn and Bacon, 1979); and Gerald Zaltman et al., *The Construction in Marketing: Some Thoughts on Thinking* (New York: John Wiley, 1982).
8. Gerald Zaltman and Christine Moorman, "Sharing Models of Inquiry," in Elizabeth C. Hirschman and Morris B. Holbrook, eds., *Advances in Consumer Research*, vol. 12 (Provo, UT: Association for Consumer Research Conference Proceedings, 1985), pp. 312–314.

  9. Gerald Zaltman and Christine Moorman, "The Importance of Personal Trust in
     the Use of Research," *Journal of Advertising Research*, vol. 28, no. 5 (1988), pp.
     16–24.
 10. Carol H. Weiss and Michael J. Bucuvalas, "Truth Tests: Decision-Makers'
     Frames of Reference for Social Science Research," *American Sociological Review*,
     vol. 45 (April 1980), pp. 302–313.

CHAPTER 7

Queries

The business of acquiring and using market knowledge is a chain of activities and like any chain is only as strong as its weakest link. Serious weaknesses may exist or develop in any of the crucial activities (e.g., the way we pose a problem, collect data, interpret it, and so forth). However, the most likely point of weakness is what we call the query stage. We use the term "query" broadly. It refers to the process of defining the basic research issue or problem, and formulating the specific operational questions that must be addressed. Three case examples illustrate problems that may arise at this stage.

CASE 1. A toy manufacturer commissioned research to learn which of two lines of dolls, each modeled after a well-known actress, would appeal most to children and to the adults who buy children's toys. Both groups clearly preferred one line and it was introduced in time for the Christmas season. The new dolls were a flop. The company had noticed that industry-wide doll sales had begun to fall off two years earlier, but it failed to ask why and whether the popularity of dolls would continue to decline. The limited discussion it had on the topic reflected a gut feeling that declining sales simply reflected the absence of a new, exciting line of dolls on the market. With the benefit of hindsight, it realized the issue could have been incorporated easily into the evaluation of the alternative lines. *Question*: Why wasn't such an obvious and important issue examined in the decision process?

CASE 2. After nearly eighteen months of mediocre performance in a period of rapid industry growth, a manufacturer of precision instruments hired an outside consultant to help determine why it was not doing better. Among other things, the consultant found that managers throughout this firm gave their superiors only the information they believed their superiors wanted. Information not solicited either was not brought forth or discounted as irrelevant. Many of the superiors receiving information suspected this behavior was happening while at the same time engaging in the same behavior when directing information to *their* superiors. It was also found that most managers would have welcomed valid information, even if the content was not what they would have liked, or even if it meant a couple of hours of additional reading per week. Thus, important information was not making its way to the right people and for the wrong reasons. When the consultant pointed this out, no one was surprised. *Questions*: Why was something so important, widely suspected, and widely practiced not addressed earlier? Why was an outsider needed to point it out?

CASE 3. The CEO of a paper materials firm was convinced that customers would accept products with a new coating material that provided better moisture protection, greater stiffening quality, and the use of thinner paper. Considerable R&D monies had been spent on the technology, and manufacturing facilities were adapted to make cups, paper plates, and other products using the coating. This required curtailing production of certain other products. The product management team developed a concept for the product and asked its advertising agency to prepare a marketing plan. Although discouraged by its client from doing research, the agency insisted on doing exploratory research if only to help understand customer reaction to the new paper products. Early in the research process it was discovered that consumers did not like the thin feeling of the new product and expressed a reluctance to buy it, even at very low prices. This surprise finding sent shudders through the product management team and created tension between it and the agency staff. When informed of the finding the CEO ordered a formal evaluation of the product through a series of consumer studies. As a result, some important product changes were made that improved the product's appeal. *Questions*: Why wasn't the product concept tested when it was first advanced in a serious way? Why did the agency meet resistance in proposing developmental advertising research? Why did friction develop between the agency and the product management team over the surprise research finding?

In each case important questions were not asked. Critical assumptions were made without their being challenged. While there may have been good reasons for making the assumptions, their validity was essential for success and, if only as an insurance measure, they should have been discussed fully and possibly researched. All three firms exhibited what we call "knowledge disavowal."

KNOWLEDGE DISAVOWAL

Knowledge disavowal refers to the avoidance of knowledge in order to maintain the status quo or to avoid a difficult choice or threatening situation.[1] It does not include the avoidance of information for reasons related to its perceived lack of relevance, timeliness, expected utility, or the cost of acquiring it. Knowledge disavowal is as systematic and pervasive as pro-knowledge phenomena and is found in all settings. For example, readers might ask themselves how prevalent in their organizations are the attitudes listed below:

Ignorance is bliss.
What you don't know won't hurt you.
Curiosity killed the cat.
No news is good news.
A little knowledge is a dangerous thing.
Don't be a know-it-all.
Silence is golden.
Let sleeping dogs lie.
Messengers with bad news lose their heads.

How many times in the past month or two have you seen these attitudes operating in disguise? Do they often characterize the behavior and/or thinking of colleagues, even yourself, with regard to potentially important information?

Knowledge disavowal contributes to groupthink, forbidden research, half-knowledge, the avoidance of exploratory and developmental research, biased interpretations of data, the rejection of surprises, and other dysfunctional behavior. Specific forms of knowledge disavowal are discussed throughout this book. The important point here is that they can be costly, as the example that follows indicates.

Failure to Examine Assumptions

Organizations that are not open to asking questions and examining important assumptions have prominent knowledge disavowal traits. One of the nation's largest producers of industrial goods was very concerned with obtaining an accurate market share estimate for a product it was introducing. Since the product was new to the firm, its production capacity would be based on this estimate. For various reasons, scales of production could not be easily altered once established. Three different methods were used to estimate market share at specified periods of time, and all three produced roughly the same estimate, which was nearly three times larger than management had expected. This information was a positive surprise, but was rejected. Production decisions were based on the preresearch expected market share.

The product was an instant success. Within six months sales reached a level that the preresearch expectation had estimated for the eighteen-month point. The firm's best guess at that time was that prior expectations were off by more than 35 percent. Unfortunately, it could not alter production quickly enough to reach the potential market and lost substantial revenues.

The knowledge disavowal in this example points to the failure to reexamine assumptions and other knowledge challenged by formal research. After this experience, the company established a procedure for examining basic assumptions whenever these are challenged by sound information.

An example from Xerox reminds us of the importance of drawing on knowledge from one area of a firm to challenge thinking in another. The firm had invested over $300 million to develop the 9200 copier duplicator and was about to approve the final business plan for the machine. The plan included a sales forecast on which other components of the plan rested. As it happened, a manager from another department was sitting in on the meeting where the business plan was being approved. He had just completed a survey of total industry production of a particular type of 8 ½" × 11" paper, which would be used in the new machine and other xerographic copiers. The executives were stunned when he announced that if the sales forecast for the 9200 was correct, the *entire* U.S. production of that type of paper would be processed by the new machine—a highly embarrassing impossibility. Here, the need for optimistic forecasts to warrant R&D and capital expenditures, combined with assumptions related to the processing capacity of the new machine, had unwittingly caused upward biasing in assumptions about the amount of material available for processing. No routine mechanism existed at the time for raising and verifying these assumptions early in the business planning process.

In fact, there were other serious failures to question assumptions about the 9200 copier.[2] For example, the financially oriented decision makers, according to one analyst, were mesmerized by the prospect that placing "an average of a single 9200 in each of the nation's 100,000 central reproduction departments" would produce an annual profit of $200 million dollars. Marketing-oriented people correctly worried that a fatal assumption was being made that a decision maker in the customer firm (disparagingly called "Charlie Printpants") would welcome the new product. "Charlie" didn't and in 1977 copier sales fell far short of expectations. "Ironically, the Xerox numbers-driven managers who ignored marketing common sense . . . saved their dream product because of other comparable mistakes of judgment."[3] For example, they seriously underestimated the number of copies people would choose to make given the ability to make more copies per second.

Avoidance of Exploratory and Developmental Research

The avoidance of exploratory and developmental research is another manifestation of knowledge disavowal. This is most readily seen in advertising research. Most firms leave developmental advertising research to their agencies, which may or may not be given the requisite research funds. When agencies do provide developmental research the client is often not involved.

Most of the client's attention and funding are aimed at evaluating the impact of advertising. According to one agency research director, "The reason so much money and effort go into evaluative research is that [client researchers and managers] tend to be tacticians, not strategists; they want numbers, not ideas." Another person we interviewed suggested that the practice of devoting so much attention to evaluation research should provide the kind of comfort that

> A patient would have going into major surgery knowing that 85 percent of the surgeon's training was devoted to learning how to assess the success of the surgery, and only 15 percent to learning what to do and how to do it.

Firms tend not to become involved in developmental research, despite the fact that the cost of a mistake in developing an advertising campaign, for example, is ultimately larger than the cost of a mistake in evaluating the campaign. There are exceptions to this, of course. As a research director from a large client company which does its own developmental research noted: "As important as creative execution is, concept development and general strategy are still more important, and for that reason we invest heavily in developmental research prior to copy testing."

This pattern in advertising research characterizes other kinds of market research, perhaps because developmental or exploratory research adds to a manager's sense of uncertainty or ignorance. A senior researcher from a major consulting company explained it this way:

> New ideas or new alternatives carry large amounts of uncertainty. You generally know a lot more about familiar ideas and a great deal less about unfamiliar ones. This means [the client] has to spend more research money or take riskier actions when what they really want is a strong signal that something they already know about is a good idea. We have managers coming in here saying they want to do [developmental] research when in truth they do not.

Biased Assimilation

Knowledge disavowal often takes the form of biased assimilation. When mixed or inconclusive evidence about a position is presented, biases in its assimilation reinforce a person's existing beliefs while lending no support for an opposite position.[4] (Biases are discussed more fully in Chapter 9.) Thus, even random outcomes can be interpreted by opposing parties as reinforcing their own positions. When research results clearly contradict our own position, the tendency is to find an error in the methodology, which leads to a reasoning process like this: If research results contradicting my position can only be produced by a faulty methodology, then a correct methodology would result in support for my position.

Biased assimilation operates not only with traditional market research but also with how we evaluate our own judgments.[5] We systematically seek confirmatory evidence that our judgments are sound and avoid disconfirming evidence. The proper strategy for learning from experience requires seeking both confirmatory and disconfirming evidence.

Forbidden Research

Knowledge disavowal also takes the form of forbidden research. Some topics and marketing actions are considered off-limits, and not because of ethical or legal considerations. For example, formal research or the collection of other information about an action that is considered politically unacceptable in a company will be discouraged or ignored. We encountered several situations in which senior management was genuinely open to an idea that its subordinates perceived to be politically unacceptable in the higher ranks of the company. Research is not conducted in a political vacuum, and often one party gains while another loses as a result of recommendations. As one senior research executive in a leading U.S. corporation told us during a personal interview:

> Most major products in our corporation have champions, i.e., people who are committed to the concept. There are also champions on the other side, i.e., those who are opposed to the product. We find it desirable to meet with both sets of champions separately . . . to extract an understanding of what market research can accomplish. We try to negotiate with them what they will accept as supporting and as negative evidence so that, when it comes, either way we won't have any arguments.

Half-Knowledge

Another interesting manifestation of knowledge disavowal is half-knowledge. This refers to a vague awareness of one's situation and the sense that it is safer not to know more because more complete information might require the opening of a can of worms.

Academic research has uncovered a phenomenon described as "vague-specifics."[6] Some managers and researchers describe wanting information that is specific enough to provide clear direction but vague enough to require at least some imaginative interpretation and application. This reflects a need to add personal intellectual value to data and to be recognized for providing added-value. For example, designers and engineers working on products that will not be introduced for four or five years want to know what people like now and what they may want tomorrow, but they do not want specifics that will tie their hands. As one research staffer put it, "Sometimes managers only need to know the direction of the wind and find information about velocity as unnecessary. And, indeed, it often is unnecessary."

Ignorance is not necessarily a bad thing. It may actually reflect—in fact be the unavoidable consequence of—the process of becoming knowledgeable. Social scientists have argued that the process of generating knowledge also produces at least as much ignorance.[7] The analogy is used in which the air in a balloon represents knowledge and the skin of the balloon represents the frontiers of ignorance. As the balloon expands with knowledge, so do the frontiers of ignorance. Thus, under some conditions, ignorance is a healthy sign—indeed a prerequisite—of learning.

ASKING VERSUS ANSWERING SYSTEMS

Some managers are reluctant to admit to not knowing everything important and necessary for a decision. This is reminiscent of a story attributed to Carl Sandburg: The white man drew a small circle in the sand and told the red man, "This is what the Indian knows"; and drawing a big circle around the small one, "This is what the white man knows." The Indian took the stick and swept an immense ring around both circles. "This is where the white man and the red man know nothing."

A leader in the public relations industry suggested that it is sometimes considered "unmanly" and "unmanagerial" to ask questions. Admitting ignorance makes a manager feel less powerful. The reluctance to ask questions results in the extensive use of limited knowledge. This runs counter to managers' complaints that they do not have sufficient and timely information. Some interviewees suggested that there is an "airy," "unnecessary" connotation to the term "research"; whereas the term "development" has a practical connotation and perhaps should be used instead. The term "market development data" has been suggested as more proactive.

Much market research is driven by an answer already in hand. Executives in several research organizations commented that managers do not know how to ask researchable questions, "But they sure know how to ask why research doesn't answer the questions they do have." A research director in a consumer products company commented, "[A vice president] doesn't want research, he wants answers." Throughout our interviews we detected a subtle but important psychological distinction between doing research and providing answers: Research may connote weakness and uncertainty; having an answer is a sign of "strength." This may be one reason why most market research is confirmatory, that is, it verifies a particular idea as a good one and avoids raising questions whose answers may suggest that the idea isn't the best one available.

One of the most significant services an inquiry center can provide is to help managers surface and challenge their own assumptions and examine alternative perspectives on what they know. This process highlights important areas of ignorance and raises uncertainty. At some level of thinking managers will freely acknowledge that the challenging of assumptions is valuable and that the risk of increasing uncertainty by uncovering important areas of ignorance is an acceptable one. However, with but three exceptions, none of the researchers and managers we interviewed engaged in formal assumptional analyses or perspective-expanding processes.

It seems obvious that asking systems are a necessary part of answering systems and that the more thorough the asking process, the better will be the answers. There is a catch, though. Researchers identify with asking systems, while managers identify with answering systems; and, although these systems are interdependent, they often clash. To some extent researchers view answering systems as unnecessary and even impossible to incorporate into the research process. In many cases managers act as if they do not understand or believe that asking systems are important. A major task, then, is to convince managers that the inquiry center is as much oriented to answering as to asking. One important way this occurs is by uncovering hidden knowledge. This is discussed below.

In many of our interviews, both managers and researchers spoke about the significance of knowledge they didn't know they had. Both groups felt that managers in particular know a great deal more than they realize. There was a general feeling that it is important to sensitize managers to what they do know as well as what they don't know. Some respondents felt that whatever helps uncover hidden ignorance should also help uncover hidden knowledge. Uncovering hidden ignorance leads to a better focus for projects, while uncovering hidden knowledge helps determine what research is unnecessary.

Of course, important areas of knowledge and ignorance may be highly visible. Whether knowledge and ignorance are hidden or visible, both need to be clearly defined. This, in itself, can reduce uncertainty in the decision-making process.

When describing the differences between good and poor research users, a senior vice president for a major research supplier suggested that good users need to know

- what is essential to know,
- what they do know,
- what they do not know, and
- what is and is not already known and available elsewhere.

While this describes a "good user," it also suggests what a good researcher might be. A good researcher is a knowledge development expert who helps managers satisfy these needs. This is a far broader view of the researcher role than typically exists. The typical view limits the researcher's task to collecting primary data. The broader view can sometimes result in a decision not to collect any primary data. This is contrary to how most researchers spend the bulk of their time.

We turn our attention now to the kinds of questions that should be raised when approaching a research issue. These questions help define what is essential knowledge, what is not, and what knowledge is available elsewhere.

PROBES TO THINKING

Listed below are several probes to thinking. These help managers and researchers to go beneath the surface questions and identify other potentially more important questions. They also help sharpen manager and researcher thinking about the use of information in making a specific decision.

How Do We Know If We've Asked the Wrong/Right Question?

The two most common ways of learning whether the wrong question has been asked are to wait until after information has been collected and analyzed and it is too late to collect more appropriate information, or to wait for feedback after a decision has been implemented. In either case, managers usually find the answer, but too late. For example, a manufacturer of high-fashion clothing planned to introduce a line of rugged outdoor sportswear and sports equipment under its trademark. It asked the important question of whether potential customers would find the clothing and equipment attractive and of good value (the answer was found to be "yes" in both cases). But it failed to ask an equally important question: Just how helpful is a trademark associated with high-fashion clothing in selling rugged sportswear and equipment? A year after its introduction sales of the new product line were extremely disappointing. Asking the important question, "Will our high-fashion brand name help us establish a foothold in the competitive rugged sportswear and equipment market?" might have saved the firm substantial money.

As we saw in Chapter 5, the best way to determine whether the right question is being asked or the right issue is being addressed is to simulate the situation. Simulating the use of information using hypothetical numbers is helpful in ensuring that the right questions are being asked and in the right way. The process consists of asking such questions as, "If sales were only XXX thousand units, what factors would most likely cause this?" "Have we sufficient information about these factors to know whether they are important and if they are, how to offset them?" The following example illustrates some of these issues.

A manufacturer of insulators for power transmission lines had an opportunity to acquire a plant outside the United States that could be adapted to produce the insulators at a low cost. A survey was planned of major utility companies that were the important buyers of the insulators and the engineering firms and other consultants that influenced their decisions. The survey was part of a larger effort to forecast the size of the insulator market over the next several years.

In the process of explaining simulated good and bad sales outcomes, the issue about the effect of perceptions about the national origin of the insulators was raised. One manager suggested that products of this sort originating from the country in question might not be perceived as having the same technical reliability as those originating from the United States, France, Japan, and Korea. Once this idea surfaced as a possible explanation, it was added as an issue to explore in a telephone survey of purchasing agents and others who were influential in the buying decision. The actual data indeed suggested that interviewees had serious reservations about buying the product if it were manufactured in that country, even knowing the facility was owned by a U.S. firm. The company decided to acquire the facility, but the knowledge of a major perceptual problem enabled the firm to take special steps to diffuse it. Had it not been alert to the problem until after it started importing and distributing the insulators, the firm would have experienced substantial losses, at least for the first two years.

Similar questions should also be asked about why the decision might be much more successful than anticipated. These questions are especially important if the firm is unable to adjust production or distribution quickly enough for the unexpected level of success. Creating demand for a product that cannot be adequately supplied opens a special window of opportunity for competitors.

What Is the Research Question?

The essential research question is not always obvious. For example, managers may ask, "How frequently should we run an advertisement?" Here, managers want a number; but researchers may have to change the question to: "What is the effect of different repetitive-message exposure strategies on learning?" The broader question helps identify relevant research on memory and learning as a guide to the selection of a message frequency strategy. Focusing on the basic issue provides a better structure for conducting the research. For example, the more basic issue stresses the need to consider alternative exposure strategies and in turn the need to consider what is feasible from a budgetary standpoint. If the "best" answer is likely to be unaffordable, then research will be wasted. The research question then becomes one of finding the best exposure strategy permitted by the budget.

Whose Question Is It?

Sometimes the individual or group requesting research has a client for the information. For example, an advertising agency may commission research on behalf of a client; or, a manager may want research done to help address a concern among dealers. It is important to understand who the third parties are and why they are of concern to the main client if their needs are to be addressed. This is illustrated by the following example.

Although it conducted no formal research, the Papercraft Corporation, a manufacturer of gift wrap material, was convinced (quite correctly as it turned out) that a new Christmas gift wrap would be a major success. However, it ran into unexpected resistance among buyers at several major retail chains when the product was first presented. Papercraft then commissioned a well-known, highly respected research organization to evaluate consumers' attitudes toward the product and the likelihood of their purchasing the product at different price levels. Buyers for major retail chains were informed that the study was to be done and were asked to discuss their information needs with the research team. Each buyer participated in two telephone discussions with the research staff. One consequence of this was a sense of ownership of the data by the buyers. It also increased their confidence in the research staff, in the objectivity of the research process, and in the final results. The research showed that the product would be favorably received at prices attractive to the retailers. After seeing the results the retail buyers became favorably disposed toward the product and increased their initial purchase quantities significantly.

The basic research questions involved here focused on the appeal of the product and price sensitivity among selected consumer groups. These were not questions for management at Papercraft; it already knew the answers. The questions "belonged" to the retail buyers. While they understood that the research was intended to support the manufacturer's position, they also understood that the research process was not biased toward that result.

Why Is It a Problem? Is There a More Basic Underlying Problem?

In the Papercraft example, the real issue facing management was not consumer acceptance but resistance from independent distributors. The research was used as a sales tool to get retailers to stock the product in quantity. In the end, this tool proved less costly than other alternatives—very low prices, unusually favorable buy-back terms, or other retailer incentives.

In other instances uncovering the real issue can lead to a decision to either not do research, or conduct *different* research. For example, a medical equipment manufacturer began production of a product for use in home care. This was a modification of a product they were selling to hospitals and clinics. The company had sound data about the size of the market, competing products, and other factors. However, it had little information about what market share they might expect. Product feature, price, and distribution decisions had already been made and could not be altered significantly by the time the firm started considering market share/sales volume issues. It was assumed that a technically superior product offered at reasonable prices would be successful. Research was initiated to provide sales estimates to guide production planning. However, early in the research process it became apparent that these data would have little impact on production plans. This became evident in discussions of how hypothetical research results might be used. The only results that would affect production plans significantly were extremely high or extremely low sales, neither of which was likely. The chance of the research producing results that might make a difference was thus so low that its expense could not be justified.

It became evident in this case that the underlying "problem" was management's discomfort with the fact that so many decisions had been made in the absence of a unit sales estimate. Thus, the research was more to give comfort than guidance and, in the case of a market failure, a basis for shifting blame from managers to the research, which all had assumed would show a high sales potential. The research director recommended canceling the research since it would have no real decision-making value or instructional benefits for the company. Her recommendation was accepted.

Have the Answers Been "Back-Translated" to Questions?

Back-translation refers to the process where, say, the English translation of a French language text is translated back into French by another person. If the two French versions agree, the English translation is considered accurate. If the two French versions are significantly different, another English translation is made and translated back into French. The process is repeated until the English version produces a French version essentially identical to the original French text. Think of the answers managers would find helpful as corresponding to the original French text, while the researcher's questions correspond to the English translation. A firm's customers are the intended English-language readers in this metaphor. The specific questions asked of customers have to be continually refined until they are capable of providing the exact kind of information managers find useful.

For a major decision requiring information, researchers can ask managers for hypothetical answers that would inform that decision. For example, a consumer electronics firm might want to learn what effect high-resolution TV might have on VCR usage and movie theater attendance. Alternative answers would be generated which would be useful in product planning and market development decisions. With respect to each answer, managers and researchers would ask, "What precise question (or set of questions) do we have to ask to get this *kind* of answer?" Care must be taken that a meaningful array of answers is generated to include both good and bad news. If a set of questions has already been generated, these should be examined to make sure that they will provide useful answers. If they do not, the questions need to be altered. This process is helpful in fine-tuning a set of research questions so that they yield actionable information.

How Challenging Is the Question?

Trivial research questions produce obvious and trivial answers. Questions that challenge basic beliefs or surface information that contradicts those beliefs are dismissed as absurd. The researcher must develop questions that probe those middle-ground assumptions that are important and fairly firmly held. These assumptions are usually correct, but when they are not they frequently lead to poor decisions. These assumptions, when challenged by sound information properly presented, are intellectually engaging for most managers.[7]

Whatever the basic research issue, managers and researchers should determine what important assumptions are being made that, were they incorrect, could result in a poor decision. Even though the assumptions are unlikely to be wrong, the consequences, if they *are* wrong, can far outweigh the cost of testing them. For example, a firm that produced pump equipment decided to add a new and expensive pumping system to its product line. In making the decision it commissioned a research effort to forecast sales for a six-year period. A thorough forecast was prepared and was instrumental in the decision to create a facility to build the system rather than acquire a manufacturer that specialized in making the system. Throughout, it was assumed that the independent dealers the firm used for its other lines, and that serviced potential customers for the pumping system, would be fully committed to the product. In fact, they were not committed at all. After nearly two years of poor sales the firm embarked on an expensive and, ultimately, successful program to obtain dealer support. Had this key assumption been tested, the firm would have saved itself the expense.

Exhibit 7-1 arrays different kinds of assumptions in terms of the probability of their being wrong and the consequences for a firm of acting on false assumptions. While these matters are not as simple as the exhibit suggests, it is a useful way of thinking about the query process. Cell 1 contains those assumptions that have a reasonable probability of being wrong and that could have a major impact if they are accepted as true but prove to be wrong. These represent fundamental and important research issues. In most instances, these assumptions receive careful examination.

Exhibit 7-1
Types of Assumptions

	Probability of Acting on a False Assumption	
Consequences of a False Assumption	Reasonably High	Reasonably Low
Serious	Fundamental Assumptions 1	2 "Snail Darter" Assumptions
Not Serious	Trivial 3 Assumptions	4 Safe Bet Assumptions

Cell 2 represents "snail darter" assumptions. The snail darter, a tiny fish thought to be extinct, was quite unexpectedly discovered in waters near a dam construction site in Tennessee. It was immediately placed on the endangered species list and that resulted in costly construction delay. Snail darter–type assumptions are very important to address and possibly research. Clearly, the cost of researching such issues and the likelihood of obtaining unequivocal answers must be considered. One problem with research on snail darter assumptions is that it is often done in ways that are biased toward confirming the assumption.

Cell 3 contains trivial assumptions. Even when there is a reasonable basis for assuming they are wrong, the consequences of being wrong are so small that research effort would be wasted. Cell 4 addresses safe bet assumptions, that is, those that are unlikely to be in error and have little consequence even if they are. Considerable resources are wasted examining the assumptions in Cells 3 and 4.

While it is desirable to challenge core assumptions, few managers and researchers do, mainly because it simply doesn't occur to them. Frequently the decision time frame is too short to permit adequate exploration of alternative viewpoints. Just as frequently there are too many of these assumptions to tackle at one time. Under these circumstances the inquiry center or market research staff or the strategic planning staffs have a special responsibility and opportunity to provide leadership in challenging thinking about assumptions and decisions. Ian Mitroff has suggested six broad principles to help managers engage in a kind of "mental judo," especially with assumptions and practices managers think absurd to challenge.[8] These principles are:

1. Seek the obvious, but do everything in your power to challenge and even to ridicule it.
2. Question *all* constraints. The most limiting constraints are usually imposed not by the problem but by the mindset of the problem solver.
3. Challenge as many assumptions about the problem as possible. Remember that what seems self-evident to you is not always evident to others.
4. Question the scope or definition of a problem. Frequently, what is omitted from the statement of a problem is as critical as what is included.
5. Question whether a problem is to be "solved," "resolved," or "dissolved."
6. Question logic. Being logical and being right are not always the same. The more logical a solution to a complex problem sounds, the more it deserves to be challenged.

These guidelines can help researchers present a broader array of ideas and understandings for possible use by managers. They also help reduce the likelihood of acting on an incorrect assumption or one that may simply not yield the best decision. The guidelines require that the researcher knows the "taken-for-granted" assumptions of clients; the intensity of these assumptions; and how to show the practical relevance of challenging assumptions and considering alternative perspectives.

There still remains a fundamental question for which there is no simple answer: "When (or where) do you draw the line between assumptions that should be questioned and those that need not, given the hundreds of assumptions we make in ordinary decisions?" Ian Mitroff provides a helpful perspective, shown in Exhibit 7-2.[9] This exhibit shows that certain assumptions considered obvious are not interesting and go unchallenged; those that have a degree of surprise are more interesting, and are apt to capture managers' attention and possible examination; those assumptions whose challenge is considered "absurd" are not interesting and receive little if any critical challenge. Mitroff and others feel that people are, at best, only marginally trained and willing to move even into just the "interesting" region of Exhibit 7-2.

Exhibit 7-2
Degree to Which One's World Is Challenged

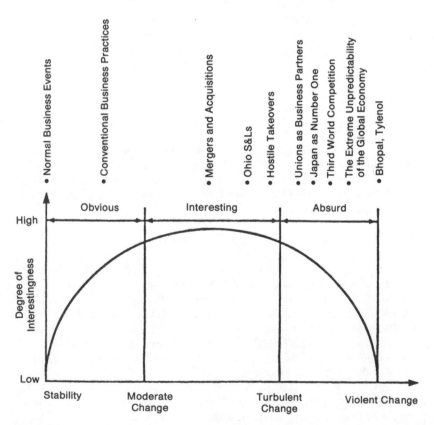

Source: Mitroff, I. I. *Business Not as Usual: Rethinking Our Individual, Corporate, and Industrial Strategies for Global Competition.* San Francisco: Jossey-Bass, 1987, p. 30 [Figure 2].

The fact that so many modern phenomena fall into the "absurd" category poses a problem for society. Mitroff claims, and we agree, that the most impressive executives are those who are mentally and emotionally prepared to deal not only with the middle region of the exhibit but also with the "absurd" region. These individuals are hard to find. Those who exist should serve as models to others in how to cope with the increasing frequency with which fundamental assumptions, our sacred organizational beliefs, must be challenged.

CONCLUSION

Defining the right problem and expressing it correctly as a set of questions are possibly the most important tasks in the overall research process. Certainly an error at this point limits the value added to the knowledge-use process by subsequent tasks. What is especially important is that there be an examination of assumptions that, if wrong, could have serious consequences for a firm. Often, because of knowledge disavowal processes, important assumptions either are not raised or are examined in biased ways. The failure of many firms to ask important and challenging questions provides a false sense of knowledge.

Notes

1. Gerald Zaltman, "Knowledge Disavowal," in Ralph Kilmann et al., eds., *Producing Useful Knowledge for Organizations* (New York: Praeger, 1983), pp. 173–187.
2. Douglas K. Smith and Robert C. Alexander, *Fumbling the Future: How Xerox Invented, Then Ignored the First Personal Computer* (New York: William Morrow, 1988), esp. pp. 186–189.
3. Ibid., p. 188.
4. Robin M. Hogarth, *Judgement and Choice*, 2d ed. (New York: John Wiley, 1987), p. 217.
5. Hillel J. Einhorn, "Overconfidence in Judgment," *New Directions for Methodology of Social and Behavioral Science*, no. 4 (1980), pp. 1–16.
6. Rohit Deshpande and Gerald Zaltman, "Factors Affecting the Consumption of Market Research: A Path Analysis," *Journal of Marketing Research*, vol. 19 (February 1982), pp. 14–31.
7. Jerome R. Ravetz, "Usable Knowledge, Usable Ignorance: Incomplete Science with Policy Implications," *Knowledge: Creation, Diffusion, Utilization*, vol. 9, no. 1 (September 1987), pp. 87–116.
8. Ian Mitroff, *Business Not as Usual* (San Francisco: Jossey-Bass, 1987), pp. 31–32; see also, Richard O. Mason and Ian I. Mitroff, *Challenging Strategic Planning Assumptions* (New York: John Wiley, 1986).
9. Ibid.

CHAPTER **8**

Data: Clues from the Market

Data are the stimuli that make us curious and provide the building blocks—the "thinker toys"—for our creativity. They are acquired from the marketplace in both planned and serendipitous ways. Data are the "stuff" from which decisions are fashioned. Although we use the term "data" freely in our daily conversation, it is a deceptively complex concept. In Chapter 6 we distinguished among data, information, and intelligence. Data were described as potential representations of reality. They are potential representations because they may or may not be accurate and may or may not be believed. As we indicated in Chapter 2, by putting data in a decision context we develop information and by applying inference (judgment) to contextual information we generate intelligence. Data range in nature from rumors all the way to the outcomes of sophisticated mathematical models.

A datum may be a single statistic—the gain or loss of market share over a period of time. Data may also consist of a detailed demographic and psychographic profile of a particular customer segment. They may also be the rumored characteristics of a new technology being developed by a competitor. In these instances and others, the data create an impression or an idea about reality. Thus, data are intellectual stimuli provoking a thought. The thought they stimulate is their content.

We will not concern ourselves here with the sources of data or the many forms of data available to researchers and managers. There are many excellent articles and books the reader may consult about these matters.[1] However, we will address some special issues about the cost and usefulness of data.

RELATIVE COSTS OF ACQUIRING VARIOUS TYPES OF DATA

Cost, of course, is an important consideration in determining the data collection method. To provide the greatest information benefit for the least cost, it is important to compare the relative cost of obtaining various types of

175

data. We can do this by looking at three different ways of generating statistical information. The first is through specific-purpose surveys, designed especially for the problem to be explored. The second is through the use of more comprehensive, or general-purpose, surveys, which provide insight into several areas of concern. The third method is through the synthesis and analysis of data already collected. The long-term costs of these methods vary greatly, as do the costs per use of the data.

Exhibits 8-1 through 8-5 identify the change in costs for the three types of information—specific-purpose (line A), general-purpose (line B), and analysis (line C). The horizontal dimension in each exhibit is simply an indication of what we expect to happen, over time, to the elements that affect cost. The vertical dimension, however, can be legitimately criticized because it focuses on costs and ignores the value of information. Cost per use, of course, is easy to calculate: Add up all the costs of collecting the information and divide by the number of uses to which it has been put. Value, on the other hand, should be measured by the extent to which the data is used and the difference (impact) that the information makes on the decision. Here, since we are not familiar with the decisions that will be made, we cannot determine the relative impact the three forms of information will have. We will, instead, simply assume that all data will have equal value and that the cost factor should be the primary decision criterion.

Exhibit 8-1
Relative Cost of Specific-Purpose Data

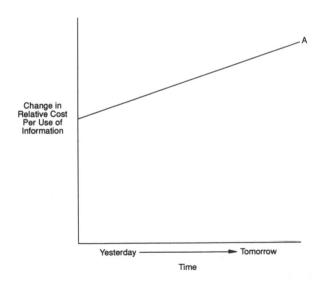

Specific-Purpose Data

Exhibit 8-1 illustrates the change in the relative costs for each use of information acquired through the collection of statistical data in a specific-purpose survey. Specific-purpose surveys are often expensive undertakings. The measurement of specific actions, attitudes, or individual characteristics requires sample survey design, questionnaire development, implementation of a collection methodology, and the utilization of analytical techniques. Surveys are people-intensive, and their costs are likely to increase over time because of rising labor costs, the use of more sophisticated and expensive methodologies, and related expenditures.

One reason for the relatively high cost of specially collected data is that the information obtained typically cannot be used for other analyses and decision-making needs. A specific-purpose survey has, by definition, a narrow range of uses and the cost of generating the idea is borne by a limited set of users. Unless a data set can be used for many purposes, the cost to the organization remains the same as the cost and value to the original user. Later in this chapter we will discuss an approach to lessening this problem.

General-Purpose Data

Exhibit 8-2 shows the relative per use cost of information collected in a general-purpose survey. Census data are a prime example of general-purpose statistics collected for a variety of uses. General-purpose data can provide insight into a variety of specific problems through proper comparison and extrapolation. In addition, general-purpose data provide benchmarks describing the general market or environmental situations; they establish and define parameters and provide a vital time reference.

A good example of general-purpose survey data is the Continuous Automobile Marketing Information Program (CAMIP) used at General Motors. CAMIP is an ongoing tracking program that surveys buyers of new GM and competing vehicles to obtain an initial reading of owner satisfaction after approximately ten weeks of ownership. The information is used in some way by virtually every entity in the corporation. Top management looks at these data to evaluate product offerings, in terms both of the competition and of GM product "norms" or averages. General quality and reliability problem areas are identified by car line and the responsible area is asked to develop an action plan to address the problem.

At a more specific level, the automotive component groups of GM also use CAMIP data. Respondents may have indicated overall dissatisfaction with an aspect of an engine such as acceleration. The CAMIP data can be used further to determine if engine problems that affect acceleration have also been reported. This enables the engine component group to identify quickly specific problem areas and to begin addressing those problems.

Exhibit 8-2
Relative Cost of General-Purpose Data

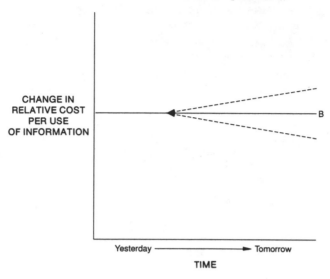

Exhibit 8-3
Relative Cost of Analysis of Available Data

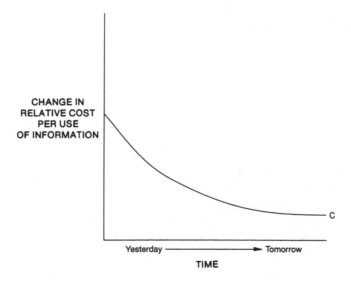

Collection and analysis of general-purpose data have the same cost pressures that we find with specific data. But, as the frequency of use increases, the cost per use is reduced.

Exhibit 8-2 tells us that if the ever-increasing cost of data collection is not offset by an increased number of uses per data item, the cost will continue to rise (upper dotted line). However, if the increased number of uses is equal to the increase in cost, the relative cost per use is unchanged over time (center line). If the increase in uses is greater than the increase in cost, the cost per use will decrease over time (bottom dotted line).

Further Data Analysis

In most corporations, a tremendous amount of data and statistical information has already been collected, and additional analyses can provide valuable information to the organization. Exhibit 8-3 shows that the relative cost of analyzing data already on hand may decrease over time. New statistical techniques help provide more meaningful measures in the further analysis of previously collected material.

In addition to the potential cost savings from not obtaining more data, the unit cost of performing analysis tasks on the computer (on the existing data) has been decreasing dramatically—from 100 to 20 percent every five years for the past twenty years. This trend is expected to continue for at least the next ten years.

Relative Cost of Different Types of Data

Exhibit 8-4 summarizes the three previous charts and clearly indicates that relative costs of all three forms of data must be carefully considered. Exhibit 8-5 illustrates that, at some point in time, when the combined costs of general-purpose data and the further analysis of that data (lines B + C) become sufficiently less than the cost of specific-purpose data (line A), the decision maker may very well decide to use the less costly approach. He or she will, however, still need to consider the quality, availability, cost, timeliness, and respondent burden in determining the type of data to select.

Even though this exhibit may indicate some cost-benefit gains through the use of other types of data, specific-purpose surveys will continue to be conducted, for there will always be the need for unique information. The exhibit demonstrates that there will be several alternatives in the selection of information needed for decision-making processes.

SHARED RESEARCH EFFORTS WITHIN THE FIRM

The cost of specific-purpose research can be reduced and its analytic payoff increased by combining or coordinating what would otherwise be independent projects. That is, we can design specific-purpose surveys that

Exhibit 8-4
Relative Cost of Specific-Purpose Data, General-Purpose Data,
and Analysis of Data

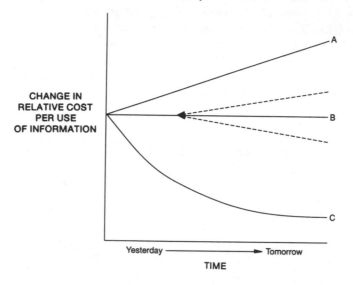

Exhibit 8-5
Relative Cost of Specific-Purpose Data and General-Purpose Data
and Their Further Analysis Combined

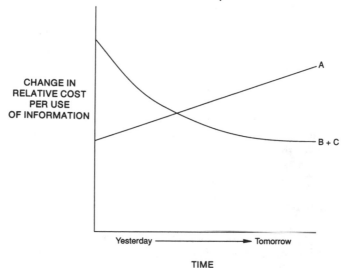

yield more general benefits. Before introducing the specific mechanics of this approach, we will comment on the extent to which this practice takes place.

Research developed for one internal client often contains information that is relevant for others. For example, research conducted for a product manager discloses a significant change in customer attitudes toward a product that is closely identified with the corporation; this may be of great importance to the public affairs staff. Conversely, attitudes toward the corporation may affect product strategy. However, many research directors feel that secondary clients pay less attention to this information than would be the case if it had been collected specifically for them. In order to lessen the not-invented-here syndrome, which may cause the nonsponsoring group to pay less attention to particular results, the researcher needs to involve the nonsponsoring group prior to the start of the research. This is important because, as we have seen, simple involvement in the research development process affects the perceived relevance and credibility of the research. Few firms routinely attempt to have multiple clients share project costs. When a project yields benefits for more than one group, it is partly a function of serendipity and partly a function of the research staff's knowledge of what would be of interest to other clients. Many researchers feel that many projects should be done as joint ventures, even as internal omnibus studies where several groups collectively gather data on a routine basis. The principal reasons they cite for joint ventures are cost savings and increased insight into the marketplace. But synergistic effects do not just happen.

Creating Synergy in Research Programs

Synergy in market research programs occurs when two or more projects can be combined or coordinated in such a way that the market intelligence yield is greater than the sum of their contributions as isolated projects. Indicators of positive synergy are

- relevant insights gained by each project that would not have been provided in the absence of their coordination;
- reduced monetary cost per project through sharing of fixed expenses;
- ability to increase sample size; and
- more efficient screening techniques to identify low-incidence respondents.

The researcher and manager efforts required to ensure that appropriate joint ventures take place represent a potential added cost.

Two Principles for Market Research Synergy

Market research synergy occurs when the principles of consistency and complementarity (discussed in Chapter 10) are followed. The consistency principle suggests that two or more projects might be coordinated if the central concerns of each are consistent with the same basic issue. The complementarity principle suggests that two projects might be coordinated when their questions and methods are compatible, that is, can be used conjunctively (see Exhibit 8-6). Thus, the following conceptual formula should guide the management of market research:

$$\text{Consistency} + \text{Complementarity} = \text{Synergy}$$

An example will illustrate this formula. Let us assume a firm has two projects: One concerns changes in movie theater attendance and the nature of the theatrical experience; the second concerns VCR purchases and usage. Both projects address the general topic of entertainment preferences and practices among the general public. Additionally, sets of questions raised by each project could complement one another in two ways. First, certain questions might be identical. For instance, in addition to the same demographic questions, each project might ask questions of various age groups about the importance of having control over the setting in which movies are viewed. A firm should not pay to have this information collected twice; each project can share the financial expense of collecting it. Resources saved might be used to increase the sample size.

Exhibit 8-6
The Principles of Consistency and Complementarity Guide Joint Ventures

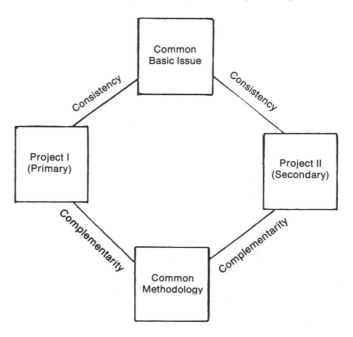

A second type of complementarity creates synergy by yielding more market insight. The project about movie attendance and the nature of the theatrical experience might be concerned with such collateral activities as dining out before/after the movie. It may be important to know about market segments for whom movie theater attendance is (and is not) part of a larger evening entertainment package. Questions about these segments may not be addressed by the VCR project because they are not apparently relevant or because it is not financially feasible to pursue all potentially relevant questions. The VCR project, on the other hand, may include questions not being pursued by the movie attendance project. It may, for example, assess the degree to which non-VCR owners are waiting for certain technology developments or the decay effect of the novelty value of a new VCR. Both sets of questions are complementary when explored in the same survey. Knowing why particular adult segments of the movie-goer market are and are not buying VCRs is important to both projects. Thus, by analyzing one project's questions in terms of the other's, new insights are provided to each one. These insights might also enrich the research staff's overall knowledge of the marketplace. Earlier detection of emerging issues may also occur.

Implementation

Implementation of joint ventures is easiest in those organizations that have a formal market research function. The research staff serves as the "broker," bringing together two appropriate projects. When two projects are to be coordinated one should be designated as the primary project and the other as the secondary project, referred to here as Project I and Project II, respectively. Each project should establish a preliminary research plan, identifying types of respondents and a preferred methodology, and communicate this to a group-level coordinator, or, alternatively, to someone in the central market intelligence unit. Project I might concern specific issues about movie theater attendance. In this instance, the likely respondent group might be very broad. The methodology might involve the use of unstructured focus groups, a semistructured technique such as the Kelly Repertory Grid which helps elicit the basic concepts people use when thinking about an issue, and a well-structured survey. Project II, whose concerns are consistent with the same generic issues of Project I, would participate in a limited way in Project I research. It would be able to add a set of complementary questions and would be expected to share a pro rata cost of the research.

The incentives for Project I and Project II staff to cooperate include the cost savings each realizes in the joint venture and the ability to invest these savings in other research projects. This should represent an increase in the amount of market information available to a line of business having a fixed research budget. Another incentive is the increase in market insight when there is synergy between the issues each group is raising. This would be measured at the data level by the number of relevant additional tabulations made possible by the joint venture.

A coordinator at the group level would determine which project is to be the primary one. The core set of Project I issues must be addressed adequately. Trade-offs to accommodate Project II should involve less central issues. This suggests that Project II issues will not require a study of broad scope. Additionally, these issues may be of the "nice-to-know" rather than the "need-to-know" variety.

It is quite possible that a joint venture would have to be abandoned early; for example, when in the beginning stages the basic issues for one project are redefined and lose their complementarity with those of the other project. Another indication would be if the reformulated research issues are best pursued by a different research methodology.

Although joint research ventures can yield synergy in the form of cost savings and additional market understanding, the possibility of such synergy is not a sufficient incentive to encourage management teams to seek out possible partner projects. Management should be aware of intended projects and the general information needs for each business unit. Brief business unit statements of research intent might suffice as a means of creating such awareness.

The broker role involves determining which projects in all areas of the firm are consistent with the same basic issues and are therefore likely to involve methodologies, e.g., sampling and data collection procedures, that suggest potentially complementary research questions. The broker may decide which project is the primary one and how many other projects might be coordinated with it. The broker also monitors and perhaps facilitates the progress of the joint venture.

The way the research function is organized can affect its ability to detect and respond to joint research opportunities. For example, a research director in a firm that has a centralized research function claims that this particular organizational structure led to many more joint ventures and facilitated client learning from prior studies. In fact, in this firm, and in certain others with a centralized research function, the research staff routinely attends divisional market planning/strategy meetings. As a consequence, they are able to identify potential joint ventures far enough in advance that they can be implemented easily.

It is worth noting that three companies that are successful in coordinating related projects are organized differently. One firm has a centralized, corporate-level research function that services the needs of its different divisions. The second has research staffs at the corporate level and in most of its many divisions. The third has a market research function in one operating division, serving the other divisions as well as corporate-level needs. In all three cases, the research staff has an independent budget but it also relies on client funding. The fact that many differences exist among firms that successfully pursue joint research ventures suggests that researcher commitment to the idea, more than organizational arrangement, is the most important factor in determining whether it occurs.

DATA RELEVANCY

Two simple questions need to be asked concerning relevance. The first is, "What data are relevant to a specific decision?" The second is, "What is the special relevance of a given set of data?" The first question focuses on defining the kinds and sources of needed data that might be relevant and available. The second focuses on the relevance of the data on hand to a specific problem (see the discussion of KNOWLEDGE USE© in Chapter 5). Often data are collected that are thought to be relevant (the first question), but when in hand and analyzed are found not to be relevant at all (the second question). This occurs most commonly when either the wrong question is asked or the right question is asked but pursued incorrectly. The right question may be operationalized improperly, asked of the wrong people, asked at the wrong time, and so forth. Data cannot be better than the thinking that goes into the framing of questions and issues, nor can they be better than the approach used to answer the question. Thus, for example, if there is a 90 percent chance of asking the right question and a 90 percent chance of pursuing it correctly, there is still only an 81 percent chance of obtaining useful data. This is why the query process discussed in Chapter 7 and the actual research process discussed in Chapter 4 are so important. When data are found not to be relevant it is often because of a faulty query process. The wrong questions may have been asked and hence the wrong problems solved. This is what Ian Mitroff calls errors of the third kind: Just as there is a probability of accepting something as true when it is, in fact, false, and a probability of rejecting something as false when it is, in fact, true, so is there a probability of solving the wrong problem?[2]

DATA RELIABILITY

Each of the basic activities in the knowledge-use process (e.g., queries, data, analysis, and so forth) adds its own unique value. The data activity adds value by establishing what representations about the marketplace are available. But the value of those data is limited by the confidence that the user has in them and in the research process used.

It is essential that the market research function create an understanding among general management that it uses accepted and well-established standards and procedures in the collection, analysis, and presentation of market knowledge. The role of the internal research staff, particularly when outside research suppliers are relied on for data acquisition and processing, is similar to the role of an accounting firm in reporting corporate results to stockholders. A large company uses the professional expertise and accepted procedures of the accounting firm in its relationship with its stockholders by saying, "You can be confident that what we're showing you is valid, because the accounting firm, whose practices we both accept as valid, has certified that we have followed accepted accounting principles in developing this report."

Managers' confidence in the rigorous standards of the research staff frees them from having to worry about the quality of the information and enables them to concentrate on assessing its meaning and developing possible actions. Similarly, senior management to whom these actions are proposed can focus on the proposals and not on the techniques of collection.

The state-of-the-art in market research is highly developed, and there are few good reasons why relevant data cannot be collected, analyzed in proper ways, and presented to users with reasonable speed. Moreover, in the knowledge provider industry there is substantial expertise in a broad spectrum of market research approaches which are appropriate for an equally broad spectrum of management issues. Thus, most (but not all) significant issues managers face are researchable. And constant progress is being made in finding more rapid and economical ways of making data available.

Despite the sophisticated state-of-the-art of market research, not all data collected are fully used. One reason is that many managers do not believe that it is possible to measure and explain customer preference or choice accurately, especially with regard to new product concepts. These managers are reluctant to approach the customer with their ideas for fear that if their ideas do not receive a good "report card" upper management will pull the plug on their projects. To protect their ideas, these managers keep them from customer studies until "it is right," which is usually at a point in the development cycle when (a) points of view have been cemented or important decisions made; (b) time pressure does not allow modifications; and (c) considerable funds have already been spent. A seasoned executive from one of the nation's leading research organizations commented that

> Time and again I've seen clients seek a study as a kind of insurance policy. They want to make sure they're not about to make a mistake with a new idea about to go to market. Apart from wondering about this at the wrong end of the decision process they sometimes [can't use] the information no matter what the results are. When you are in a last minute situation it is sometimes cheaper to follow through with a bad idea than to "can" the project.

Of course, other managers do understand that accurate measures of customer preferences can be obtained through research. However, many of them are wary of the research staff. They have had experiences that condition them to believe that staff groups, especially at the corporate level, are predisposed to interpret research results in ways that support their own positions.

This either discourages operating managers from requesting research from a staff function or encourages them to do it on their own. It is necessary to avoid situations in which managers are skeptical of the ability of research to provide accurate and relevant data or suspect that the research staff has a special position of its own.

CONCLUSION

Data are representations of reality and come in a variety of forms. They may range from highly quantitative descriptions of events to intuitive feelings based on past experience. The cost of acquiring data varies according to the type of data and how readily they can be used on multiple occasions. The value of data is affected by the number of different users. It is important that standard, accepted practices be followed in the collection, processing, and presentation of data, and that managers understand that these practices are being followed. This frees managers to think less about the validity of data and more about their meaning and applications.

Notes

1. See, for example, Harper Boyd et al., *Marketing Research: Text and Cases*, 7th ed. (Homewood, IL: Richard D. Irwin, 1989), pp. 168–207; and Bob Shaw and Merlin Stone, "Competitive Superiority through Data Base Marketing," *Long Range Planning*, vol. 21, no. 5 (October 1988), pp. 24–40.
2. Ian I. Mitroff, *Business Not as Usual* (San Francisco: Jossey-Bass, 1987).

THE REALITY OF KNOWLEDGE USE

In Part IV we investigate the world of the information user. Chapter 9 discusses the interpretation of data, which is at least as important to the user as it is to the provider of information. The special focus on biases is particularly important to managers, both with respect to the development of their own analyses and in their evaluation of analyses provided by others.

Chapter 10 addresses the problem of generating alternative actions and selecting the best one. This problem is approached in a unique way. First, we stress the fact that critical decisions made in an organization are often related to one another. We then present a special framework for coordinating decisions so that they reinforce one another. This creates positive synergy in the firm's decision network.

Chapter 11 is of equal concern to information users and providers. It addresses the issue of how to improve whatever inquiry center is already in place in an organization. The inquiry center "champion" is likely to be a manager as most organizations do not have a formal research function. This chapter emphasizes the importance of the champion as change agent and recommends an incremental approach to improving how the organization currently hears the voice of the market and balances it with the voice of the firm.

In Chapter 12 we address the concept of learning, especially learning about how a manager thinks about a problem. Particular emphasis is given to uncovering theories-in-use, or the implicit models managers use more or less automatically when making decisions. The more the implicit theories or models can be made explicit the easier it is to improve them and increase the likelihood of an enduring improvement in the decision process. We use as an example the collaboration between Mr. Burton and Ms. Reynolds, whose correspondence began this book.

CHAPTER 9

Developing Analyses and Breaking through Biases

Analysis is the process of using data to arrive at and interpret ideas. It is the thinking that follows statements such as, "These data say . . . ," "What this tells me is . . . ," or "This indicates that . . . " Although stimulated by data, interpretive ideas are like hunches, far-out theories, and tentative hypotheses. They don't just suddenly emerge full-blown from data.

Analyses are based on different kinds of data. For example,

- After examining certain statistics involving a sample of nearly 1,100 people, a product manager concluded that customers were not willing to sacrifice performance on a particular product attribute in favor of improved performance on another attribute.
- On viewing several focus groups, a service manager concluded that the ambience of the customer waiting area had a far greater impact on customer satisfaction than originally thought.
- After hearing a speech by a senior scientist from a competing firm, an R&D manager concluded that his competitor was much further along in the development of a new waste treatment process than had been believed.

We begin with a discussion of how to stimulate the development of analyses. As is true with so many issues in this book, identifying and then challenging key assumptions is an important part of the process. We then discuss the behavioral biases that shape our interpretations of data. The last section of the chapter is concerned with the logical inconsistencies and fallacies that frequently creep into our analyses.

Even with considerable data available managers may do little analysis. This is due in part to the "failure-of-success" syndrome. When something works well, one naturally tries to repeat it; but when the situation changes, a successful blueprint for analysis and action can lead to error. When an important market condition has changed, managers often fail to detect it, or, if they do, they fail to analyze it properly. They fail to see that past thinking and actions, although successful, may need to be altered.

DEVELOPING ANALYSES

Effective data analysis depends heavily on the ability to recognize patterns that tell a story. The more precise the statement of the basic query, and the more careful the data collection process, the easier it is to recognize and describe patterns.

Managers use at least four basic types of analyses:[1]

- *Alert analyses* create an awareness of important events that have just happened or are about to happen. The event could be a major but unexpected action by a competitor or a regulatory agency or a product tampering crisis.
- *Current analyses* provide basic operating information such as daily or weekly sales figures, inventory assessments, periodic measures of market share, and other tracking studies.
- *Basic analyses* go beyond executive summaries and provide detailed information about an issue. The user may rely on the executive summary primarily but will have the detail necessary to implement a decision.
- *Estimate analyses* relate to future events such as the training required by office personnel to function in the "office of the future" or the nature of home entertainment systems in the year 2000. These analyses may be scenarios of unfolding events or simply a snapshot picture of a future situation.

The same set of data may provide multiple kinds of analyses. For example, to help make expansion plans, a firm prepared an estimate analysis concerning the demand for certain paper products in the late 1990s. These same data helped the firm expand its current market for an existing product line by identifying a user group never before considered. This enabled the firm to use more of its production capacity and achieve certain cost efficiencies. An alert analysis was serendipitously provided. While developing the estimate analysis the company discovered that a competitor was evaluating the same paper product market. To raise the necessary funds to enter this market, it was considering selling one of its subsidiaries. The subsidiary's major product line was a formidable competitor in one of the company's other markets. Thus, the company was alerted to a potentially important change in its competitive environment and was able to develop contingency plans. The estimate analysis provided unexpected analyses of value to other managers in the firm.

The ability to derive a story, that is, to see meaningful and coherent patterns in data, depends as much on the robustness of thinking in the early stages as it does on the technical aspects of how data are obtained, processed, presented, and evaluated. In fact, careful yet imaginative thinking *prior* to a research effort is a condition for making effective use of that research in the decision-making process. And part of that up-front effort involves challenging our own prejudices and preconceptions. We must guard against the possibility of deriving a story that is more coherent with our beliefs than it is with reality.

Thinking Probes

To challenge existing thinking researchers and clients need to use certain "thinking probes," or truth tests when approaching a research problem (see also Chapter 7). The examples below are drawn from specific market situations, hence their conclusions may not be universal.

Form. What appears to be a single dimension of market behavior may be more complex. We must ask, then, whether there are more dimensions than meet the eye. For example, a small manufacturer of plastic materials established a market development plan based on the assumption that price was the sole determinant in customer purchase decisions. A newly hired manager convinced senior management to test this assumption. It was found that while price was important, so, too, were the supplier's dependability, ability to respond to unusual requirements, and ability to provide technical consultation.

Sufficiency of evidence. Here the question is whether what was considered sufficient evidence to support a position is sufficient after all, or whether what was considered insufficient evidence might not in actuality be sufficient. In the example above, the new manager had worked for a firm selling other materials to essentially the same customers. His experience enabled him to question the evidence his new colleagues used to support their belief that price was the only significant customer decision variable.

Subjectivity. Is what seems to be an objective assessment in fact highly subjective (or vice versa)? A regional investment brokerage company planning a major promotional program targeted at individual investors hired an outside firm to conduct the necessary developmental research. The brokerage staff assigned to work with the research firm believed that client loyalty to the brokerage company versus loyalty to individual account representatives was a critical issue. The broker firm's CEO, however, insisted that account representatives were not influential in a client's decision to select and remain with a brokerage house; thus, he felt the issue of relative loyalty should not be researched. Insights about this contention were readily available from existing records, yet the CEO felt that even this simple documentation effort was unnecessary. The brokerage staff was concerned about the CEO's objectivity on the issue but felt it necessary to drop the loyalty issue from the study. However, the research project director pursued the matter with the CEO and eventually found an acceptable way to address the issue. As it turned out, the research (as far as this company was concerned) largely supported the CEO's position. This was a surprise to the research team and brokerage staff, which had developed a number of reasons why the CEO was acting so "defensively."

Co-relation and co-variation. It is useful to challenge the assumption that events or factors are or are not related to one another. Mistaking an "associational" relationship between factors for a "causal" relationship is common. A distributor of plumbing supplies and equipment assumed that its sales force compensation plan was highly effective in encouraging sales staff to develop new business. The plan had been in place for about two years, during which time new-business development increased significantly. When this activity began to drop off noticeably, top management was puzzled. No change in compensation arrangements had occurred. A specialist in sales force compensation was asked to assess the situation. It was found that the system had not, in fact, stimulated the earlier increase in new-business development. At best, the two factors were unrelated. In fact, there was some evidence that the system might even have resulted in less of an increase had not other factors been present.

Composition. What appears to be homogeneous events and situations are often not. The management of a limousine service in the New York City area believed its clients couldn't be differentiated from one another in a meaningful way. It decided to test this assumption. Using certain market segmentation techniques, it discovered that its clients could be divided into three basic groups. This resulted in better (and differentiated) service to each group and enabled the firm to expand services to a new user group.

There are several other tools to challenge existing thinking.[2] These are described briefly below. In addition, recall the techniques we discussed in Chapter 5, which are also helpful in surfacing and addressing a variety of biases in the use of information.

1. *Methodology.* Challenging the idea that a given methodology is appropriate for a given task.
2. *Separation.* Challenging the idea that what appear to be separable or inseparable phenomena are not.
3. *Supply.* Challenging the idea that what appears to be a fixed or variable resource is not.
4. *Organization.* Challenging the idea that what seems to be a disorganized (unstructured) or organized (structured) phenomenon is not.

5. *Generalization.* Challenging the idea that what appears to be a unique (local) or general (global) phenomenon is not.
6. *Stabilization.* Challenging the idea that what appears to be a stable or unstable phenomenon is not.
7. *Function.* Challenging the idea that what is a good means or a bad means to an end is not.
8. *Opposition.* Challenging the idea that what seem to be nearly identical or opposite phenomena are not.

BEHAVIORAL BIASES

Biases are distortions in the way we evaluate events. They reflect special orientations in the perception and processing of data. There are two major types of bias. One stems from the methodological and statistical procedures used to acquire and process data. Most biases of this sort are avoidable but a few are not. Standard procedures exist for identifying, measuring, reducing, and even eliminating methodological and statistical bias. For this reason, problems can be minimized, and where biases exist, they can be made explicit.

The other type presents a much greater problem and is the primary concern of this chapter. These biases have sociological and psychological origins. They are rarely explicit, often subtle, and relatively few procedures exist (see Chapter 5) to detect and eliminate them. They can also cause methodological and statistical bias.

Biases reside in our frames of reference, that is, in our assumptions, decision rules, and expectations. They are often consistent with one another and thus mutually reinforcing. We may conceptualize a problem in a biased way, collect data about the problem in a biased way, interpret the data in a biased way, and then conclude in a biased way that we have developed a clear picture of reality.

It is difficult if not impossible to avoid all biases. In fact, many experts say that the idea of an "objective" reality is a chimera; that all data are value laden and biased. This is one reason why managers and researchers need to examine an issue from multiple perspectives, which often means from the standpoint of multiple biases.

In the discussion that follows, we describe biases that are especially important to understand when implementing the knowledge-use process.[3] These are the biases that influence how we evaluate proposed and ongoing ideas and actions and the data on which they are based. For better or for worse, they are an integral part of the development of market analyses. After reading this section readers are urged to review the Appendix at the end of the chapter. It is an excellent and more detailed summary, prepared by Robin Hogarth, of the main sources of bias as reported in the research literature.[4]

Biases in the Evaluation of Information

There is a tendency to give more emphasis and greater credence to information that is concrete, retrievable, and salient.

Concreteness. People place disproportionately greater emphasis on concrete information than on more abstract and yet possibly more reliable information. For example, a focus group in which customers make explicit comments provides visual and verbal "concreteness" to the observing manager. In contrast, the results of a large telephone survey about the same issue which the manager doesn't monitor are seen by the manager as more abstract, even though it is a more reliable and accurate measure of customer thinking and behavior. Concreteness bias arises when the focus group information contradicts that of the phone survey and the manager instinctively acts on the information provided by the focus group. (This runs counter to the conventional and questionable wisdom that qualitative studies are vague and "soft.") A major complaint among researchers is that managers too often act on the basis of focus groups conducted for exploratory purposes and ignore their unreliability as confirmatory research.

Retrievability. This bias exists when our ability to recall an event influences our judgment about it. For example, our ability to recall one set of data better than another may cause us to place more emphasis on that set of data as a guide in decision making. However, the reason for recalling it better may be unrelated to its validity or decision-making value. The convenient-light syndrome described in Chapter 6 is a special version of the retrievability bias.

Salience. This exists when certain data—or even certain people—are especially prominent and lead us to overrepresent the significance of those data. For example, a surprising research result may be given undue attention simply because it stands out, not because of its reliability. The way in which a person presents information can also affect how it is evaluated. The presenter can influence how the audience will later evaluate the information by making certain elements more salient than others without having to make his or her own evaluations obvious.

Hypothesis-Confirming Biases

Hypothesis-confirming biases were discussed in earlier chapters. They concern the tendency to seek confirmatory evidence in what questions are asked, how they are asked, or in the kinds of data being collected. One field of study, "expectancy theory" addresses this type of bias. It explores the tendency for people to act in ways that actually bring about the results they expect. For example, there is an expectation in a firm that customers are unhappy with a product feature. Sales personnel (or researchers) may then unintentionally phrase questions in such a way as to elicit unfavorable statements from customers about the feature, even if customers are relatively satisfied with it. These expectancy-related processes are powerful and yet sufficiently subtle that managers and researchers are generally unaware of them.

A related bias is referred to as "cognitive dissonance" or "post-decision doubt." Once a commitment is made, doubt may arise about the wisdom of the decision—a doubt so strong that it produces tension and a consequent need to reduce it. This is especially likely when alternative decisions were attractive or when there was considerable ambiguity about which was the best decision. Thus, managers may seek supportive evidence confirming that a choice already made was the best decision, or at least a very wise one. This is one reason why studies are done on actions already decided upon. The need to reduce dissonance heightens the selective processes operating on what information we expose ourselves to, what we perceive, and what we recall. There will be a strong bias toward finding information supporting the decision and a bias away from information suggesting it was not a good one.

Observer and Participant Biases

There can be different biases depending on whether one is an observer or a participant in the decision process. For example, researchers (observers) become committed to a new-product idea based on their personal judgments about it and the enthusiasm of managers. The bias arises out of a desire to see it succeed simply because the idea is intrinsically appealing. This positivity bias may lead to confirmatory biases. Similarly, when research staffs are too closely tied to a brand management group or are rewarded in the same way as these managers are, they may develop product commitments that unintentionally lead to biased methodologies. One of the reasons for insisting on accepted and standard research practices is to avoid this kind of researcher bias and even the suspicion of it among managers.

Observer and participant biases may surface in other ways. In looking for the cause of, say, poor product performance, the product manager (the participant) is more likely to attribute it to situational factors, such as competitor tactics, dealer problems, acts of God, and so forth, than to one over which he or she had some control. An outside observer, such as a consultant, is more likely to trace the poor performance to its true source.

Insensitivity to Statistical Principles

We frequently generalize from a very small sample even when we know that in a technical sense it is incorrect to do so. For example, one bad experience at a restaurant may influence the diner never to return. However, the same person might strongly object to not pursuing a new-product idea simply because of the negative results of a single focus group.

We often make important judgments about a person's capabilities on the basis of a limited and highly controlled interaction. We may be unsure of our judgments but want to act on them. Similarly, we may decide that what three or four customers say is representative of the larger population and not seek further opinions.

Statisticians use a concept called "regression toward the mean" in which there is an especially high (or low) number of individual outcomes that are unlikely to recur. Outcomes likely to repeat will tend toward a mean that may be well below (above) the high (low) number of individual outcomes. This is a common pattern. Despite knowing this, we tend to ignore it and have continued high levels of expectation as a result of a single or few cases of unusually strong (weak) performance. Thus, when managers or salespeople perform well in one or a few instances we continue to view them as stars, even though they never achieve that level of performance again.

Ex Post Facto Judgment

A special kind of bias arises when we try to determine the causes of an event after it has happened. We typically seek a simple, sufficient explanation and reject complex necessary explanations.[5] The procedures of formal research lessen the incidence of ex post facto judgments. However, in other ways of learning about and understanding the marketplace, we run a higher risk of making this kind of error. In fact, this kind of post hoc thinking is common in our interpretation of personal experiences. While intuition, experience, and expert opinion are valid and important sources of knowledge, they are apt to cause us to generalize from a few data points, focus on the least complicated explanation, and not look for more powerful underlying causes of events.

Information Preferences

The circumstances under which a decision is made can bias the use of information.[6] In a situation where there is no risk associated with either an action or its alternative, the tendency is to be indifferent to both supportive and nonsupportive information.

Another set of biases occurs when all options involve serious risks and a sense that no good solution can be found. Here, if there is no deadline, the manager may procrastinate and avoid data that require serious thinking. When there is a close deadline and the manager can shift responsibility to someone else, there will be relatively little information seeking and efforts will be made to find an outside expert or a superior to make the decision. When concerned by an approaching deadline and no opportunity to shift responsibility, the decision maker will seek information that supports his or her inclination and will avoid information that does not.

In the ideal situation, the decision maker is aware of the risks associated with decision options, has sufficient time and resources to evaluate options, and seeks both confirming and disconfirming information, while selecting only the most relevant data from reliable sources. The ideal situation rarely occurs. Even positive outcomes do not confirm that the right research and analysis were done. When asked how they knew they were selecting the best option, managers frequently responded that they knew only after the decision was made, implemented, and then evaluated. In other words, because a decision produced good results, it is somehow assumed to have been the best decision, even though there is no sound evidence that other options wouldn't have produced even better outcomes. Unfortunately, this common way of evaluating actions contains elements of many of the biases we have identified.

The situations leading to possible bias are unavoidable. Some problems by their very nature make it difficult to collect both confirming and disconfirming evidence. In addition, problems can't always be anticipated early enough to conduct the kind of inquiries that would provide helpful and reliable information. Furthermore, acquiring both confirming and disconfirming data can be costly and not justifiable. Thus, the absence of the ideal circumstance does not necessarily imply poor researcher or manager practice. What is important, however, is that managers and researchers be sensitive to the kind of less-than-ideal situation they are in. This sensitivity can create an awareness of the biases that are most likely to arise. Forewarned . . . forearmed.

FALLACIES

Incorrect explanations or analyses that have the power to persuade us are called fallacies.[7] There are many kinds, and most are accepted unwittingly. Below we describe some of the more common ones.

Distraction

Magicians have raised "sleight-of-hand" to an art form, distracting our attention from reality to the illusion they would have us embrace. Managers and politicians are no less skillful in this art, which has three variations: false dilemma, slippery slope, and straw man.

False dilemma. A broad array of alternatives is often narrowly defined, using either/or terms, to involve only two, drastically different, alternatives when, in fact, many other options are available. For example, consider the statement, "We either go ahead with the product launch or we kill it." The "either/or" terminology should prompt us to ask whether there are any other alternatives.

Slippery slope. This reasoning claims that if we follow a particular course of action, other events will naturally follow, ending in an undesirable situation. For example: "If we offer rebates now, our competitors will start offering them; and then future customers will expect incentives and defer purchases until we offer them again." Here it is important to ask whether there are ways of implementing a decision that can avoid unintended and undesirable consequences, and to challenge the implied inevitability of these consequences.

Straw man. A third distractive sleight-of-hand is the straw man, which involves making an opposing position appear weaker in order to make one's own position appear stronger by focusing attention on a single, unattractive feature of the opposing position. Yet there may be other, more important, reasons to favor the opposing argument. One way of responding to this is to elicit arguments for and against each position. For example, a research study indicated that the initial acceptance of a new consumer durable good would be lukewarm at best. A product manager who feared that the new product would cannibalize her product used these data to build a persuasive argument against launching the new product. The "champion" for the new product brought forth other data from the same research showing that the prospects for longer-term success warranted its introduction. The champion's argument was bolstered by competitor intelligence that showed other reasons for entering the market.

Counterfeit Reasoning

In this fallacy, certain props are used as substitutes for a sound analysis. An interesting example is a study of sales promotion budget-setting practices in the office furniture business. Nearly all firms used the same approach— essentially, the sales promotion budget would be based on a percentage of sales; many used a similar percentage. The main reason given by managers for using this approach was, in effect, "Experts, that is, other experienced managers, are in complete agreement. Since they all follow the same practice, it must be a good approach." Indeed, consensus among experienced managers can be an important indicator. However, the study also uncovered the fact that with but one or two exceptions, managers had no other justification for setting budgets as they did.

Begging the question. Another form of counterfeit reasoning is begging the question. Here, the conclusion that follows the premise is simply a restatement of the premise. It might be true, but it doesn't add insight. For example, "If managers have relevant information, they will feel it is appropriate to the problem they face" is a true statement. However, appropriateness to a problem is simply an indicator of relevance. It is not independent of it.

Emotional Appeals

Emotional appeals can be legitimate or improper, depending on the motivations of the arguer and the consequences of the position being advocated.

Appeal to force and appeal to pity. An appeal to force is the threat of incurring disfavor if certain data are brought forth. It is offered in lieu of logical or legitimate reasons. A related improper use of emotional appeal is an appeal to pity. Here, a researcher is asked to "hide," or downplay, certain data because they may make a manager look bad. This is often expressed by some variant of the following statement: "You really shouldn't present this because it is misleading and will be used as a report card against me." Data, of course, can be misinterpreted and used wrongly, in which case the appeal may be appropriate. For example, in response to complaints from some sales personnel, a major pharmaceutical firm hired a consultant to help it reorganize its method of monitoring company and industry sales and to come up with a better way of analyzing data on sales force performance. One outcome was the discovery that some sales personnel believed to be high performers (even winners of company awards) were actually doing quite poorly, while others believed to be poor performers were actually doing very well. The firm had been misinterpreting data because they hadn't been processed or organized in the most insightful way, and wrongly using the data as "report cards."

Prejudicial language. Another form of emotional appeal in lieu of support involves the use of prejudicial language, which may appear quite innocent. One manager commented that whenever she hears the term "clearly," as in, "These data clearly show . . . ," she immediately suspects that the data may not be clear at all. At other times the prejudicial language may be more evident. This same manager, when describing her firm's overly cautious management style, suggested that a favorite ploy among some staff was to introduce a less-preferred action or alternative with phrases such as, "A more risky approach that could work . . . " or "A more imaginative option that hasn't been tried yet is. . . . " Management in her firm had the same degree of comfort with the terms "risky," "imaginative," and "untried" as it had with "death," "taxes," and "leprosy." When prejudicial language is used for deceptive purposes, the intent is to stigmatize alternatives.

CONCLUSION

Developing ideas or analyses from data is a challenging and important task when the issue or the decision to be made is not routine and is neither clearly defined nor well structured, a characterization of most decisions that have significant consequences. This is also the kind of situation that brings forth multiple and conflicting interpretations of data and where differences in managers and researchers' frames of reference—the viewing lens— become most evident. It is important in all decision situations to probe and challenge existing thinking and to be sensitive to the presence of biases in the analysis of data. Biases are unavoidable and not necessarily bad. Being sensitive to the nature and presence of biases helps guard against their undesirable effects.

Notes

1. Arthur S. Hulnick, "Managing Intelligence Analysis: Strategies for Playing the End Game," *International Journal of Intelligence and Counterintelligence* (August 1988), pp. 321–343.
2. Gerald Zaltman, Karen LeMasters, and Michael Heffring, *Theory Construction in Marketing* (New York: John Wiley, 1982).
3. This discussion uses a schema suggested by Richard M. Perloff et al., "Socio-cognitive Biases in the Evaluation Process," *New Directions for Program Evaluation*, vol. 7 (1980), pp. 11–26.
4. Robin M. Hogarth, *Judgement and Choice* (New York: John Wiley, 1987).
5. Perloff et al., "Sociocognitive Biases in the Evaluation Process," p. 20.
6. I.L. Janis and L. Mann, *Decision Making: Psychological Analysis of Conflict, Choice, and Commitment* (New York: Free Press, 1977).
7. Jerry Cederblom and David W. Paulsen, *Critical Reasoning: Understanding and Criticizing Arguments and Theories*, 2d ed. (Belmont, CA: Wadsworth Publishing, 1986), p. 9.

APPENDIX TO CHAPTER 9

Bias/source of bias	Description	Example
ACQUISITION		
Availability	—Ease with which specific instances can be recalled from memory affects judgements of frequency.	—Frequency of well-publicized events is overestimated (e.g., deaths due to homicide, cancer); frequency of less well-publicized events is underestimated (e.g., deaths due to asthma and diabetes).
	—Chance 'availability' of particular 'cues' in the immediate environment affects judgement.	—Problem-solving can be hindered/facilitated by cues perceived by chance in a particular setting (hints set up cognitive 'direction').
Selective perception	—People structure problems on the basis of their own experience.	—The same problem can be seen by a marketing manager as a marketing problem, as a financial problem by a finance manager, etc.
	—Anticipations of what one expects to see bias what one does see.	—Identification of incongruent objects, e.g., playing cards with *red* spades, is either inaccurately reported or causes discomfort.
	—People seek information consistent with their own views/hypotheses.	—Interviewers seek information about candidates consistent with first impressions rather than information that could refute those impressions.
	—People downplay/disregard conflicting evidence.	—In forming impressions, people underweight information that does not fit a consistent profile.

Appendix continued

Bias/source of bias	Description	Example
Frequency	—Cue used to judge strength of predictive relations is observed frequency rather than observed relative frequency. Information on 'non-occurrences' of an event is often unavailable and frequently ignored when available.	—When considering relative performance (of, say, two persons), the absolute number of successes is given greater weight than the relative number of successes to successes *and* failures (i.e., the denominator is ignored). Note, however, that the number of failures is frequently unavailable.
Concrete information (ignoring base-rate, or prior information)	—*Concrete* information (i.e., vivid, or based on experience/incidents) dominates *abstract* information (e.g., summaries, statistical base-rates, etc.).	—When purchasing a car, the positive or negative experience of a *single* person you know is liable to weigh more heavily in judgement than available and more valid statistical information, e.g., in *Consumer Reports*.
Illusory correlation	—Belief that two variables covary when in fact they do not (possibly related to 'Frequency' above).	—Selection of an inappropriate variable to make a prediction.
Data presentation	—Order effects (primacy/recency).	—Sometimes the first items in a sequential presentation assume undue importance (primacy), sometimes the last items (recency).
	—Mode of presentation.	—Sequential vs. intact data displays can affect what people are able to access. Contrast, for example, complete listed unit-price shopping vs. own sequential information.

Bias/source of bias	Description	Example
	—Mixture of types of information e.g., qualitative and quantitative.	—Concentration on quantitative data, exclusion of qualitative, or vice versa.
	—Logical data displays.	—Apparently complete 'logical' data displays can blind people to critical omissions.
	—Context effects on perceived variability.	—Assessments of variability, of say a series of numbers, is affected by the absolute size (e.g., mean level) of the numbers.
Framing	—Outcomes are evaluated as deviations from reference points or levels of aspirations. This can interact with the way people evaluate outcomes that are 'framed' as losses or gains.	—Loss versus gains frames can induce reversals in expressed choices.
PROCESSING		
Inconsistency	—Inability to apply a consistent judgemental strategy over a repetitive set of cases.	—Judgements involving selection, e.g., personnel/graduate school admissions.
Conservatism	—Failure to revise opinion on receipt of new information to the same extent as Bayes' theorem. (Note this may be counterbalanced by the 'best-guess' strategy and produce near optimal performance in the presence of unreliable data sources.)	—Opinion revision in many settings, e.g., military, business, medicine.

Appendix continued

Bias/source of bias	Description	Example
Non-linear extrapolation	—Inability to extrapolate growth processes (e.g., exponential) and tendency to underestimate joint probabilities of several events.	—Gross underestimation of outcomes of exponentially increasing processes and over-estimation of joint probabilities of several events.

'Heuristics' used to reduce mental effort:

—Habit/'rules of thumb'	—Choosing an alternative because it has previously been satisfactory.	—Consumer shopping; 'rules of thumb' adopted in certain professions.
—Anchoring and adjustment	—Prediction made by anchoring on a cue or value and then adjusting to allow for the circumstances of the present case.	—Making a sales forecast by taking last year's sales and adding, say, 5%.
—Representativeness	—Judging the likelihood of an event by estimating degree of *similarity* to the class of events of which it is supposed to be an exemplar.	—Stereotyping, e.g., imagining that someone is a lawyer because he exhibits characteristics typical of a lawyer.
—Law of *small* numbers	—Characteristics of small samples are deemed to be representative of the populations from which they are drawn.	—Interpretation of data, too much weight given to small sample results (which are quite likely to be atypical).
—Justifiability	—A 'processing' rule can be used if the individual finds a rationale to 'justify' it.	—When provided with an apparently rational argument, people will tend to follow a decision rule even if it is really inappropriate.

Bias/source of bias	Description	Example
—Regression bias	—Extreme values of a variable are used to predict extreme values of the next observation of the variable (thus failing to allow for regression to the mean).	—Following observation of bad performance by an employee, a manager could attribute subsequent improvement to his or her intervention (e.g., warning to the employee). However, due to regression effects, improvement (performance closer to the mean level) is likely *without* intervention.
—'Best guess' strategy	—Under conditions involving several sources of uncertainty, simplification is made by ignoring some uncertainties and basing judgement on the 'most likely' hypothesis. (Note, people simplify by ignoring uncertainty.) More generally, tendency to discount uncertainty.	—Ignoring the fact that information sources are unreliable.

The decision environment:

—Complexity	—Complexity induced by time pressure, information overload, distractions lead to reduced consistency of judgement.	—In decisions taken under time pressure information processing may be quite superficial.
—Emotional stress	—Emotional stress reduces the care with which people select and process information.	—Panic judgements.

Appendix continued

Bias/source of bias	Description	Example
—Social pressures	—Social pressures, e.g., of a group, cause people to distort their judgements.	—The majority in a group can unduly influence the judgement of minority members.

Information sources:

—Consistency of information sources	—Consistency of information sources can lead to increases in confidence in judgement but not increased predictive accuracy.	—People often like to have more information, even though it is redundant with what they already have.

—Data presentation: See items under the ACQUISITION section.

OUTPUT

Response mode:

—Question format	—The way a person is required or chooses to make a judgement can affect the outcome.	—Preferences for risky gambles have been found to be inconsistent with the prices for which people are willing to sell them.
—Scale effects	—The scale on which responses are recorded can affect responses.	—Estimates of probabilities can vary when estimated directly on a scale from zero to one, or when 'odds' or even 'log-odds' are used.
—Wishful thinking	—People's preferences for outcomes of events affect their assessment of the events.	—People sometimes assess the probability of outcomes they desire to be greater than their state of knowledge justifies.
—Illusion of control	—Activity concerning an uncertain outcome can by itself induce in a person feelings of control over the uncertain event.	—Activities such as planning, or even the making of forecasts, can induce feelings of control over the uncertain future.

Bias/source of bias	Description	Example
FEEDBACK		
Outcome irrelevant learning structures	—Outcomes observed yield inaccurate or incomplete information concerning predictive relations. This can lead, *inter alia*, to unrealistic confidence in one's own judgement.	—In personnel selection you can learn how good your judgement is concerning candidates selected; but you usually have no information concerning subsequent performance of rejected candidates.
Misperception of chance fluctuations (e.g., gambler's fallacy)	—Observation of an unexpected number of similar chance outcomes leads to the expectation that the probability of the appearance of an event not recently seen increases.	—So-called 'gambler's fallacy'—after observing, say, 9 successive Reds in roulette, people tend to believe that Black is more likely on the next throw.
Success/failure attributions	—Tendency to attribute success to one's skill, and failure to chance (this is also related to the 'Illusion of control'—see above).	—Successes in one's job, e.g., making a difficult sale, are attributed to one's skill; failures to 'bad luck'.
Logical fallacies in recall	—Inability to recall details of an event leads to 'logical' reconstruction which can be inaccurate.	—Eyewitness testimony.
Hindsight bias	—In retrospect, people are not 'surprised' about what has happened in the past. They can easily find plausible explanations.	—The 'Monday morning quarterback' phenomenon.

Source: Robin M. Hogarth, *Judgement and Choice*, 2d ed. (New York: John Wiley, 1987), pp. 216–222.

CHAPTER **10**

Knowledge and Wisdom

To be determined and accepted, the meaning of data has to be integrated with judgment. Once that is done it becomes necessary to identify the alternative actions that the meaning suggests and to select the most appropriate one. As indicated in Chapter 2, knowledge and wisdom are the two stages of the information hierarchy that inform the world of the information user. Identifying alternatives is a knowledge activity: the translation of intelligence reports into feasible action alternatives. Wisdom concerns the selection of the action likely to work best.

The process of interpreting data, translating meaning into alternative actions, and selecting the most appropriate is as much art as science. There are many helpful decision aids for generating alternative actions and selecting among them. (These are discussed in the Appendix to the book, organized around the three dimensions of an inquiry center. Because technology is changing so rapidly, specific decision aids are not discussed.)

Ultimately, final decisions are based on managerial judgment. The quality of these judgments depends, in turn, on the quality of information managers have, the quality of their decision support tools, and their creative use of both the tools and the information.

We have been impressed time and again by the fact that the most successful managers are those who are deeply concerned with how information is used to reach decisions. These managers recognize that it is the quality of the thinking process leading to a decision that determines the quality of the decision. They also recognize that they often have far more control over the quality of the decision-making process than they have over the consequences of a decision. That is, there are many things beyond management's control that affect the ultimate success of a decision. The majority of these factors are external to the firm and come into play after a decision has been made.

In many ways the quality of a decision might best be evaluated in terms of how well researchers and managers perform with respect to what it is they can control. They clearly have far more control over the information-use/decision-making process than they do over the many independent forces in the marketplace that influence the success of a particular decision. Put somewhat differently, managers influence the market consequences of their decisions largely through control over the quality of their decision making and risk analysis.

This chapter presents an overall framework, supplementing that provided in Chapter 4, for identifying and selecting actions. It is overarching in the sense that it may be used with whatever decision tools or decision-making approaches managers customarily employ. The framework is not meant to replace or even to stimulate manager creativity; it is a general perspective which helps raise the quality of decision and risk analyses by recognizing that important decisions and the resultant actions are linked with other important decisions and actions. The framework is intended to create a healthy form of synergy in this network of decisions. Before introducing it we will discuss the idea of organizations as decision networks or decision systems.

ORGANIZATIONS AS DECISION NETWORKS

There are many perspectives on the nature of the organization.[1] An organization can be viewed as a set of factors of production, a power system, a network of stakeholders, a decision-making body, a hierarchical arrangement, or a clustering of line and staff personnel. However, the basic idea is that an organization is a network, or system, of decisions. This is much more than saying it is a network of decision *makers*, with a focus on people and departments. Viewing a firm as a network of decisions stresses actions or judgments and the connections among them, which are the ultimate expression of the voice of the firm in the marketplace.

Viewing an organization as a network of decisions highlights two important facts. First, decisions made in one area of a firm frequently affect and are affected by decisions made in another area. Constraints or needs in one area often influence decisions in other areas. Thus, financial accounting decisions affect human resource decisions and vice versa. Second, each functional group often makes decisions that are normally associated with those of other functional groups. Thus, human resource management makes important financial accounting decisions within its function just as financial accounting management makes important human resource decisions within its functional area.

Because so many decisions are part of a network in which each decision directly or indirectly influences another, major decisions must be **consistent** with the goals of the corporation, its business units, and its products and services. Decisions must **complement** one another to maximize their overall impact. These notions of consistency and complementarity, introduced in Chapter 8, are important elements of our framework and create synergy among diverse decisions.

Organizations are networks of decisions that help the organizations respond well to the voice of the market. To do so it becomes essential to generate options and make choices that will lead to positive synergy within the network. Our framework provides basic guidelines for achieving this.

A FRAMEWORK FOR IDENTIFYING AND SELECTING ACTIONS

Our framework is derived from extensive analysis of marketing successes and failures and refined through careful evaluations of formal applications. It is based on two simple principles that can be applied in nearly all decision-making situations. Successful decisions tend to have this framework; failures do not. A more complete presentation of our framework can be found elsewhere.[2]

As we mentioned above, the principles of consistency and complementarity guide the generation and selection of alternatives.

The Consistency Principle

The consistency principle requires that each component of an action plan—say, the marketing mix—be consistent with the plan's overall objective. That is, if the objective of the plan is to provide state-of-the-art technology to customers, then all elements within the marketing mix must be logically derived from (i.e., be consistent with) that objective. On another level it means that all product and service offerings be consistent with (i.e., logically derived from) the goal of the business unit. On still another level, the consistency principle suggests that all business units have goals that are consistent with the overall corporate mission.

One roadblock to the application of the consistency principle is the absence of a well-defined mission within the mindset of the firm. Business units often lack distinctive goals; and their product or services often lack clearly specified concepts, or these concepts change so frequently that they never take root in the customer's mind. The corporate mission, the business unit goal, or the product concept is the essential idea that customers should associate with the firm, the business unit, or product. In generating alternative actions for a particular product, a fundamental criterion must be whether the action is a logical derivative of the product concept. The action must be a reinforcing statement of that concept.

The Complementarity Principle

Decisions in a network of decisions must reinforce each other positively. For example, in conveying the concept of durability a brand manager should be certain that the array of actions being considered with respect to product content, texture, name, packaging, and so forth, all be consistent with durability.

The consistency principle allows managers to identify and select among numerous possible alternative decisions. However, product, promotion, and other decisions that are consistent with a marketing objective are not necessarily complementary with each other. The complementarity principle further reduces options to a single set of actions that are more complementary or reinforcing to one another than is true for any other set of actions. The result is a set of actions that are not only logically derived from or supportive of a higher objective, but also help each other be more effective in achieving that larger objective.

An example of the two principles is provided by one of the world's most reputable manufacturers of camera equipment. High manufacturing costs had put the company under pressure to raise prices significantly on its medium-format camera bodies (cameras that use a larger negative than the conventional 35mm camera). An extensive survey was made of serious amateur and professional photographers to ascertain, among other things, their likely responses to price increases. One analysis showed that the price increase would likely cause many people planning to buy a medium-format camera body in the next four months to switch to another brand. It was also found that an increase now would probably not have this effect on buyers who planned a purchase at least five months away.

The firm needed to raise prices and yet did not want to lose near-term sales. It realized that customers who might be willing to pay higher prices in five or six months would react negatively if they saw a price increase closer to the time of their actual purchase. The firm was truly between a rock and a hard place. Its marketing staff generated a variety of possible actions based on its interpretations of the data.

Each proposed action had to satisfy two important criteria. First, it had to be consistent with the basic product concept that had been established for the camera. Tactics or strategies that might detract from the concept of the camera body or cause confusion among potential buyers as to its craftsmanship and technology were rejected. Second, each proposed pricing action had to complement other marketing decisions. That is, it had to reinforce product, promotion, and distribution decisions already in place or under consideration. (Some product modifications were being introduced and a new promotional program was being developed at this time.) After extensive evaluation of several options the marketing staff selected a fairly routine but highly effective solution to their pricing problem: Announcing a price increase but creating rebates for an extended period which kept the real price the same. However, because it had carefully thought through this and other alternatives, the staff understood why it should work and why it might not, and were thus able to develop an accurate evaluation of the likelihood of success.

It is clear from this example that the decisions of different functional areas affect one another. When decisions are made with the principles of consistency and complementarity in mind, synergy within the organization is enhanced. Synergy is always present in an organization. The thoughtfulness of decisions plays a big part in whether that synergy is positive or negative. This is reflected in part by other comments made by senior members of this camera company.

A member of the research team that had participated in the decision-making process shared with us a very important insight, a version of the convenient-light syndrome:

> One of the fascinating things that occurred in these meetings, and I've seen this in so many other companies and projects, is the tendency to interpret data in ways that favor courses of action we are comfortable with and think we can pull off successfully . . . . [The senior product manager] had to work very hard to get the team to generate alternative actions from what we eventually agreed the data meant and not to agree on what the data meant based on our priors about what actions were feasible. His efforts in this case and in other decisions have started to make a difference. The team is being a lot more creative in how they interpret data and in the array of feasible action implications they develop. We're also seeing marketing programs that are more coherent and successful.

One of the senior executives in this company also shared an important observation concerning staff development: "I expect my managers to be more concerned with how they use information and reach decisions than with the actual decisions." Actual decisions, of course, are of great concern to this person and to his staff. He was exaggerating to make a very important point: It is precisely because final decisions are so important that the process of reaching them demands considerable care and constant improvement. The executive went on to explain:

> For years we were driven by a need to have [answers] fast and to present them with great certitude. We call it now, the "knee jerk planning and fervent prayer affliction." We got pretty efficient at it. Once in a while we even had a success. Well, you know what happened when [the new CEO and president] were brought in to turn things around . . . . A few people were let go because they couldn't drop the habit of grabbing at one or another familiar answer and then becoming its champion. They couldn't develop the ability to think through an answer, be it a creative or conventional one. They

couldn't understand that possible actions or decisions had to be understood in terms of their relationship to other decisions past, ongoing, or likely in the future. [The president] has been especially effective in getting [division directors and product managers] to see how one another's decisions should be reinforcing.

This executive was pointing to the difference between grabbing at an available action and developing an action that clearly conveys product concepts, is consistent with that concept, and reinforces other initiatives. The very same action may be chosen, in the first instance without thought but in the second with care and deliberation. The real danger is the manager's tendency not to reflect but to act—an enshrined virtue in our business culture.

Top-Down and Bottom-Up Processing

Top-down and bottom-up processing are part of the procedure for achieving synergy through the consistency and complementarity principles. Exhibit 10-1 presents four levels at which decisions are made. Each lower level is a set of decisions nested within the decision network of the preceding level. Thus, each level consists of a network of interacting decisions, chosen according to our two basic principles.

We use the marketing mix to illustrate the top-down and bottom-up processes in Exhibit 10-1. As shown in Level II, the components of the marketing mix (the marketing decision network) are product, promotion, distribution, and price. These components, as illustrated by promotion, consist of a submix (Level III). The component parts of promotion are advertising, publicity, sales promotion, and personal selling. Finally, these may have further submixes. For example, the advertising submix consists of theme, copy, auditory cues, and visual cues (Level IV). At each level, components interact with one another to produce positive or negative synergy for two tasks, communication and operations. The communication task conveys the concept of the product, which is congruent with customer needs and preferences. The operating task helps remove transaction barriers between buyers and sellers. (These two tasks are performed at each level in Exhibit 10-1 and will be discussed further.)

The top-down process. When the alternatives for the marketing mix at Level II are developed, the marketing objective specified at Level I must be kept in mind; all the alternatives being considered with respect to promotion, distribution, and so on should be consistent with the Level I marketing objective. The process of moving from a higher-level objective to the identification of consistent lower-level alternatives is a top-down process. Thus, at the top level, Level I, marketing provides guidance for activity at the next level, Level II (see arrows in Exhibit 10-1). Similarly, the basic objective established for the

Exhibit 10-1
Creating Positive Synergy by the Top-Down Process for Consistency and the
Bottom-Up Process for Complementarity

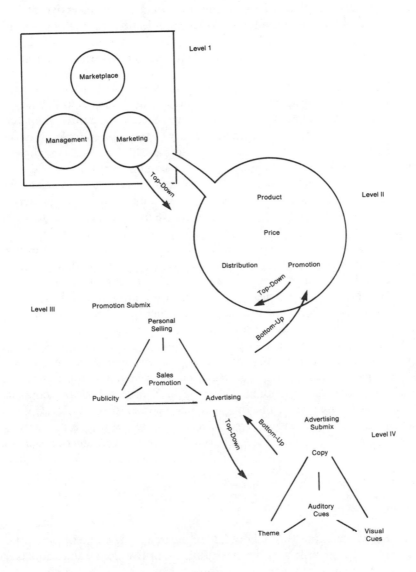

Source: C.W. Park and Gerald Zaltman, *Marketing Management* (Hinsdale, IL: Dryden Press,
1987), p. 29.

promotion component at Level II provides guidance for activity at the next lower level, Level III. Here, too, alternatives chosen at Level III with respect to advertising, personal selling, and so on must be consistent with the objective established at Level II for promotion. Finally, the objective set for advertising at Level III provides guidance in selecting alternatives for its component parts at the next lower level, Level IV; that is, alternatives for copy, theme, and so forth must be consistent with the advertising objective.

The bottom-up process. Once alternatives are specified at each level, the marketing manager must, starting at the bottom (Level IV), select those alternatives most complementary to one another. Stated differently, the alternative chosen for copy must be complementary to that chosen for each of the other components that make up Level IV. This basically involves a juggling of alternatives to find the final choices (one per component) that provide the highest degree of complementarity. This done, the manager proceeds to the next level, Level III, where the process is repeated. Thus, a single set of alternatives is chosen consisting of one alternative from advertising, one from personal selling, and so on. The set should provide the highest degree of complementarity at that level. A similar procedure is followed at Level II before moving on to Level I, where the process is again repeated. When a set of lower-level decisions does not lead to satisfactory complementarity at a higher level, the process is repeated at the lower level to find that lower-level set leading to favorable complementarity at a higher level. Moving from Level IV to Level I is the bottom-up process.

Together the two processes will lead to a high degree of positive synergy. They are not as unwieldy as they may appear. At any given time the firm will have in place at each level a set of decisions, even if the top-down and bottom-up processes are ignored. One way or another, through action or inaction, choices are made concerning each component on every level. What we advocate is simply assessing current decisions in terms of their consistency with a higher-level objective and their complementarity with decisions about other components at the same level. This procedure is one of the most likely to yield positive synergy within a decision network.

Communication and Operating Tasks

Nearly all decisions throughout a firm include at least one of two tasks: the communication task and the operating task. The communication task conveys the product in a way that customers perceive it as being congruent with their needs and preferences. The operating task removes barriers to customer transactions. The five types of transaction barriers are place, time, ownership, perception, and value.

1. *Place* (product accessibility). Goods are generally produced in physical isolation from customers (a place barrier). Making the product or service

available to customers in the right place is one of the important operating tasks. Thus, assembly, distribution, and other marketing activities can reduce the place barrier between buyer and seller.

2. *Time* (product availability). Not having the product or service available at the right time can be another transaction barrier. Stores that are open long hours and on Sundays overcome time barriers for customers who are employed full time.

3. *Ownership* (usability). Ownership barriers are obstacles to owning and/or using a product or service. They include, for example, the difficulty of product installation, unavailability of rental or lease arrangements, a long product delivery period, absence of an installment plan, and the lack of product warranties.

4. *Perception* (identifiability). A perceptual barrier may occur when customers cannot recall the name of the product when needed, and/or have difficulty in identifying the product among competing alternatives. Product design, packaging, brand name, advertising, and salesperson activity reduce these perceptual barriers.

5. *Value* (differential utility). We've already seen how customers compute value. When the price is higher than the amount they are willing to spend, their perception of the value of the product becomes negative (a value barrier). The range of prices customers are willing to pay is often influenced by their perceived utility of the product. While price changes can affect value barriers, so, too, can other marketing mix components.

Coordinating Tasks and Specifying Marketing Objectives

Because communication and operating tasks are related, they should be coordinated in a deliberate way. For example, when a firm does a good job in communicating how a product addresses customer needs, certain transaction barriers are lessened. Customers will think of the product more readily and have higher perceived worth for it, thus lessening value barriers. The selection of distribution outlets is an operating task that helps bring the customer into convenient contact with a product or service. At the same time, the type of outlet used may have a communications implication; jewelry sold by Tiffany's is perceived differently from jewelry sold at J.C. Penney's. The same candy given to a loved one in an attractively wrapped box on Valentine's Day doesn't carry quite the same meaning if given in a brown paper bag.

Communication and operating tasks are like two end points on a hierarchical continuum leading up to a purchase. At one end customers must be interested in the product and understand how it fits their needs. Therefore, a product or service must be presented to them in a way that is consistent with their needs and preferences. This is the task of communication activities. Customer interest may not, however, be transformed into an actual purchase when there are transaction barriers along the way. Operating activities are needed to remove these barriers. When the two tasks are coordinated, with the communication task preceding and subsuming the operating task, a successful exchange is more likely.

As this suggests, marketing objectives must contain an explicit statement of the communication and operating goals. One example of such a marketing objective may be "to increase the awareness of the product concept among a specific target market and to remove specific time, place, and value barriers in 1995 by 10 percent."

Besides specifying communication and operating goals, marketing managers should understand the extent to which accomplishing their objectives will contribute to an increase in sales and/or market share. They should know what support from other functional departments of the firm is necessary to reach particular sales and market share goals. This understanding is critical for the adjustment and control of marketing management activity. Without it, it is difficult to identify possible sources of a problem.

Traditional Statements of Objectives

Specification of marketing objectives in terms of product concept communication and the removal of transaction barriers are departures from common business practice, where marketing objectives and the evaluation of performance are normally based on sales volume, market share, or other readily measured outcomes. There are three reasons why primary marketing objectives should not be expressed in these forms.

First, sales/market share as objectives do not speak to the activities intended to bring them about. Objectives should embody guidelines for subsequent operations and implementation. A 10 percent sales increase as an objective, for example, provides no guidelines, nor does it recognize that the efforts of more than one functional department may be required to accomplish it. On the other hand, product concept communication and the removal of those transaction barriers that are under marketing control should directly guide the development and implementation of the marketing program. For example, formulating and arranging the four components of the marketing mix are directly determined by the product concept offered to prospective customers and the specific operating tasks to be performed. Each set of marketing decisions (product, distribution, promotion, and price) must be consistent with the product concept and the operating task, and complementary to one another.

Second, there is a difficulty in the relative difference in control that marketing managers have over sales and market share, on the one hand, and the communication and operating tasks on the other. As we pointed out earlier, sales and market share are heavily influenced by other forces. When a desired outcome is not within the direct control of marketing managers, it does not serve a useful purpose to include it among marketing objectives. Communication and operating tasks, on the other hand, are within their control.

Third, product concept and corporate mission must be linked. Communicating a firm's mission to the marketplace is ultimately accomplished through its product concepts. Marketing objectives are more readily and logically linked to the corporate mission when they are stated in terms of product concept communication and operating tasks rather than in terms of sales level or market share.

DESIGNING THE MARKETING MIX AS A DECISION NETWORK

The marketing mix—the network of product, price, distribution, and promotion decisions—must include both communication and operating tasks. Although the tasks reinforce one another, communication activities have more initial impact. Customers must understand what they are getting before they will consider a transaction. Examples of successfully communicated concepts are not difficult to find. They include Crest's "tooth-decay prevention," "the superior engineering" of Mercedes-Benz, "the friendly skies" of United Airlines, and "a piece of the rock" as offered by Prudential Insurance Company.

The operating task should aim to remove transaction barriers under marketing's control so that the customers' interest can be transformed into actual transactions. Potential customers who are interested in the firm's product cannot purchase it when it is priced too high or is unavailable.

The manager should see to it that each of the four components of the marketing mix help remove transaction barriers and support one another in doing so. These conditions are likely to lead to positive synergy among the marketing mix components. For example, advertising as a part of promotion not only removes perceptual barriers, such as customer difficulty in identifying or recalling the product, but also lessens value barriers by highlighting the benefits of owning the product. Increased awareness leads to better identifiability and brand name recall, which reinforces packaging strategy for a distinctive product. This, in turn, further reduces perceptual barriers. The distinctiveness created by brand name awareness and packaging increases the likelihood of retailers buying the product. Thus, reduced perceptual barriers also reduce time and place barriers. Knowledge of the benefits provided by a product also reinforces the perceived fairness of the established price, thus lowering value barriers. When each component of the marketing mix supports the others, the total effect becomes far greater than the sum of each effect in isolation.

An Application

To communicate a product concept well (see Exhibit 10-2), the marketing mix should be consistent with each component of it. Some components of the marketing mix have subcomponents. For example, product includes product design, trademark, packaging, and augmented product features such as installation services and warranties. Together they constitute a submix: the product mix. Some submixes even have component parts. For example, packaging has color, graphics, size, materials, and shape components. These constitute the packaging mix. The marketing mix, its submixes, and their components should be designed to be consistent with the product concept to be communicated. This is a top-down process and is reflected by circled numbers 1 and 2 in Exhibit 10-2.

Successful communication of the product concept is not likely unless the submixes at the most detailed (lowest) level are properly managed. The presence of positive synergy at the lower level is required to produce positive synergy at the next higher level (bottom-up process, reflected by circled numbers 3 through 7 in Exhibit 10-2). Therefore, synergy in the packaging mix, for example, must be achieved before synergy in the overall product mix can be obtained, and so on up the ladder. The consistency principle guides the top-down process and the complementarity principle guides the bottom-up process. Specifically, while the principle of consistency aids marketing managers in identifying possible alternatives for each component in the mix, complementarity helps them select a single alternative for each component at each level. In this way, each component of the marketing mix, individually and jointly, communicates the product's relevance to customer needs and preferences. Customers understand and appreciate the product concept quickly and accurately.

The same process described for the communication task applies to the operating task. The five transaction barriers are listed in Exhibit 10-3. Using the top-down process, the manager should identify alternative actions or decision at each level that are consistent with the removal of transaction barriers at that level. The complementarity principle is then used to select the most complementary set of alternatives at each level, following the bottom-up process. Positive synergy is most likely to occur at each of the higher levels if it has first been achieved at their respective lower levels.

Some elaboration concerning the operating task will be helpful here. The five transaction barriers must be removed or lessened by the four components of the marketing mix. Just as no one component is sufficient for communicating product or service concepts, neither is any one sufficient for removing all barriers or even a single one. However, certain submixes are appropriate for particular barriers. As shown in Exhibit 10-3, the product mix is especially helpful in lessening value, ownership, and perceptual barriers, although it removes only a portion of these barriers. It contributes to the removal of

Exhibit 10-2
Interactions among Marketing Mix Components
for the Communication Task

Levels of Purpose	Concept to Communicate	Process (Top-Down)	Process (Bottom-Up)	Customers' Reactions
Marketing Mix: Product, Distribution, Promotionj, and Price	Product concept is communicated via marketing mix	Consistency between · Product Concept and Marketing Mix Components Product Distribution Promotion Price ① ↓	⑦ Complentarity among: Product Distribution Promotion Price ⑥	Appreciate and Understand the Product Concept through Marketing Mix
Marketing Mix Component: Product Mix	Determine the specific composition of product mix components to communicate the product concept	Consistency between Product Concept and Product Mix Components Product Design Mix Trademark Brand Name Logos Product Functions Packaging Mix Augmented Product Features ② ↓	⑤ Complentarity among: Product Design Mix Trademark Brand Name Logos Product Functions Packaging Mix Augmented Product Features ④	Appreciate and Understand the Product Concept through Product Mix
Product Mix Component: Packaging Mix	Determine the specific composition of packaging mix subcomponents to communicate the product concept	Consistency between Product Concept and Packaging Mix Components Size Shape Materials Color Graphics	③ Complentarity among: Size Shape Materials Color Graphics	Appreciate and Understand the Product Concept through Packaging Mix

Source: C.W. Park and Gerald Zaltman, *Marketing Management* (Hinsdale, IL: Dryden Press, 1987), p. 79.

Exhibit 10-3

Interactions among Marketing Mix Components
for the Operating Task

Levels of Purpose	Controllable Transaction Barriers to Be Removed	Process (Top-Down)	Process (Bottom-Up)	Customers' Reactions
Marketing Mix: Product, Distribution, Promotionj, and Price	Perceptual Time Place Ownership Value	Consistency between Removal of Transaction Barriers and Marketing Mix Components Product Distribution Promotion Price ①	Complentarity among: Product Distribution Promotion Price ⑥ ⑦	Be more likely to engage in the actual exchange
Marketing Mix Component: Product Mix	Determine the specific composition of product mix components to remove perceptual, ownership, and value barriers under their control	Consistency between Removal of Transaction Barriers and Product Mix Components Product Design Mix Trademark Brand Name Logos Product Functions Packaging Mix Augmented Product Features ②	⑤ Complentarity among: Product Design Mix Trademark Brand Name Logos Product Functions Packaging Mix Augmented Product Features ④	Be more likely to overcome barriers under the control of product mix
Product Mix Component: Packaging Mix	Determine the specific composition of packaging mix subcomponents to remove perceptual and value barriers under their control	Consistency between Removal of Transaction Barriers and Packaging Mix Components Size Shape Materials Color Graphics	③ Complentarity among: Size Shape Materials Color Graphics	Be more likely to overcome barriers under the control of packaging Mix

Source: C.W. Park and Gerald Zaltman, *Marketing Management* (Hinsdale, IL: Dryden Press, 1987), p. 80.

ownership barriers by providing installation and product delivery services and warranties. Whenever needed, these services must be provided as a part of the product mix. However, the product mix cannot remove other aspects of ownership barriers associated with payment method or product use. They must be removed by other submixes.

CONCLUSION

The introduction to this book referred to the silo effect in which different functional groups work as if they are independent of one another. A major concern that has emerged recently, especially with regard to the development of new products, is how to overcome this effect and foster greater coordination across functions. This chapter introduced the idea that many important decisions made by one group affect and are affected by those made by another. This suggests that an organization can be viewed as a network of decisions. We've introduced a framework to help managers foster more positive synergy among decisions in this network. The inquiry center can play an important role in fostering this synergy by making sure the voice of the market is heard by the managers whose decisions are part of the organizational decision network.

Notes

1. Gareth Morgan, *Images of Organizations* (Beverly Hills, CA: Sage Publications, 1986), esp. Chapter 4; see also William N. Dunn and Ari Ginsberg, "A Socio-cognitive Network Approach to Organizational Analysis," *Human Relations,* vol. 40, no. 11 (1986), pp. 955–976.
2. C.W. Park and Gerald Zaltman, *Marketing Management* (Hinsdale, IL: Dryden Press, 1987).

CHAPTER 11

Implementing the Inquiry Center Concept

Inquiry centers are the learning systems used by individuals, organizational units, and firms as a whole. Specific functions that facilitate both formal and informal learning, such as market research, competitor intelligence staffs, and economic planning departments, are often thought of as formal inquiry centers. But inquiry centers exist everywhere in one form or another, and anyone who wants to tap into the marketplace must improve them.

Making firms more market-based through the better use of market information requires organizational change—often fundamental change. This chapter deals with a special aspect of this task: how to introduce inquiry center improvements.

An "ideal" inquiry center reflects the size, internal structure, learning systems, organizational culture, product markets, and managerial competencies of a firm. It is a concept that can be achieved for any firm, but to expect to do so in a single step is unrealistic. Only newly created organizations, or ones facing severe crises, are open to such major change. For most researchers and managers, the most fruitful course to follow is to implement change incrementally. Incremental changes that produce modest improvements enhance credibility and justify further changes. But even such a benign approach may appear radical to some. Change is always discomforting, and all innovations have the potential for altering organizational equilibrium. What is a small change to some may be a major change to others. In fact, seemingly small, isolated changes can have unexpected multiplier effects.[1] Even the act of considering change is not without its consequences.

Ideally, the design and implementation of an inquiry center would go hand-in-hand with the formation of other company systems. But the inquiry center is not usually recognized as being central enough to warrant this approach. Unfortunately, this situation becomes a self-fulfilling prophecy, reinforcing the idea that the inquiry center doesn't have much to contribute and hence need not be given much prominence. For this reason, it is unusual for major improvements to occur in a short time.

Inquiry Center Champions as Change Agents

In identifying the true customers of market research (Chapter 3) we suggested that researchers and other champions of formal inquiry centers should view themselves as the product or service managers for their function within the company. In this role, they must

- convey to clients the essential concept of an inquiry center,
- demonstrate how it addresses important client needs, and
- reduce barriers between knowledge providers and knowledge users.

In doing so they are agents of organizational change and must view themselves as such.[2]

SIX KEY QUESTIONS

The successful introduction of an organizational innovation requires an understanding not only of the issues but also of the people involved—as individuals and as groups. To understand people as individuals, we need to know several things. What is their ability to understand and handle sophisticated tools? How secure are they in their positions? What are their values? Can they influence others?

To understand people as a group, we need to understand how they interact. How traditional is the group? Does it follow the well-trodden path or is it willing to try new ideas? It is important to remind ourselves that acceptance of an innovation does not necessarily ensure its use.

There are six key questions to answer before deciding whether to try to introduce change in an organization.[3] The first is the "mega question." If it is not possible to answer "yes" to both its parts, then it is probably inappropriate to institute the proposed change. The first part of the mega question is: **Have top managers agreed that there is a need for the proposed change?** The second part is: **Has the organization designated a champion?** Has a specific person or group been given both the responsibility and the authority to make the change happen?

If the answer to both parts of the mega question is "yes," we can proceed to the second question: **Who has participated in planning for the change and who has not?** Little will be gained if the parties that will be affected by the change have not been consulted or their inputs solicited.

The third question asks: **What, if anything, does the change modify or replace . . . and how will personnel make the transition from the old to the** new? Nearly every change implies the discontinuance of some way of thinking and behaving. That is why change is discomforting. A simple change in the software used to analyze and present data may, for example, require changes in how managers access data and interpret them. Managers may have to lessen their reliance on data specialists and get used to doing more of their own analyses. For the change agent, it means that attention must be paid to helping clients discontinue prior ways of thought and behavior, thereby providing a bridge to new ways.

The fourth and fifth questions are two sides of the same coin: **Who will benefit immediately from the change and who will benefit in the longer term?** and **Who will suffer immediately and who will suffer in the longer run?** Some people may suffer initially but benefit over the longer term. For others it may be the reverse. For example, when an innovative data-tabulating system was introduced at the U.S. Census Bureau it was perceived by many as eventually diminishing the bureaucratic status, and possibly the job security, of certain programming managers, even though their importance was enhanced initially because they were central in training users in the new system.

The final question is, **How will the change affect major relationships in the organization?** These include individual job relationships as well as organizational, social, and other informal contacts. Many inquiry center changes are specifically intended to affect major relationships in the organization by bringing together functional groups, surfacing their different assumptions and perceptions, and using market data to broker these differences.

For example, how does the centralization of a research function or its decentralization alter researcher-user relationships? How does the current trend toward downsizing or eliminating research staffs and using outside suppliers affect researcher-user interactions? Changes that increase the frequency of interactions among researchers and users and involve researchers more actively in the early stages of the decision-making process clearly alter informal job relationships.

Because of increased direct access to data, brand managers may take data out of context. This possible misuse of data makes some researchers nervous and clearly affects relationships between researchers and users. Some researchers feel that it places them in a policing role.

SENIOR MANAGEMENT COMMITMENT

We would like to return to the first part of the mega question. An important factor in the process of becoming market-based is the level of commitment of senior management and how well this is communicated throughout the organization. When senior management takes a strong and well-communicated position that the organization will be market-based and makes appropriate use of information in doing so, market information tends to be valued highly and used effectively. This greatly facilitates the task of making inquiry center improvements. Thus, critical tasks for the inquiry center champion are to elicit commitment at the top and make sure that commitment is clearly communicated and understood throughout the organization.

The articulation and communication of this philosophy may be a statement such as that in Exhibit 11-1. This statement was made by J. Philip Samper, then vice chairman of Eastman Kodak, at the beginning of a workshop to develop a market intelligence system. The ideas contained in it are appropriate for small organizations and for organizations in any product and service market.

Exhibit 11-2 contains comments excerpted from a speech by Robert Stempel, now CEO of General Motors, at a corporatewide market research conference involving senior staff of all divisions of GM. Here, too, the issues addressed are those that should be addressed by senior personnel in organizations of all sizes and cultures and in all product markets.

If senior management lacks the commitment expressed in Exhibits 11-1 and 11-2 or the willingness to communicate it forcefully, the firm has a serious problem. We call this the "thinking-to-follow" problem; understanding it requires making a distinction between thinking-to-lead and thinking-to-follow.

Thinking-to-Lead versus Thinking-to-Follow

Thinking-to-lead involves the sensing of important market changes in their early stages and developing creative responses. Thinking-to-follow involves learning how to respond quickly and effectively to important changes in their advanced stages. Both kinds of thinking are necessary and important and require intelligence and creativity to be done well. However, the critical issue concerns the relative dominance of the two kinds of thinking among the firm's leaders.

In many companies the thinking-to-follow mentality dominates. This posture may not be too costly in stable markets. However, the half-life of product markets is becoming increasingly brief. Markets are changing more rapidly and thus the average time for which a given practice is relevant is getting shorter. Rapid technological change is bringing new ideas to market more quickly. Information technologies permit faster evaluation of marketing strategies and tactics, making possible more rapid marketing mix adjustments. Customer behaviors and attitudes are changing with greater frequency. Under these conditions, the half-life of a given marketing strategy is also shortening.

Firms that follow the lead of others are finding their "wait-and-see" approach costly. By the time they see which way the market is headed, and get their product development and marketing up to speed, they find themselves in mature product markets where competition is intense and margins razor-

Exhibit 11-1
Eastman Kodak's Policy on the Use of Information

It is imperative that the information be kept in a manner which ties it to business objectives and issues. This is important because, in my mind, it will facilitate the timeliness of your ability to respond and enhance the relevancy of response.

. . . We need to review how well we are doing compared to the objectives, opportunities, and threats. I would appreciate it if your plans included ways for us to have signals that would show, sometimes upon demand and sometimes in a proactive way, where we are and how the "gap" between what we are and should be doing seems to be progressing . . . . I also believe that the assumptions that underlie possible strategic options would be identified, tested, and included as part of the analysis as options are considered for future strategy. The Market Intelligence concept should consider these critical assumptions and appropriate information necessary for determining final business strategy . . .

If we have done our job well . . . we probably have paved the way toward evolving a preliminary business strategy that has high credibility and is much more "fact-based."

The final business strategy can be tested with the help of the Market Intelligence system by looking at the business objectives and making comparisons of anticipated performance. Again, the final test of any business strategy will be its success in the marketplace. The Market Intelligence system's role of anticipating information needs and having information readily available will be very important.

. . . I have a few general comments to make about my expectations for the Market Intelligence system. It's important that we remember to manage information within and between the many elements of our planning process in a systematic way. The same is true within and between organizations. We must be able to move appropriate information through organizations, through geographic locations, and through changing world or regional conditions.

An appropriate degree of discipline should be implanted in the planning process so that effective information can be gained by those users when they need it. The design of the Market Intelligence system should complement the discipline built into the planning process.

The thing I like best about the concept of the Market Intelligence system that is embodied in this conference is our understanding that the system is more than hardware and software. The human component, in developing business strategy, is primary. The computer is a potentially valuable tool and its value will depend upon the people who want to use it and know how to work with it effectively. I have confidence in this group and in your plans, and I know you will give serious consideration not only to the role of the users and providers of the information, but also to those other stakeholders who will benefit from the success of this program. I appreciate your undertaking the process of learning from each other and outside experts about decision support systems and business planning needs.

Exhibit 11-2
GM's Commitment to Hearing the Voice of the Market

Understanding the voice of the customer or the voice of the market is absolutely essential in today's marketplace. The product development process all grows from the voice of the customer.

We have a blueprint for product development. It's one single process; we call it the Four Phase Process. It really works as a good road map on how to bring the car from the designer's dream to the gleam in the customer's eye on the showroom floor. We've got a lot of honing to do on that process to make it work, and one of the pieces we're honing is right up front with the market research . . .

. . . We need to be drawing on our customer research that's already on hand. You heard [the research director] say that his objective was to have answers to three out of four questions available when the questions are asked. We also need to be thinking about different times for different programs. Is it a body program; is it a total new vehicle; is it a niche-market vehicle? Each one will have its own market research. But the object of all of it should be to shorten that total process. So for the market research people, the challenge is how do I have accurate, timely information in the shortest possible time?

We have to keep working to get a better focus on the customer. As we get closer to that, we have to stay focused. I think the customer focus links very closely to Dr. Deming's idea on quality and to many other processes going across the organization today.

We talk about commitment. It's easy to say, and it's hard to do. We all have opinions. Some are very strong about GM and what we need to do to make great cars and trucks. We even have different opinions on what great cars and trucks are. But we have an obligation to discuss the ideas and come up with some shared ideas of what GM is and what its vehicles should be. It's not enough to say, "It's my opinion, do it my way." You have to work together, there has to be a plan, a process, one voice, and that can only happen when we talk to each other and listen to each other and find the common language and commitment.

You heard the word "listening" today. A lot of people think they listen, but they don't. They're the types who seem to listen and say, "I hear you, but I know better. I know how to build a great car or truck. And you've never really built one, so let me do it my way." Well, you can't really work that way. We do have to listen to what the customer is telling us. When he talks about ride/handling, we really have to understand what he means. He might be talking about bumps in the road, and he calls that ride/handling. When he talks about acceleration, does he mean flat-out acceleration, or does he mean getting onto expressway ramps. There are hundreds and hundreds of differences between what the customer says and what he really means.

Obviously, this is going to mean a cultural change at GM. They'll tell you in the past that GM was successful without market research. Well, [the vice president of marketing] put that myth to rest . . . . We've been listening to the market for a long time when you think about it. We have listened better some times than others. That's where the self-starter, the automatic transmission, and turn signals came from. In fact, as I review some of the history in Design Staff, it says that's how we literally got rid of the headlights sticking out on the fender and finally put them inside and managed to hide them altogether.

There have been a lot of reasons for our success over time, and for a long time we were a manufacturing company. Everything we made, we could sell. GM cars were durable and affordable. We had the best designs. We met many of the customer's criteria. Now the environment that we operate in has changed. The demands on us are much different. The winner today is going to hear the voice of the customer, hear it clearly, and offer the products sooner than any of the competition. It's not just how you collect the data. Everybody can collect the data. It's how you use the data once you have it. It takes work.

If we're going to satisfy customers, we've got to hear the voice of the market. So it's the job of the market research function to make sure the voice of the market is heard. It's the job of marketing, technical, and design communities to make sure the voice of the market is used along with their own ideas to give us the very competitive advantage we need to win in the marketplace.

---

thin. Not too many years ago a firm could wait, say, eighteen months to see how it should respond to a competitor's technological improvement. This strategy allowed pioneering firms to incur the risks associated with being first and to make errors that the follower could avoid. As markets become more and more dynamic, however, the period for which an imitation or adaptation is valid is much shorter. Also, evidence suggests that being first has decided market-share advantages over the long term.

The thinking-to-follow posture reflects an absence of a commitment to being market-based and a lack of commitment to the use of market information.

The six key questions identified above assess the feasibility of making a change to an inquiry center. From these we turn our attention to questions that are relevant when putting an inquiry center change into effect.

THE "A VICTORY" MODEL

Several factors must be considered when implementing change. These factors are summarized by the acronym A VICTORY and have been useful in a variety of organizational settings over a long period of time.[4] The A VICTORY factors and the questions they raise focus the change agent's attention on what is required to implement change successfully.

A = Ability. What are the abilities and inabilities with respect to accepting changes in the inquiry center? Are the necessary resources and capabilities (e.g., staff training, facilities, funds, and so forth) available to implement, sustain, and evaluate the changes? For example, managers may need training in how to surface assumptions, formulate issues, and interpret statistics in order to make effective use of new information systems. These same skills are helpful in creating a problem-*sensing* as well as a problem-*solving* orientation among managers.

V = Values. How compatible with management's attitudes and practices are the values, cultural norms, and attitudes required by a proposed change? For many managers the idea of planning ahead for future research needs is foreign territory. Do managers prefer an inquiry center that produces better thinking? better decisions? better products or services? more satisfied customers? Focusing on any one of these will result in a different orientation within the inquiry center. Each orientation requires a somewhat different supportive value. For example, a unit at Ford Motor Company was very innovative in adopting a new way of assessing customer satisfaction but resistant to a technique to help it think differently about those data.

I = Idea/information. How clearly understood is the nature of a proposed inquiry center change and the reasons for it? Some inquiry center changes result in managers getting more information presented in more complex ways. This raises the "more-is-less-and-less-is-more" paradox. When introducing changes, researchers and managers must provide complex information simply, through the use of special visual displays or other information packaging strategies. This is not to criticize managers' abilities to process complex information nor their willingness to try to understand it. Rather, the need for less complex presentations of complex information reflects problems of information overload, time pressures, and the need to separate the wheat from the chaff in any set of data expediently. We will return to the "idea" component of the A VICTORY model later in this chapter.

C = Circumstances. What factors or features in the organization may affect the acceptance and implementation of the inquiry center concept? Have there been significant personnel changes? Recent reorganizations? How does the structure of a company affect its response to new ideas? Organizations that are highly centralized and formal in their procedures may be slow to make a decision on some innovation but quick to embrace it once the decision is made. The reverse is true for organizations that are decentralized and less formal.

T = Timing. How ready is the organization to consider the proposed change? Is it "an idea whose time has come"? Are current circumstances advantageous for introducing the change?

There is nothing as energizing as a crisis for creating a readiness to change. But this readiness does not last forever. A senior manager at AT&T shared an experience we've encountered in many companies:

When [the crisis] happened we agreed that we needed to change [an aspect of the research program] as soon as possible. Unfortunately we had no good idea of what the change should be. By the time a consensus developed that what we needed was a mechanism for examining our basic assumptions early in the research process, some of the sense of urgency created by [the crisis] had receded . . . . It also took a long time to figure out how to make this change. By the time we found an acceptable procedure people around there had become indifferent again. At least now we've got a good solution which we'll implement quickly as soon as the problem occurs again. And it certainly will. . . . One thing I learned, "timely" may be a brief window of opportunity in a division like ours.

O = Obligation. What is the perceived need for change among relevant decision makers and potentially influential "champions"? What is their level of commitment?

We spoke earlier about the "we-should-but-don't" paradox. This raises the question of how the inquiry center can help resolve the discrepancy between what managers know they should be doing and what they actually do. How proactive should inquiry center personnel be in pointing out these discrepancies? The tolerance level of managers to reminders that they could be doing better is not particularly high. For that matter, neither is the same tolerance level of researchers.

A leading information-use expert, Alden Clayton, has commented that the role of experts is changing. Formerly they were expected to produce standardized information products that could be entered into the decision-making process at particular times. Now, experts are expected to keep their clients informed at all times. This implies a very different way that experts and clients relate to one another. It raises questions related to the tolerance issue: To what extent should experts, in or outside the firm, wait to be called upon? To what extent should they be proactive, even at the risk of being intrusive, with information they feel is relevant but not known by the client? How can this be done without experts overstaying their welcome?

R = Resistance. Where are the loci of resistance to change? Consider the following example. The research director for a multinational corporation based in Sweden had managers participate in a process designed to elicit their procedural knowledge. (Procedural knowledge is concerned with decision rules that say, in effect, "If this, then that, except when . . . unless . . . " See Chapter 12.) That action was met with heavy resistance on the part of managers, based partly on their thinking that their procedural knowledge couldn't be mapped because it wasn't systematized. There was additional resistance because managers were reluctant to surface assumptions they only vaguely sensed and were uncomfortable acknowledging. As one manager admonished,

"Let sleeping bears lie!" This reflected a certain fear that deficiencies would be uncovered in thinking and decision-making processes.

Y = Yield. What are the benefits of the change for those who are asked to approve it or implement it or who are otherwise affected by it? Can these benefits be measured? For managers, the benefits may be tied to the kind of "products" the inquiry center would produce. For example, some companies emphasize state-of-the-art reports on key issues such as productivity, motivating personnel, and market segmentation techniques. Other companies emphasize developing questions and answers based on current knowledge about particular issues. More often emphasis is on providing basic statistics on current operations and serving a library function.

The A VICTORY model in various forms has been applied successfully in a number of traditional business organizations of various sizes operating in industrial and consumer markets: Papercraft, Shell Oil, Tender Care, Eastman Kodak, and Air Tool Products. It has been used most extensively among public and private health and social service organizations as a guide for improving the use of research, particularly research that evaluates marketing programs. An application developed for the federal government's National Institutes of Mental Health in evaluating its research-use processes and those of the numerous organizations it assists is presented in Exhibits 11-3 and 11-4. The lower set of column headings in Exhibit 11-3 presents a slightly different labeling of the knowledge-use process than the one we used earlier. The upper set of column headings are the five functions of a market intelligence framework we discussed in Chapter 4.[5]

Each cell in Exhibit 11-3 implies a set of questions and issues that managers and researchers in both for-profit and not-for-profit organizations have found extremely useful when introducing improvements in inquiry centers. These questions are helpful in identifying factors affecting the implementation of an inquiry center innovation. Exhibit 11-4 illustrates some of the issues raised by each cell in Exhibit 11-3. Naturally, the specific issues will reflect the specific situation in the reader's department or firm. For instance, the relevant questions about "ability" with respect to changes in information storage and retrieval systems may vary among departments in the same organization because of differences in the kinds of data needed, the frequency with which they are collected and used, and so forth.

We have found in our own work and in the experiences of others that most inquiry center problems and solutions, at least where a strategy of incremental change is involved, are limited to one or two of the cells found in Exhibit 11-3. Thus, the subset of questions that need to be addressed by the inquiry center champions is generally a manageably small number.

Exhibit 11-3
Introducing Change in a Market Intelligence Function

Change Factors	Assess Market Information Needs		Measure the Marketplace	Store, Retrieve, and Display Data	Analyze and Describe Data		Market Information Process Quality
	Client Need Assessment	Translation of Needs into Research Questions	Conduct of Usable Research	Storage of Research Information	Translation of Research into Action Implications	Implementation of Action Implications	Evaluation of Research Applications
Ability							
Values							
Idea							
Circumstances							
Timing							
Obligation							
Resistance							
Yield							

Exhibit 11-4
An Audit for Introducing Change in an Inquiry Center
Using the A VICTORY Model

ABILITY

Assessing Market Information Needs

Client Need Assessment. Is the organization capable of defining its information needs, or would outside help be required/beneficial/disruptive?

Translation of Needs into Research Questions. What factors influence the capacity and inclination of different parties to translate user needs into questions that can be readily researched? What kinds of skills are needed? Who has them?

Measuring the Marketplace

Conduct of Usable Research. Does the client have the resources to fund market research? How can engineers or R&D managers use organizational resources to increase the relevance of research to them?

Storing, Retrieving, and Displaying Data

Storage of Research Information. How can an organization enhance the storage, awareness of, and retrievability of research information? What influences the effectiveness of departmental or organizational libraries?

Analyzing and Describing Data

Translation of Research into Action Implications. If research is done internally, how is it translated into action implications? Is the translation limited by the organization's structure or procedures?

Implementation of Action Implications. Does the user have the skills and the fiscal and personnel resources to carry out the best alternative?

Enhancing and Assessing Market Information Value

Evaluation of Research Applications. Can the organizational user or client evaluate the effectiveness of its research applications? Does the organization have the resources to provide evaluation by a person or persons external to the user system?

VALUES

Assessing Market Information Needs

Client Need Assessment. Is there a norm in the organization supporting critical self-assessment (as opposed to self-congratulation or rationalization)? Is asking for help encouraged or viewed as an admission of failure?

Translation of Needs into Research Questions. Does the organization reward those who try to state their needs in terms of researchable questions? Do organizational members emphasize the complexity and insolubility of problems?

Measuring the Marketplace

Conduct of Usable Research. Does the organization reward or punish research (or researchers) that is forward-looking and oriented toward strategic issues?

Storing, Retrieving, and Displaying Data

Storage of Research Information. What is the status of the storers of information? Are they considered drones, or do they command respect? Do they encourage users to use existing search and retrieval systems to solve problems?

Analyzing and Describing Data

Translation of Research into Action Implications. Will research that is easily translated into action implications be more highly valued by project managers than research that appears difficult to translate but may be more relevant?

Implementation of Action Implications. Is the organization politically open to the new knowledge, or does knowledge threaten existing interest groups?

Enhancing and Assessing Market Information Value

Evaluation of Research Applications. Does/should an organization place more value on internal or external evaluations? Are the values of the evaluating group compatible with those of the user? If not, what problems might emerge in evaluation?

IDEA

Assessing Market Information Needs

Client Need Assessment. What quality/value of data is needed before a problem can be defined or clearly stated? Have enough sources of data for need assessment been tapped to help avoid a biased assessment?

Translation of Needs into Research Questions. Knowledge needs differ in terms of how easily they can be phrased as researchable questions. Also, users and researchers vary in their facility in translating a user need into a researchable question. Is this a problem? Can either group be trained in this skill?

Measuring the Marketplace

Conduct of Usable Research. How easily are ideas actually researched?

Storing, Retrieving, and Displaying Data

Storage of Research Information. What information would managers like to see stored, and how would they like to see it stored?

Analyzing and Describing Data

Translation of Research into Action Implications. Is the new knowledge sufficient to derive action implications, or are additional data needed? This might be asked in terms of how comprehensive the data are. Also, new knowledge may have characteristics that affect its translation into action implications. Is the knowledge complex, divisible (only parts being usable), and easily communicated to those who can translate it into action implications?

Implementation of Action Implications. How much knowledge or expertise do managers or other users feel they have in implementing change? What types of action implications (if any) do different users feel they need outside help with in implementing?

Enhancing and Assessing Market Information Value

Evaluation of Research Applications. Are information users familiar with the principles of sound evaluation?

CIRCUMSTANCES

Assessing Market Information Needs

Client Need Assessment. What factors external and internal to researchers and users prompt need assessment activities? How do factors such as the availability of funding or slack resources in an organization influence what information needs are assessed? Are there critical thresholds that a need has to exceed for it to receive attention?

Translation of Needs into Research Questions. Do organizational relationships influence project personnel's abilities to translate organizational needs into researchable questions? To what extent does the availability of resources affect the production of applications-oriented research?

Measuring the Marketplace

Conduct of Usable Research. Can organizational traits such as complexity, formalization, and professionalization affect the production of applications-oriented research?

Storing, Retrieving, and Displaying Data

Storage of Research Information. Does changing technology make most stored information obsolete? Can decentralization influence the effectiveness of information storage and retrieval systems? If so, under what circumstances is each structure most or least appropriate?

Analyzing and Describing Data

Translation of Research into Action Implications. How does the structure of a firm or unit (its complexity, formalization, and centralization) affect its decision to act on new knowledge?

Implementation of Action Implications. How does the structure of a firm or unit affect implementation of its decisions? How does the external environment affect the willingness and speed with which an implication is implemented?

Enhancing and Assessing Market Information Value

Evaluation of Research Applications. What factors produce resistance to evaluation? Can they be countered or minimized? Do organizational variables such as professionalization affect evaluation efforts?

TIMING

Assessing Market Information Needs

Client Need Assessment. Are user needs assessed on a regular basis or only at the beginning of a project? How readily can the user define the problem for which information is required? Can this process be accelerated?

Translation of Needs into Research Questions. How much time is required to translate user needs into a form that can be easily researched? Is the time lag such that the nature of the problem itself may change? How much time is lost when needs are incorrectly translated?

Measuring the Marketplace

Conduct of Usable Research. If the information requirements of users change during the course of a project, are changes communicated to researchers in time for them to modify the research?

Storing, Retrieving, and Displaying Data

Storage of Research Information. What storage factors influence when information is used? Are storage and retrieval systems more user- than researcher-oriented?

Analyzing and Describing Data

Translation of Research into Action Implications. Do users have enough time to derive action implications from research? Is the decision-making ability of the user hampered by not getting information in time to consider alternatives?

Implementation of Action Implications. Is information available to the user when required, or is it frequently late? If the latter, how can the currency of information be ensured?

Enhancing and Assessing Market Information Value

Evaluation of Research Applications. What determines the timing of research evaluations? Is there an objectively best time to evaluate the primary and secondary effects of knowledge use? What accounts for deviations from this best time?

OBLIGATION

Assessing Market Information Needs

Client Need Assessment. What creates a discrepancy between what a user knows and what the user feels he or she ought to know?

Translation of Needs into Research Questions. To what extent are users responsible for translating their information needs into researchable questions?

Measuring the Marketplace

Conduct of Usable Research. How great must an information need be felt among users before they are willing to experiment with new ways of acquiring it? How willing is the organization to innovate in using research information?

Storing, Retrieving, and Displaying Data

Storage of Research Information. What factors influence the decision to search or not to search existing data bases for a solution to a problem?

Analyzing and Describing Data

Translation of Research into Action Implications. How willing are users to hire specialists to translate research information into action implications or to acquire these skills for themselves?

Implementation of Action Implications. How much motivation is required on the part of users at different organizational levels before they feel obliged to implement action implications?

Enhancing and Assessing Market Information Value

Evaluation of Research Applications. Are users prepared to evaluate how well research information has been applied? How much of a willingness exists to use new methods of evaluating whether information has been applied correctly?

RESISTANCE

Assessing Market Information Needs

Client Need Assessment. Do some users dislike having their needs assessed by external specialists? Do these users fear lack of control, discovery of substandard performance, or other factors?

Translation of Needs into Research Questions. What are the bottlenecks in translating needs into research questions? Are they semantic, operational, or attitudinal?

Measuring the Marketplace

Conduct of Usable Research. Is there resistance to having a specialist facilitate information flows and transfers?

Storing, Retrieving, and Displaying Data

Storage of Research Information. What are the time, energy, and financial costs of alternative means of storing information? What are the barriers in the organization to innovations in research information storage systems?

Analyzing and Describing Data

Translation of Research into Action Implications. Many researchers are reluctant to participate in the translation of research into action implications. Why?

Implementation of Action Implications. Are researchers encouraged to assist users in the implementation process? Is this process resisted by researchers or users?

Enhancing and Assessing Market Information Value

Evaluation of Research Applications. What personal and organizational factors account for resistance to evaluating knowledge applications?

YIELD

Assessing Market Information Needs

Client Need Assessment. Do project managers and other users appreciate the value of accurately assessing and defining problems? Are needs defined within the user's organization or outside it? How does this affect the accuracy of problem definition?

Translation of Needs into Research Questions. Do users perceive a relationship between the quality of information and the accuracy with which their needs are translated into researchable questions?

Measuring the Marketplace

Conduct of Usable Research. Are potential users of knowledge more apt to understand and perceive benefit in research in which they participate?

Storing, Retrieving, and Displaying Data

Storage of Research Information. Do different kinds of information storage systems affect the amounts and kinds of information that is retrieved from them?

Analyzing and Describing Data

Translation of Research into Action Implications. Are users more likely to use information that they themselves have translated into action implications?

Implementation of Action Implications. Is there a self-fulfilling prophecy effect whereby the expected yield or benefit of knowledge influences the way in which—and hence the success with which—that knowledge is implemented?

Enhancing and Assessing Market Information Value

Evaluation of Research Applications. Who is ultimately responsible for evaluating whether knowledge has been correctly applied?

ATTRIBUTES OF CHANGE

The "idea" component of the A VICTORY model merits further discussion. The idea or innovation is either

- a change in the inquiry center a researcher would like current clients to accept; or
- an established feature of the inquiry center which is perceived as new by current or prospective clients.

In each instance, the change or innovation has attributes that affect its acceptance. These attributes are features of inquiry center services that should be given special attention as potential customers are encouraged to make more use of existing services or first use of new services.

Here we discuss the attributes of inquiry center changes that we have often observed as important in many different organizations. As with any change, what is critical is how the inquiry center is perceived by its clients. From the clients' viewpoint, making first use or simply greater use of formal market research may be a major change involving new attitudes and behaviors. Similarly, clients may view changes in how they are expected or required to use market research as a major innovation, even if the kind or amount of research is unchanged. The inquiry center champion must be sensitive to these perceptions and to the fact that they may differ from his or hers. Especially important are client perceptions of the innovation's relative advantage, complexity, compatibility, ease of trial, adaptability, and cost.[6]

Relative Advantage: Incremental, Curative, Preventive, or Combination

The relative advantage of an innovation concerns the benefits it provides that existing arrangements do not, and may be presented in four ways. First, it can be shown to increase the magnitude of a desired event. For example, it could be presented as enhancing the quality of information, its timeliness, its retrievability, and so forth. It should stress that an added level of service is being made possible by the change. Second, some changes are curative in nature. They are intended to reinstate a desired level of performance. This quality, too, should be stressed where relevant. Third, an inquiry center change can also be presented as preventive, that is, as lessening the likelihood that an undesired event will occur, such as being caught by surprise by a major change in customer preferences.

In general, incremental and curative innovations are accepted more readily than those that are preventive. Therefore, fourth, innovations presented as having all three attributes will be accepted even more readily. It is important that the champion of change convey all four attributes or incorporate these benefits into the planned change.

Complexity

This attribute concerns the difficulty in using the change and/or in understanding how it works. A major obstacle in getting managers to use new information technologies is the perception that they are too complicated to understand or use effectively.

Advocates of a new tool or practice, being familiar with it, often fail to see through the eyes of someone exposed to the innovation for the first time. The advocates are often so enamored of its elegance and benefits that they forget that it may not have the same salience and appeal to others. It is important that a change not be more complex than necessary, and that its perceived complexity to neophytes be anticipated.

Compatibility

This attribute concerns how well a change fits with managers' thinking and practices, and their organizational circumstances. For example, managers may have an expressed need for more information and may be willing to invest time and resources in acquiring and using it. However, if the information is not presented in a compatible format, it may be underused or ignored. Researchers in a major bank, for example, have user codes for key managers which automatically provide those managers with data in the form of pie charts, bar graphs, and so forth, depending on the managers' preferences. These codes even include their personal preferences for color graphics.

Trialability, Divisibility, and Reversibility

These attributes concern, respectively,

- how easily a change may be implemented without a long-term commitment,
- how readily it may be tried in one location, and
- how easily it may be discontinued without adverse effect.

These can be facilitating factors if a change can be limited to a single demonstration project or tried in one department. Thus, whenever possible, every inquiry center "reform" might be presented as a limited "experiment," conducted in a way that permits clear evaluation, and pursued in a manner that makes discontinuance easy. Also, not every inquiry center reform is appropriate for all clients; thus, only certain client segments might be targeted and care exercised to prevent spillover to inappropriate client groups.

Adaptability

This feature concerns the ability to alter or modify an inquiry center change to suit the unique circumstances of the user. It is necessary to consider the needs of different clients and to adapt the change, much as products and services are often differentiated for different external customers. For example, a technique for "back-translating" (see Chapter 7) possible actions at the product management level into research questions may not work the same way when applied to strategic planning issues at the corporate level or when applied to engineering decisions.

Cost: Financial and Nonfinancial

The financial cost of a change generally receives the most attention because it is easier to "objectify" than are the benefits of changing how managers think and use information. For example, it is easier to measure the

cost of a two-day training program in assumptional analyses than the anticipated future benefits of having acquired the ability.

Financial costs are usually evaluated accurately before a decision is made
to implement a change; when they cannot be assessed, the change effort
usually does not proceed. Thus, financial issues do not typically serve as
barriers during the implementation stage. It is generally the nonfinancial costs
that determine the success of a change at this stage. Nonfinancial costs include
the perceived loss of influence by a manager or researcher, the added energy
and time required to initiate and maintain the change, the risks associated
with the failure of the change to work as planned, and the unanticipated,
dysfunctional consequences of change.

There are also opportunity costs involved. There may be other changes
forgone or delayed because of limited resources. There is another opportunity
cost: A negative experience with a given change may make clients resistant to
future improvements. The failure can be costly, creating a performance gap,
or discrepancy, between a current state and a desired and feasible alternative
state. This discrepancy is the cost of not making change. The greater the
discrepancy and the greater its understanding among inquiry center clients,
the more likely clients are to make a change. It is the task of the inquiry center
manager to document and communicate the existence of a costly performance
gap.

Consider the example of a major credit card company making extensive
use of market research but having very limited staff. The research director
realized that once the main issue in a specific project had been addressed, her
staff was always pressed to move on to another urgent project. She sensed that
important lessons for the firm were contained in a project's data set but were
never developed because of time constraints. Additionally, time pressures
precluded experimenting with new analytic techniques which could yield
additional insights of value to the firm, though not necessarily relevant to the
core issue of the project.

Her staff agreed and felt frustrated that the cost per "lesson" from the
research was much higher than necessary because so few lessons were learned
from the data collected. Put somewhat differently, the information content of
much of the data was greater than actually realized.

Using a few representative past projects (and a lot of weekends), she and
her staff were able to demonstrate a sizable discrepancy between valuable
lessons learned and those actually available in the same data. Again, many of
these missed lessons were related to issues not central to the particular projects
but still of importance to the firm. She was able to demonstrate that at least
two major errors the firm had recently committed might have been averted
had the undeveloped lessons been learned. The performance gap in this
example was sufficiently large and easily communicated that the research
director was authorized to hire an additional analyst to conduct "secondary
data" analyses among the various projects.

CONCLUSION

Introducing change in any organization requires careful planning and a sensitivity to a wide variety of forces affecting the acceptance or rejection of new ideas and practices. This is especially true when the change involves something as fundamental and important as how the organization uses information in decision making. Thus, the person or group responsible for improving the firm's ability to hear and use the voice of the market must view themselves as change agents. Since most firms do not have a formal research function, this responsibility will often fall on managers. This chapter identified several important questions and criteria to consider when introducing change, and how they can be used to facilitate the process of improving quality in the decision process by improving quality in the market information process. It also stressed the importance of obtaining from the most senior management a clear commitment to improve the firm's existing inquiry center.

Notes

1. Charles Gleick, *Chaos: Making a New Science* (New York: Penguin Books, 1987).
2. Edward M. Glaser, Howard H. Abelson, and Kathalee N. Garrison, *Putting Knowledge to Use* (San Francisco: Jossey-Bass, 1983).
3. Vincent P. Barabba, "Steel Axes for Stone Age Men," in Robert D. Buzzell, ed., *Marketing in an Electronic Age* (Boston: Harvard Business School Press, 1985), pp. 107–133.
4. Howard R. Davis and Susan E. Salasin, "Change: Decisions and Their Implementation," in S. Feldman, ed., *The Administration of Mental Health Services*, rev. ed. (Springfield, IL: Thomas, 1979), pp. 117–130.
5. Vincent P. Barabba, *Market Intelligence: The Critical Issues—and Some Answers*, 14th Annual Albert Wesley Frey Lecture, Graduate School of Business, University of Pittsburgh, June 1982.
6. Everett M. Rogers and Floyd Shoemaker, *The Communication of Innovation* (New York: Free Press, 1971).

CHAPTER 12

Learning

In this chapter on learning we emphasize two approaches. One approach is helpful in gaining a perspective on the basic thinking processes underlying decisions. It is closely related to the concept of the viewing lens discussed in Chapter 2. The second approach involves learning more about the nature of uncertainty when making decisions. The importance of both kinds of learning is rooted in our perspective that organizations are networks of decisions, and that an inquiry center can help firms learn so that their decisions represent the best balance between what customers want and are willing to pay for and what a firm is realistically able and willing to do. We will use the Global Technologies Company, whose problems were described in Chapter 1 by its president, Mr. Burton, to illustrate both types of learning.

The idea of an inquiry center is based on the need to learn as a means to improving thinking and action. The concept of hearing the voice of the market and making constructive use of it with respect to the voice of the firm is a learning process:

- learning what we need to know;
- learning the relevant facts;
- learning what they mean;
- learning what to do about it;
- learning about the consequences of decisions;
- learning why certain results occurred and not others; and
- learning if we need to change our basic thinking.

Few terms are used as often as "learning," and so it is not surprising to find an abundance of definitions of it. We define learning as creating useful understanding or insight by processing experience. This includes the acquisition of new understandings and/or new ways of thinking based on the transformation of experiences into something meaningful and useful.

Processing Experience

Experiences arise from our exposure to stimuli and may assume many forms. When an engineer from Rockwell spends a day at an important trade show listening to customers talk about their needs, experiences arise that yield insights contributing to the modification of a product feature.

When manufacturing personnel from the 3M company view focus groups of purchasing agents discussing their perceptions of quality control among competing vendors, that experience contributes to a decision to bring in major industrial customers for plant tours and meetings with quality control personnel. When a senior loan officer from Chase Manhattan Bank overhears a chance remark at a fund-raiser about personnel changes in a firm currently seeking a loan from them, she may decide to seek further information. Data concerning a significant change in imaging technology prompted an Eastman Kodak staff group to reexamine important assumptions to determine what changes, if any, in basic thinking might be required with respect to strategic planning issues.

In these examples, customer opinions, a chance remark, or technology data are "experienced"; that is, they are registered in someone's mind and "processed" within the context of other information. As a result, a change in thinking occurs. This change in thinking may increase or decrease certainty about the nature, existence, or importance of an event. For example, we may become less confident in our estimates of market share as a result of a new trade association report.

Much learning comes to us secondhand—from other people's or firms' experiences. We learn of new-product opportunities by evaluating the ad hoc product changes or adaptations made by customers or suppliers.[1] For example, 77 percent of innovations in scientific instruments are generated by users.[2] We also learn through our assessments of another firm's success or failure.

Creating Understanding

Our definition of learning also included the idea of useful understanding, or insight. The many ways in which information is useful were discussed in Chapter 5 and will not be repeated here. We simply remind the reader that usefulness has many manifestations but that the most useful information is that which helps us think about a problem rather than telling us what to do.

Not every experience with data provides positive learning. We may, for example, gain understanding about customer attitudes toward shipping services from our data, but if the basic problem is incorrectly defined (e.g., as shipping personnel indifference), we may not learn anything useful. The real problem could be unrealistic delivery dates promised by sales personnel, container design problems, and so forth, rather than the behavior of shipping department personnel. There is an assumption in our definition of learning that the understanding we acquire from experience is valid and reliable. But if there is an error or bias in either the collection of data or its analysis, we may not learn anything helpful. Even scrupulously derived data may lead us astray. Because blind taste tests show one product to be superior to another does not mean that identical consumers will show the same preferences in the actual consumption context, where brand labels may alter their perceptions.

KINDS AND LEVELS OF LEARNING

As we've noted, there are many kinds and levels of learning among managers. Some further elaboration will be helpful here. Although we will describe them separately they may occur more or less simultaneously, evolving out of the same experience.[3]

Explanatory

First, we may learn at a simple descriptive level. For example, studies that track changes over time in market share, corporate images, brand attitudes, and so forth describe important aspects of the market. Descriptive learning creates an awareness of certain features of our environment. Through descriptive learning we may, for example, discover that purchasing agents think our product quality is below industry standards.

Second, we may learn at a deeper level why purchasing agents believe our product quality is substandard. They may, for example, too often receive damaged goods, or have no firsthand familiarity with our manufacturing process. They may have the general impression that we are an unusually cost conscious company willing to take manufacturing shortcuts, or that we have poorly trained or motivated production workers.

Third, we may learn that these factors, as judged by purchasing agents, interact with and reinforce one another so that an even stronger negative impression is created. Thus, we learn about patterns among factors and may be able to develop a model describing the relative importance of these factors; which ones cause others to become important, and how this varies among different purchasing agents.

Fourth, we may learn further how purchasing agents developed these perceptions and exactly how they reinforce one another.

Thus, one kind of learning, explanatory learning, can range from a simple description of events, to an explanation of what causes them, to how these causes interact and contribute to other events.

Prediction

In a similar way we can learn to reduce uncertainty about future events. We can say that purchasing agent perceptions of our product quality will likely be of a certain level in the future because we can expect certain factors (now improving) to interact in specified ways for specific reasons. Obviously, the better we can describe and explain what factors affect purchasing agent perceptions, and how these factors operate, the less the uncertainty about our predictions.

Control

There are corresponding levels of understanding with respect to control, that is, to our attempts to alter purchasing agent perceptions by manipulating factors that influence their perceptions. At the first level is the simple understanding that purchasing agent perceptions can be manipulated. The next level is the understanding that they may be partially influenced by our manipulation of certain factors. The third level of understanding concerns how these factors can be manipulated. The fourth level of understanding concerns why we believe these manipulations will work; it concerns our underlying assumptions, decision rules, and expectations about purchasing agent behavior. These form our theories of action.

Being able to describe an event does not necessarily mean we can explain, predict, or control it. In fact, it is easy to imagine situations where we might be able to do any one of these things well but none of the others adequately, if at all. Accurate description is an essential condition for performing the other functions. Generally speaking, though, the better we can describe an event, the better we can explain it, the more accurately we can predict it, and the more we can control it. As important as learning to explain, predict, and control events is, there is a far more important type of learning managers may experience. Unfortunately, it is the least frequently occurring form of learning. This more significant learning has to do with understanding our frames of reference—our "theories-in-use"—as a way of improving other kinds of learning.

THEORIES-IN-USE

Chapter 10 discussed the value of viewing organizations as networks of decisions. Decision networks exist at every level. Each manager has his or her own network of decisions (see Chapter 6); so do departments and divisions and the corporation itself. While not every decision is ultimately linked to every other decision, groups or clusters of decisions fall together.

Just as a decision involves variables, a network of decisions involves a network of variables. Linked together, they define a theory. A theory is, in effect, a set of connected variables that help us to describe, explain, predict, and/or control an event. Thus, it is important to understand our decision networks from the perspective of our implicit theories. This helps those responsible for analyzing decisions to lessen the recurrence of bad decisions, increase the repetition of good decisions, and facilitate the development of even better decisions through continuous improvement of the implicit theories.[4]

The importance of examining our implicit theories or theories-in-use must also be understood from another perspective. Theories-in-use are simply representations of the viewing lens described in Chapter 2, through which we perceive the voice of the market and project the voice of the company. For better or worse our theories-in-use determine how successful we are in becoming an effective market-based company.

The theory-in-use approach to theory development is different from that customarily described in the scientific literature. It is a more inductive, inferential process of thinking about phenomena.[5] The basic idea is simple: If you want a good theory of, say, selling, you should understand what a successful salesperson thinks and does. Underlying this idea is the recognition of the complexity of real-world problems, the diversity of human behavior, and the dynamic nature of the voice of the market. As a consequence, deterministic relationships (which can be described by equations) among the variables that comprise a theory will be rare. More often the relationships among the variables or the variables themselves will have a degree of uncertainty and be more appropriately described by the degree of correlation.

An important implication is that our real-world theories will not produce a single-number forecast or prediction of the future. Instead, each prediction or forecast is accompanied by a probability distribution which reflects our degree of confidence in the theory and our knowledge of the dependent variables.

An Illustration

Let's use personal selling as an illustration. Effective salespeople employ a number of theories-in-use in their interactions with customers. A highly successful office furniture salesperson may initially consult about the customer's problem rather than advocate particular products. What principles underlie his theory? One principle is that of being customer-oriented. A second is being a consultant or adviser. Implicit in this principle is that a consultant may be perceived as being on the side of a client. An advocate in this context would be perceived as being on the side of the office equipment supplier. These principles suggest the following theory:

> If I appear to be concerned with understanding the client's problem, and if I offer general advice about solving that problem, the client is more likely to perceive me to be on his or her side, and, thus, more objective. Hence, the customer is more likely to accept suggestions I make about the office equipment and furniture I represent.

Exhibit 12-1 represents this simple theory displayed as an influence diagram.[6] The diagram accommodates theories that are intended to be used in complex real-world problems, where the diversity of human behavior and the dynamic nature of the voice of the market cannot be ignored. For these problems a deterministic connection among the variables that comprise a theory is relatively rare.

An influence from one variable to another means that knowledge of the state of the influencing variable changes the likelihood of various states of the influenced variable. For example, in Exhibit 12-1, the arrow from "Display of consultant behavior" to "Customer acceptance of purchase advice" means that learning the degree to which a salesperson displays consultant behavior changes the likelihood of a sale. The diagram indicates that even when a salesperson displays consultant behavior, and when the salesperson is concerned with understanding the customer's problem, customer acceptance of purchase advice may be uncertain, because of other unidentified variables that may influence the customer's decision.

Exhibit 12-1
A Simplified Theory

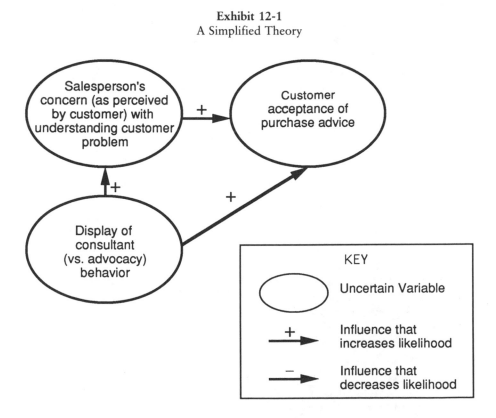

For example, consider one other principle: use of referrals. The unstated reasoning behind this principle is:

> If I refer to other firms I've helped, then my advice will be taken more seriously, and if I refer to firms that have followed my advice which did not involve my line of equipment, my role as consultant will be enhanced and I'll be perceived less as an advocate and more as a helper.

Two propositions worth noting here are: (a) The larger the number of other firms advised, the more credible the salesperson's advice; and (b) the more that advice is perceived as not being linked to the salesperson's line of equipment, the greater his or her overall credibility as a consultant (see Exhibit 12-2).

Undoubtedly additional concepts and propositions could be developed from the same principles, but our purpose is simply to indicate that the salesperson in our example does have a successful theory. Had we suggested

Exhibit 12-2
A More Elaborate Theory

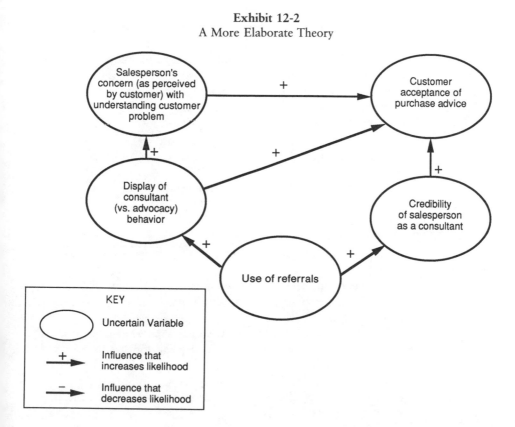

to him that he possessed a rich, complicated, and well-developed theory, he would probably have taken offense. The term "theory" often implies something abstract and perhaps not especially helpful or relevant. The principles this salesperson uses are hardly abstract. Neither are they unhelpful or irrelevant; they provide him with a comfortable living and a sense of personal accomplishment. He would also be surprised if we were to enumerate the large number of concepts implicit in the selling principles he operated on, and he might be puzzled if we claimed they formed a theory of what influences customer acceptance. This surprise and puzzlement merely illustrate the fact that few people ever bother to identify the theories they use in everyday life. Because of this, we are typically not conscious of the richness of our thoughts and how commonly they are used. Thus, the old dictum, "There is nothing so applied as a good theory," has considerable truth. Also, the process of creating theories from principles may involve a gradual transfer from conscious to subconscious thought. After much experience, consciously developed principles become embedded in the subconscious as habits. The behaviors these principles give rise to become customary, perhaps even automatic ways of doing things.[7]

Before we discuss the rationale for a theory-in-use approach and outline the specific steps in using a theory-in-use strategy, we should note that:

- Not every successful salesperson in the same industry uses the same principles. Others may have different theories that work well for them.
- Even if basically the same principles were identified, different salespersons might use them differently.
- Other observers might identify principles other than those we identified.

Steps for Identifying Theories-in-Use

Below we describe several steps involved in identifying theories-in-use. More detailed descriptions of these steps can be found elsewhere.[8]

Step 1. Identify appropriate theory holders. A theory holder is a person or group of people who are effective practitioners in the subject at hand.

Step 2. Specify the indicators of effective practice. These may be verbal statements or behaviors. The best indicators are those that may be observed unobtrusively.

Step 3. Develop principles that describe the observed behavior or practice. This involves creating a statement that appears to govern what is observed.

Step 4. Identify the concepts involved in each governing principle.

Step 5. Describe the linkage(s) between concepts in each principle in propositional terms.

Step 6. Identify and describe possible linkages between concepts in sep-
         arate principles.
Step 7. Know how the theory holder perceives or experiences reality.
Step 8. Know how the theory builder perceives or experiences reality.
Step 9. Collect several cases and develop syntheses.
Step 10. Identify ineffective practitioners and perform Steps 3 though 9.
Step 11. Identify the propositions that are common to both successful
         practitioners and those who are not.
Step 12. Determine whether the unsuccessful practitioners are simply
         overwhelmed by the "wrong" propositions or principles or
         whether other variables are operating that haven't been specified
         yet.

MR. BURTON AND MS. REYNOLDS REVISITED

Chapter 1 began with an exchange of letters following Ms. Reynolds's
presentation to senior management at Mr. Burton's company. Reynolds and
her staff eventually became more involved with senior management in the
firm. Specifically, she addressed their two primary concerns: how to improve
the value of research staff activities; and how to make better use of information in corporate decision making. Reynolds's task was to assess senior managers' theory-in-use with respect to using information in making important
decisions. Once this was done, decisions and actions could be taken to further
strengthen the positive elements where necessary, and change the dysfunctional elements to the extent possible. This would also lead to an improvement in the value of research staff activities.

We shall present the theory-in-use among senior managers in the form of
a progress report letter sent to Burton.

EVALUATING THEORIES-IN-USE

It is fine, of course, to say that managers and researchers have implicit
theories about their responsibilities; that all social science research agrees that
having such theories is, in fact, unavoidable; and that they have a major
impact on manager and researcher performance and ultimately on that of the
organization. It is another matter to know how to evaluate and improve these
theories. To address this issue, we describe two useful approaches below.

One way of evaluating implicit theories is to surface them as Reynolds
does, present them in a descriptive form, and then determine how well they
are functioning in a particular firm or business unit. This procedure is useful
in developing a normative model or theory. However, it requires beginning
with a description of the current environment and how it might ideally
function.

KNOWLEDGE USE CONSULTANTS

Mr. George Burton
President
Global Technologies
1990 Century Blvd.
Los Angeles, CA 91342

RE: Progress Report Request

Dear George:

As you know, we have completed the mapping of the theories-in-use which describes how key managers use information in making decisions. I was pleased to hear that you and the other participants found the exercise to be professionally stimulating and even fun.

We are in the process of assembling a set of research-use models reflecting what I call the three "mosts"; that is, descriptions

- of most of the thinking,
- of most of your managers/researchers,
- most of the time.

We have been sharing preliminary versions of these models with small groups of managers and researchers to receive their feedback about the descriptive validity of the models (e.g., Is this what they told us?) and to give them a chance to provide further ideas.

While these discussions inevitably stimulate thinking about making normative improvements in these theories for the future, I prefer to have separate sessions for this purpose. It is very clear that the participants are eager to get involved in more prescriptive, what-do-we-do-about-it sessions.

This letter is a response to your request for a sample descriptive model. At the *end* of this letter I have attached a "map" [Exhibit 12-3, p. 263] It needs to be understood from these perspectives:

1. It presents several general propositions which are relevant to your company. These are not "laws"; that is, they are not necessarily applicable or valid for other companies. They are, however, general information-use propositions which I believe are valid for you and companies very much like yours.

2. The relationships between variables in each proposition describe probabilistic tendencies. That is, "A" tends to, or is likely to, result in "B," other things being equal. Just how much influence A has on B and how likely it is to occur will vary depending on a number of circumstances that are not even shown. The A-B relationship does, however, represent an important tendency that merits careful consideration.

3. I am also assessing in a very preliminary way your actual performance with respect to these general propositions.

My evaluation of how the general model is working in your company has a certain discouraging quality to it. This must be understood from the following perspective:

- Even modest improvements in how the model operates can yield substantial improvements in corporate performance, and
- while the rethinking and reorientations necessary to make these improvements are not trivial, they are not fiscally costly in your case.

More important, I think there is considerable motivation among your staff to make these improvements. You are receiving some discouraging information against one of the most positive backdrops that you could hope for; you have some serious problems which are matched or even exceeded by a serious commitment among your staff to correct the problems. That is about the best news a CEO can hear about a recognized problem.

The general propositions are shown schematically in the map. This map presents the network of some of the more important variables or factors influencing the use of information by managers in your company. It is not your normal flow diagram or model with clear independent and dependent variables. One of the special and valuable qualities of the human mind, even if a frustrating quality for descriptive or communication purposes, is that our ideas exist and function more in the interwoven manner of threads in a finished Oriental carpet, rather than as isolated threads wound on spools before the carpet is begun. This is what makes our thinking so rich, varied, and creative, and also so difficult to articulate at times. Let me walk you through a portion of the map before proceeding to the general propositions and my evaluations. The path is shown in bold lines for convenience. It starts with the asterisk.

The more skilled a research staff is in the use of decision and risk analysis techniques with managers, the more open managers are to considering diverse sources of information. The more open managers are to diverse sources of information, the greater their ability to reconcile diverse viewpoints among them. This, in turn, can increase the incidence of their having ideas giving them competitive advantage. It also lessens the likelihood that they will uncritically use prior ways of thinking, which may have been successful but may no longer be fully appropriate. Thus the less frequent the incidence of the "failure-of-success" syndrome. The lower the incidence of the failure-of-success syndrome, the more likely a "thinking-to-lead" mentality is to arise. (This is still more likely the greater the incidence of ideas giving you competitive advantage.) In turn, managers are more likely to value the activities of your research staff.

Of course, there are other connections not shown that could be made among the various ideas in the diagram. So, too, are there important variables missing, including those that might influence how much of an effect one variable or factor has on another and whether it has any effect at all. It is also important to point out again that what are being described here are not absolute relationships or ones for which equations can be written.

It is precisely this dynamic, complex quality that makes organizations and individuals so fascinating and challenging to study and why it is so important that they study themselves. Roman numerals are used to help you locate the principal factor in each proposition.

General Proposition I:

The more dependent a research staff is on internal clients for its total operating budget, the more biased in support of the client's initial position the results will be perceived to be. ("When things are perceived as real, they are real in their consequences.")[9]

Evaluation

Your central market research group, though small, appears to be quite competent. They are constrained, however, in developing new methods and surfacing new issues, because they are entirely dependent on your individual operating managers for budget support. Additionally, because each study requires a specific interest sponsor, other potential users of the study tend to distrust the results, particularly if they conflict with programs they wish to bring forward. There is a perception that the research department will not "bite the hand that feeds it." My own impression is that it is quite unwarranted and hence unfortunate since important information is discounted.

General Proposition II:

More openness by managers and researchers to diverse sources of information leads to

1. greater ability to reconcile diverse viewpoints within the team;
2. greater ability of the team to identify critical information and avoid unnecessary research; and
3. greater ability of the team to develop novel syntheses of diverse information.

Evaluation

There appears to be relatively little effort to seek alternative viewpoints about an issue. Moreover, when they are brought forward a strong adversarial atmosphere tends to develop, which discourages open assessments of different positions. There seems to be an "entirely right" or "entirely wrong" mentality with respect to different positions. This, of course, discourages creative syntheses that add even more value to available information.

General Proposition III:

Following the above idea, the greater the ability to develop novel insights from varied information sources, the greater the incidence of ideas giving competitive advantage.

Evaluation

In speaking of particular competitors, so many of your managers commented, in effect, "Why didn't we think of that? We had the same data they did." This is one of the reasons why you are following rather than leading the competition.

General Proposition IV:
The greater the ability to reconcile diverse viewpoints,

1. the lower the incidence of the failure-of-success syndrome, and
2. the greater the incidence of ideas giving competitive advantage.

General Proposition V:
The greater the incidence of ideas giving competitive advantage, the greater the incidence of a thinking-to-lead versus a thinking-to-follow management planning process.

General Proposition VI:
The lower the incidence of the failure-of-success syndrome, the more likely a thinking-to-lead management planning process.

Evaluation
For reasons already indicated, there seems to be an overreliance on thinking and planning processes that worked well in the past with little examination of their appropriateness to current or anticipated situations. Something that worked in the past is assumed to work now, or later. In dynamic markets such as yours, this can lead to failures. Waiting to see what the competition does isn't always wrong, but it can lead to trouble, as I believe it has for you. This relates very much to your expressed concern that your sales have been essentially flat for an extended period of time despite general industry growth.

General Proposition VII:
The greater managers' understanding of the research process (in terms of what it can and cannot do and when it is and is not necessary to use), the greater the level of trust between managers and researchers.

General Proposition VIII:
The more knowledgeable researchers are about managers' issues and their specific task and decision constraints, the greater the level of trust between managers and researchers.

Evaluation
There is a lack of familiarity even among your marketing staff with the basic mechanics of market research, and what it can and cannot do. This understandably lessens the perceived value of formal research as a learning tool. We noted some cases where this same lack of familiarity resulted in an overconfidence in market research and an inappropriate disparagement of other equally valid and important ways of learning. In either case, this contributes to the perception that information is often used to support the perspectives of one group versus those of another. We also found a level of unfamiliarity among researchers about client circumstances, and that compromised the value of the information made available to managers.

General Proposition IX:
The greater the level of personal trust managers have in researchers,

1. the greater the use of research, and
2. the more open managers are to new and perhaps surprising research results.

Evaluation
We found considerable variation in the levels of trust your managers have in researchers. In some instances, related in part to researchers being perceived as biased in favor of a particular client, but for other reasons as well, there is considerable distrust and hence ignoring of potentially important information.

General Proposition X:
The better trained the research staff is in assumption surfacing techniques and other decision and risk analysis tools, the more open managers will be to diverse sources of information and methodologies.

General Proposition XI:
The earlier researchers and managers begin working as a team on current and future issues,

1. the better the managers' understanding of the research process, and
2. the better the researchers' understanding of manager issues and research needs.

Evaluations
Your market research staff is usually not involved in the early stages of decision making, especially in problem diagnosis efforts. This contributes to their failure to understand user needs and abilities. Also, you do not have the best thinking possible in the early stages of issue definition, sometimes collect unnecessary data, often collect data that aren't as helpful as they could have been, and collect information that is available rather than what is needed. The incidence of post-survey regret is very high. This fosters the complaint among managers about their not receiving relevant, cost-effective, or timely information.

You can also see in the map that manager perceptions of the value of research staff activities are influenced by the incidence of their thinking-to-lead, by the perceived relevance, cost, and timeliness of information, and by the perceived quality of thinking about an issue as part of the research process.

Sincerely,

Mary L. Reynolds

Exhibit 12-3
Influence Diagram

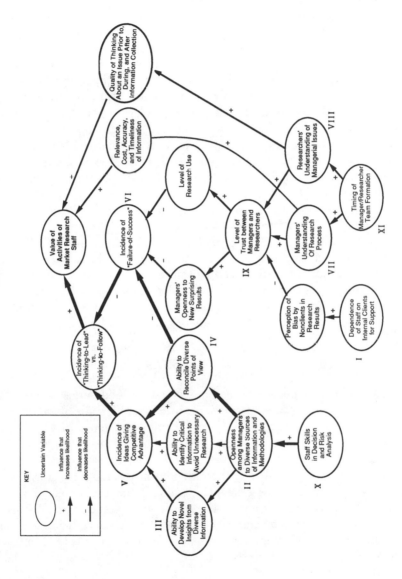

Market inquiries, especially formal studies, represent a second approach to evaluating and improving theories-in-use. These assess the importance and functioning of variables considered relevant to a decision. Variables that share a relationship to a decision are also likely to influence one another. Managers' maps of the potential relationships among "independent" variables and their influence on the "dependent" variable, that is, the basic decision, represent their theories-in-use about the decision situation.

Chapter 5 suggested some ways of evaluating and improving theories-in-use with respect to specific decisions and general thinking. In that chapter we discussed the concept of comfort zones and ways of estimating them. Important clues about the adequacy of particular elements in theories-in-use are provided by the discrepancy between an actual finding and the expected finding prior to the research, especially if the actual result falls outside a comfort zone. The further the actual result is from expectations, the more likely it is that our implicit theory contains an error, even if only with respect to one variable.

Recall our example concerning Tender Care Learning Centers in Chapter 5. Most of the many variables contained in its larger survey comprised the directors' theory for marketing their services. One of the variables the directors considered important concerned transportation services. Research showed that their perceptions about customer satisfaction with such services were wrong. There was a considerable discrepancy between actual and expected results. In fact, the actual results fell well outside their comfort zone, which indicated that the directors' theory needed to be changed.

CONCLUSION

Many kinds and levels of learning were identified in this chapter. While all are important we placed particular emphasis on the value of identifying the basic models or theories-in-use managers employ when involved in decision making. Systematic improvement in these models can yield systematic improvement in the quality of decision making. The improvements may consist of learning about critical factors missing from the usual theories, learning about factors that should not be included in the theories, or learning how to think differently about relevant factors under consideration. Because the theories are implicit, managers are not accustomed to surfacing and understanding them, even though it is probably the most valuable kind of learning that can occur in an organization.

Notes

1. Eric Von Hippel, *The Sources of Innovation* (New York: Oxford University Press, 1988).
2. Ibid., p. 73.

3. David A. Kolb, *Experiential Learning: Experience as the Source of Learning and Development* (Englewood Cliffs, NJ: Prentice-Hall, 1984); Gerald Zaltman, Christian R.A. Pinson, and Reinhart Angelmar, *Metatheory and Consumer Research* (New York: Holt, Rinehart & Winston, 1973).
4. Jeffrey M. Keisler, "Implementing Decision Analysis," paper presented at the Managerial Economics Luncheon Colloquium, Harvard Business School, Boston, November 16, 1989.
5. See, for example, Chris Argyris, *Reasoning, Learning, and Action: Individual and Organizational* (San Francisco: Jossey-Bass, 1982), p. 83; Chris Argyris, R. Putnam, and D.M. Smith, *Action Science* (San Francisco: Jossey-Bass, 1985); Donald Schon, *The Reflective Practitioner: How Professionals Think in Action* (New York: Basic Books, 1982); Donald Schon, *Educating the Reflective Practitioner* (San Francisco: Jossey-Bass, 1987); and Gerald Zaltman, Karen LeMasters, and Michael Heffring, *Theory Construction in Marketing* (New York: John Wiley, 1982).
6. Daniel Owen, "The Use of Influence Diagrams in Structuring Complex Decision Problems," in Derek W. Bunn, ed., *Applied Decision Analysis* (New York: McGraw-Hill, 1984).
7. The reader interested in pursuing this idea further should consult the literature on psychological scripts. A good introduction may be found in R.C. Schank and R.P. Abelson, *Scripts, Plans, Goals and Understanding: An Inquiry into Human Knowledge Structures* (Hillsdale, NJ: Lawrence Erlbaum, 1977), esp. Chapter 3.
8. Zaltman, LeMasters, and Heffring, *Theory Construction in Marketing*.
9. W.I. Thomas, cited in Robert K. Merton, *Social Theory and Social Structure*, rev. ed. (New York: Free Press, 1963).

Glossary

Accountable Management. Persons held accountable for the decisions of what the organization is capable of and willing to present to the marketplace. They are responsible for ensuring that the right data are collected for decision making.

Action Audit. A technique whereby managers brainstorm about actions they may take regarding the issue being researched. For each action a corresponding set of research questions is developed to ensure that adequate information will be obtained about that action.

Adaptability. The ability to alter or modify an inquiry center change to suit the circumstances of the user.

Alert Analysis. Creating an awareness of important events which have just happened or are about to happen (e.g., a major but unexpected action by a competitor or a regulatory agency, or a product tampering crisis).

Analytical Process. The separation of a whole into its parts to determine their nature, proportions, functions, relationships, and so on.

Appeal to Force. The threat of incurring disfavor if certain ideas or data are brought forth or if certain decisions are made.

Appeal to Pity. An occurrence in which a researcher is asked to hide, or significantly downplay, certain data because they make a manager look bad.

Assertion Probe. Method used to highlight the fact that often a decision is justified by a reason that is not, in fact, the primary reason supporting the decision.

A VICTORY Model. A model derived from learning theory to account for the implications of change. It examines eight factors (ability, values, ideas/information, circumstances, timing, obligations, resistance, yield) that can act as either barriers or facilitators to customers' responses.

Basic Analyses. These go beyond executive summaries to provide detailed information about an issue.

Begging the Question. A form of counterfeit reasoning that occurs when a conclusion following the premise merely restates the premise.

Bias. Distortion in the ways we evaluate events. It reflects special orientations in our perception and processing of data.

Bottom-Up Process. Once alternatives are selected at each level of decision making, those most complementary to one another are chosen, starting at the bottom level. This involves juggling alternatives to find the final choices that provide the highest degree of complementarity among them.

Box-Jenkins. A forecasting method based on time series models which relies on the ability to capture systematically the trend, cycles, and other characteristics of the series.

Box-Plots. Graphic techniques that provide information about the central tendency, variability, and shape of the distribution of data.

Cluster Analysis. A statistical analysis that groups people or objects on the basis of common characteristics. The groups are mutually exclusive and relatively homogeneous.

Cognitive Dissonance. A post-decision doubt about the wisdom of a decision.

Collaborative Design. The preparation of the survey instrument not only by those responsible for conducting the survey, but also by those responsible for storing, retrieving, and analyzing the data.

Comfort Zone. The acceptable range within which managers would find the results of research easy to believe.

Communication Task. Conveying to customers the relevance of a product or service to their needs and preferences.

Company Push. *See* Voice of the Firm.

Competent Curiosity. A healthy need to know about markets and knowing how to satisfy that need competently.

Competent Wisdom. The ability to find the most valid and relevant meaning of data, developing plausible alternative actions based on that meaning, and selecting and implementing the right action in the right way.

Complementarity. The state achieved when each decision or component in a mix reinforces the effect of every other component.

Conceptual Information Need. A need for information that will aid general thinking about an issue rather than provide a specific solution or identify alternative actions.

Confirmatory Research. Research that verifies whether a particular idea is a good one and that tends to avoid raising questions whose answers may suggest that the idea isn't the best one available.

Conjoint Analysis. A set of techniques used to derive the relative preference respondents assign to each attribute when selecting from several alternatives.

Consistency. The state in which each component of a decision in a mix is logically derived from a higher-level decision.

Constructive Conflict. Conflict emanating from different interpretations of agreed-upon facts is beneficial to decision making because it sharpens the analytical skills and encourages use of the intuitive and experiential strengths of the participants.

Convenient-Light Syndrome. The phenomenon of searching for answers to problems where it is easiest and not necessarily where the answers may be found.

Correlation and Covariation Probe. This thinking probe suggests that it is useful to challenge the assumption that events or factors are or are not causally related to one another.

Counterfeit Reasoning. In this fallacy, deception arises because misleading props such as pseudo-consensus, equivocation, and "begging the question" are used.

Current Analysis. This provides basic operating information such as daily or weekly sales figures, inventory assessments, periodic measures of market share, and other kinds of tracking studies.

Data. Representations of reality that may or may not have meaning, accuracy, or believability. Examples may include rumors, forecasts, intuitive feelings, personal observations, recommendations, and opinions.

Data-Poor Thinking. Thinking about an issue without the added stimulus of formal data.

Data Reduction Technique. Method of reducing large amounts of data into smaller groupings that reveal the structure and interdependencies of the data. Techniques such as factor analysis, principal components analysis, multi-dimensional scaling, cluster analysis, and product position maps fall into this category.

Data-Rich Thinking. Thinking about an issue with the aid of relevant data.

Decision Analysis. A method of achieving decision quality by combining aspects of systems analysis and statistical decision theory to form a body of knowledge that can deal pragmatically with making choices in complex, dynamic, and uncertain situations.

Decision and Risk Analysis. A process for assuring quality in decision making with special emphasis being placed on areas of uncertainty about a problem.

Decision Quality. A quality decision is irrevocably tied to allocations of resources, including capital and operating budgets, personnel, time, and so forth.

Descriptive Information Need. A situation characterized by the need for information that helps define what managers know and do not know of importance for a decision.

Descriptive Statistics. Collected data described by such techniques as calculating the mean and variance of sample data, preparing box-plots of the data, and calculating correlations of variables in the data set.

Discrepancy Analysis. The difference between the managers' prediction of a research finding and the actual result. The greater the discrepancy between the actual and predicted results, the more valuable is that item of information.

Distraction. The swaying ("sleight-of-hand") of one's attention from the "true" picture to the "reality" that the source of distraction would like its audience to embrace.

Equivocation. A form of counterfeit reasoning occurring when a phrase or concept changes meaning from one part of an analysis or argument to another.

Error of the Third Kind. Precisely solving the wrong problem when you should have been working on the right problem.

Estimate Analysis. A description of future events such as the training required by office personnel to function in the "office of the future" or the nature of home entertainment systems in the year 2000. It may be a scenario describing the unfolding of a sequence of events or simply a snapshot picture of a future situation.

Expectancy Theory. A theory exploring the tendency for people to act in ways that actually bring about the results they expect.

Explanatory Learning. A type of learning ranging from a simple description of events to an explanation of what causes the events, how the causes interact, and the reasons why the factors are important.

External Customer Commitment. The sense of partnership between a firm and its customers which involves sharing information and participation in one another's important activities so a common mindset is established.

Factor Analysis. A set of statistical techniques that study the interrelationships among the observed variables. Its intent is to determine if a large number of variables have a small number of common factors that account for their intercorrelation.

Failure of Success. The tendency to rely on past analyses and actions that were successful but that are no longer appropriate and hence fail when used again.

Fallacies. Incorrect explanations or analyses that have persuasive power.

False Dilemma. When an array of alternatives is narrowly defined using either/or terms involving drastically different alternatives, there may be many other options available.

Formative Evaluation. Evaluation that helps to improve the value of a specific research project while it is unfolding.

Frame of Reference. This reflects our perceptions of the world. A frame of reference has three components: a set of general assumptions (what we are willing to take for granted and need not bother testing); decision rules (guidelines for responding to different situations or stimuli); and expectations (patterns and processes we believe are taking place). It influences our orientation toward problems, the way we conceptualize problems, and the kinds of solutions we prefer.

Fundamental Assumption. Assumption that has a reasonable probability of being wrong and that could have a major impact on the firm if it is accepted as true and in fact proves to be wrong.

Future Shock. The disorientation and decision overload produced by high-speed change.

Good Research User. Such users have a need to know: What is essential to know, what they do know, what they do not know, and what is and is not already known and available elsewhere.

Hard-to-Be-a-Prophet-in-Your-Own-Land Syndrome. Acceptance of an idea is based at least in part on who is perceived as originating the idea, encouraging the acceptance of an idea by appealing to an outside authority whose broad experience lends greater weight to the idea.

Hypothetical Data. Simulated findings presented in a way actual findings will be.

Inquiry Center. The ideal mindset in a company for effectively and efficiently reconciling the voice of the market with the voice of the firm. While the term "center" denotes an organizational unit, it is as much an attitude, ethic, or creed as it is a formal entity. In the inquiry center are the various data bases, facilitating tools, processing equipment, and human resources that enable information users to function well in the three dimensions of logic, energy/collaboration, and imagination.

Instrumental Information Need. The information-use need that is characterized by information collected in response to specific needs which have a direct application and thus an explicit, instrumental role in making decisions.

Knowledge Disavowal. The avoidance of knowledge in order to preserve or maintain the status quo or to avoid a difficult choice or threatening situation.

Law of the Lens. The tendency to use our existing way of thinking to find what we are looking for.

Market Back–Company Forward Mechanism. An environmental dimension that refers to what the market indicates it needs and is willing to pay for *and* what the firm is capable of and willing to provide to the market.

Market-Based. Hearing and using the voice of the market in decision making throughout a business.

Market-Based Firm. A company whose decision making is based on the reconciliation of differences between the voice of the market and the voice of the firm.

Marketing. The process of planning and executing the conception, pricing, promotion, and distribution of ideas, goods, and services to create exchanges that satisfy individual and organizational objectives.

Marketing Mix. The blend of the four marketing tools: product, promotion, distribution, and price.

Marketing Research. The process of monitoring issues of special interest to the marketing function such as advertising effectiveness, sales force development, site selection, customer reactions to product changes, and so forth.

Marketplace Reality. A statement of what the market indicates it needs and is willing to pay for—the voice of the market.

Market Research. The process of collecting accurate, timely, and relevant information regarding the needs and wants of the market and conveying this information to appropriate management. Its goal is to learn about important stakeholders so that more knowledgeable decisions can be made.

Multidimensional Scaling. A body of techniques for representing graphically the locations and interrelationships among a total set of observed variables. The techniques uncover how individuals perceive the relationships among products by identifying the relevant dimensions along which products or brands are compared.

Needs Assessment. The process of determining what the ultimate users of research, such as human resource managers, R&D, or product managers, need to know about the marketplace.

Network of Decisions. A perspective that emphasizes that decisions made in one area of a firm frequently affect and are affected by decisions made in another area.

New Marketing Myopia. The perception that the marketing function is primarily responsible for marketing, when, in fact, virtually all groups make decisions that affect how customers and others view the firm's offerings.

90-Day Syndrome. The tendency to confine thinking to the current quarter.

Nonprobabilistic Data. Data obtained from surveys for which a probability sample has not been constructed.

Not-Invented-Here Syndrome. The tendency to systematically reject ideas, recommendations, or decisions perceived as originating outside the company, reflecting a bias against solutions based on their origin.

Old Marketing Myopia. Viewing one's market too narrowly.

Operating Task. Removing barriers to transaction so that customers who want a product can purchase it with minimum effort.

Perceived Price. The price customers expect to be charged for a product or service.

Perceived Value. A customer's summary evaluation of a product, taking into account the benefits and price. Perceived value equals perceived worth minus perceived price. When perceived price is lower than perceived worth, the perceived value is positive and customers feel they "got a good deal." Conversely, when perceived price exceeds perceived worth, customers conclude that the product is not a good value and they were "ripped off."

Perceived Worth. What customers feel they should pay for the benefits they receive from a product or service.

Post-Survey Regret. The feeling, after the collection of information, that different research procedures should have been used, that certain questions were not asked or not asked differently, that the wrong information has been collected, and so forth. Often it reflects a failure to think about the use of information early enough in the research process.

Prejudicial Language. The inappropriate use of adjectives or qualifiers in the description of information to appeal to the emotions of the user.

Probabilistic Sample Survey. A survey of a representative sample of the market from which the research can generalize with some "probability" of accuracy. The sample is achieved by selecting elements or groups of elements from a well-defined population by a procedure that gives each element a calculable nonzero probability of inclusion in the sample.

Product Concept. The meaning of the product relative to consumer needs or preferences. It reflects a firm's basic competency in meeting particular market needs in ways that differ from that of competitors.

Product Planning Matrix. A Quality Function Deployment (QFD) structure within which a program team can consolidate the necessary information for reconciling the voice of the market with the voice of the firm. *See* Quality Function Deployment.

Product Position Maps. Maps that represent the perceived relationships among brands, with shorter distances between brands indicating greater similarity in perception of relevant attributes. *See* Multidimensional Scaling.

Pseudo-Clairvoyance. A phenomenon, also referred to as hindsight bias, demonstrated by managers concluding that had they been asked to predict an outcome they would have correctly done so, when, in fact, they would not have done so. This may lead to the conclusion that the research was unnecessary or uninformative, since, "It is only telling us what we already know and could have predicted."

Quality Function Deployment (QFD). A process providing a framework for effective and direct interaction between market researchers, program managers, and engineers, thereby minimizing the ambiguity or discrepancy that often exists between market information and product specifications.

Regression. A statistical tool that quantifies the relationship between a dependent variable and one or more independent variables.

Relative Advantage. The benefits that an innovation provides that existing arrangements do not. It may be incremental and curative (intended to reinstate a desired level of previous performance), or preventive (lessening the likelihood that an undesired event will occur).

Reversibility. How easily a change may be discontinued without adverse effect.

Silo Effect. Major functional areas do not talk with one another in situations where they should.

Slippery Slope. A line of reasoning claiming that if we follow a particular course of action a succession of other events will follow naturally, ending in something quite undesirable, when there are ways of implementing a particular decision that avoid unintended or undesirable consequences.

Smoothing Technique. A technique that uses a series of historical data to predict the value of a future event in the series. The process assumes that there is some pattern in the series that will repeat.

Snail-Darter Assumption. Assumption that has a reasonably low probability of being wrong but which could have a serious impact on the firm if it is accepted as true and proves to be wrong.

Social Construction of Reality. This concept holds that people in different positions in a social system such as a company tend to have different understandings of the same phenomena and hence different ways of "knowing that they know" because of different frames of reference.

Straw Man. Making one's position stronger by making the opposition seem weaker.

Subjective Expected Utility Theory. A sophisticated mathematical model of choice that lies at the foundation of most contemporary economics, theoretical statistics, and operations research.

Summative Evaluation. Evaluation that helps to assess the value of a research project after it has been completed.

Synergy. Joint effects or the interactions among the parts of any system. Positive synergy occurs when component parts of a system result in added effectiveness or efficiency, or both. Negative synergy results in less effective and/or efficient decision outcomes.

Theories-in-Use. Implicit theories that represent the viewing lens, the filter through which we perceive the voice of the market and through which we evaluate options and project the voice of the firm.

Thinking-to-Follow. Learning how to respond only after important changes are already in their more advanced stages.

Thinking-to-Lead. Sensing important market events in their early stages and developing creative responses.

Top-Down Process. The process of moving from a higher-level objective to the identification of consistent lower-level alternatives.

Transaction Barrier. Factor that inhibits a successful exchange between the firm and the customer.

Trialability. How easily a change may be implemented without a long-term commitment.

Trick 'em Approach. When managers in one group anticipate how managers in another group will respond to their analysis, and then change their analysis so that when the second group adjusts the first group's report, it will come out the way the first group wanted it to in the first place.

Truth Test. Also called a reality test, it comprises the rules or guidelines used to assess the accuracy of a particular experience or observation. It influences the kinds of data that are collected, how they are collected, and how they are interpreted and acted upon.

Unequal-Opportunity Methodology. A methodology that does not give an unwelcome answer (bad news) the same opportunity to show up as it does a more welcomed answer (good news). The methodology favors the more welcome answer. It is not usually the result of a deliberate effort to skew results, but is more often the consequence of not thinking about potential responses.

Viewing Lens. A frame of reference, that is, the assumptions, expectations, and decision rules used to evaluate and respond to a situation.

Voice of the Firm. What the firm is capable of and willing to provide to the market.

Voice of the Market. What the market indicates it needs and wants and is willing to pay for.

Walking the Floor. The direct observation of what key stakeholders such as customers, dealers, and suppliers are doing.

We-Should-But-Don't Paradox. Knowledge among managers that they should be behaving one way while knowingly avoiding that behavior.

Appendix

Chapter 2 introduced the concept of an inquiry center as a knowledge loom. In this Appendix I demonstrate how to use current and near-term technologies to implement the three dimensions of the inquiry center—logic, energy/collaboration, and imagination/creativity. The technologies proposed are not meant to replace the human dimension of organizations. This has long been the fallacy of technology. Technology, like any tool, is meant to augment the human dimension.

It will be helpful to begin with a look at the levels of the inquiry center that are supported by state-of-the-art technology. In my discussion I will use the components of the Haeckel hierarchy as benchmarks (see Exhibit A-1).

Exhibit A-1
Evaluation of the Status of Computing Technology
in Relation to the Haeckel Hierarchy

Level	Elements Manipulated	Status
Data	Numbers, Words	Available
Information	Statements	Available
Intelligence	Rules	Available
Knowledge	Knowledge Bases	Near-Term
Wisdom	Combined Knowledge Bases	Long-Term

This Appendix was prepared by Marc B. Itzkowitz.

From the exhibit one sees that the technology for manipulating data and information is available and has been so since the earliest days of computing. The ability to manipulate intelligence at the computer level has been a more recent innovation. This ability is the function of expert systems. The main goal of expert systems is to encapsulate the intelligence of those deemed "experts" into systems that can be used by nonexperts to raise the level of their effective intelligence. As a result, nonexperts can act like experts. A dictionary is a commonly used expert system. A dictionary, like other expert systems, is composed by an individual or team that is knowledgeable in lexicology. Their intelligence is pooled into an output—in this case in the form of a book—that is readily accessible to those with a certain minimal set of basic skills (i.e., a moderate level of spelling ability). With this basic ability the user is able to access and make use of the intelligence of those far more knowledgeable than him- or herself.

AN INTRODUCTION TO EXPERT SYSTEMS

In the most basic sense, expert systems contain two major components. The first component is a set of conditional statements commonly known as rules. These rules are statements of intelligence. The complete set of rules is often referred to as "knowledge," or a "knowledge base." For example, if one were constructing an expert system to assist inexperienced doctors through a medical examination, one might make a rule that says, "If patient looks flushed, take his or her temperature." This rule, combined with other rules, would form a medical knowledge base.

The second component of the expert system is the inference engine, which is needed to manipulate the rules. Its job is to take an initial set of inputs from the user and infer from the knowledge base either a conclusion or what other data the user must provide before a conclusion can be reached. If a conclusion is reached, then the user is given a course of action; if a conclusion is not reached, then the user is asked for more information and the iterative process continues. Continuing with the medical example, the initial question an expert system might ask of the doctor is how the patient looks. If the doctor responds that the patient looks flushed, the above-mentioned rule would be triggered. The doctor would then be asked, "What is the patient's temperature?" and the process would continue. Again, it is the responsibility of the inference engine to take data and infer what other data are needed from the knowledge base. Thus, the combination of the inference engine and the knowledge base allows for a formal treatment of intelligence.

Knowledge, the next step in the Haeckel hierarchy, is given the status of near-term, since research on constructing knowledge bases and inference engines is still in its early stages. For complex problems, we know little about how to construct these critical components; moreover, the large knowledge bases required for complex problems can bring current inference engines to a standstill. Therefore, the level of certitude required by the Haeckel hierarchy to pass from intelligence to knowledge is not yet satisfied. Advances will need to be made in processing power and inference engine theory before certitude is reached and before using complex knowledge bases becomes the norm. However, the research in this field is accelerating at such an enormous rate that the status of near-term is encouraging. Expert systems are already being introduced into the mainstream home computing market to perform such functions as grammar checking and tax preparation.

The final stage in the Haeckel hierarchy, wisdom, earns the status of long term because, before one understands how to combine knowledge bases, one must understand better the workings of individual knowledge bases. Research in the construction of knowledge bases has been going on for many years; however, research into how to link these knowledge bases has been practically nonexistent.

THE DIMENSIONS OF THE INQUIRY CENTER

At this point one might well wonder, "How do I go about developing these rules?" This is where the concept of the inquiry center as a multidimensional knowledge loom comes into play. Chapter 2 states that a successful inquiry center must incorporate three dimensions: the logic of decision making, energy/collaboration, and imagination/creativity. The three dimensions show how the weaving of rules will feed the knowledge bases of future inquiry centers. The following sections discuss the technologies that facilitate the use of each dimension.

Logic

The most commonly addressed dimension is the logic of decision making, and it is along this dimension that computing technology has been fully exploited. This is because logic has been the forte of computing technology ever since the creation of the world's first computer—the abacus—many thousands of years ago. This primitive computer was designed to simplify the use of the logic-driven science of mathematics. Every computer invented since then has had at least the ability to do simple math and logic. If you look at some of the most common uses of computing technology today, you will see that math and logic are somehow involved. Spreadsheet programs are a prime example. There is not a business computer today that does not have a spreadsheet loaded or nearby. What is the reason for such proliferation? Spreadsheets are immensely popular because they appeal directly to the logic dimension and allow the nonexpert to apply complex statistical and mathematical treatment to a given set of numerical data. It allows the application of the scientific method to a series of "what-ifs" and brings out the Sherlock Holmes in all of us.

Other popular computing technologies that allow the user to manipulate and utilize logic are games, graphing programs, and data bases. Treasure hunts, chess, football, business simulations (i.e., for eliminating post-survey regret), and other such games are rich in strategy. Graphing programs are merely natural extensions of the spreadsheet concept. After all, graphs give the power of visual interpretation to the otherwise overwhelming chaos of numbers on a spreadsheet. Finally, there are data bases. These are the most vivid example of how to deal with the logic dimension in the computing environment. Consider the two most popular ways data have been organized over the past three decades: hierarchical and relational. In the hierarchical model, data are organized first by category and then by subcategory and so on in an ever-widening pyramid-shaped structure. Take, for example, the organization of a components list for an automobile (see Exhibit A-2). The topmost level might be the name of the car, whereas the bottom level would consist of the smallest components under consideration. Moving from top to bottom the level of detail increases. Another pyramid would be formed for a different automobile, and so on. In some cases, two or more automobiles may share a common part.

Unlike the hierarchical model, the relational model groups similarly structured data into the table (similar to a spreadsheet), and tables of related information are kept in the same data base (see Exhibit A-3). By using a series of "logical operators" (and, or, nor, not) a parts list for each automobile can be reconstructed from this compact structure.

Exhibit A-2
A Hierarchical Data Base Model Using an Automobile Components List

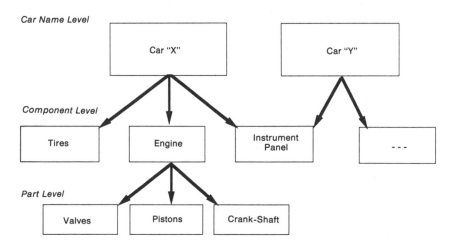

Energy/Collaboration

The next, and more complex, dimension is that of energy/collaboration. This is a dimension that, in terms of technology, has come a long way since the advent of electronic mail (email). In fact, creating more of a sense of community among users is the current direction in computer-based communication. This is different from the original concept of email as an alternative to the telephone. The advantage of email was that you could leave a message for a person who was hard to reach by phone. The introduction and subsequent widespread use of answering machines eliminated the need to compose electronic letters, so this advantage disappeared.

The next use of email was for sending letters to people on a distribution list. This clearly had advantages over the phone. It saved the letter writer the hassle of making the same phone call to many people, and it was faster than sending off multiple copies of the same letter through interoffice mail. While this system was useful for the dissemination of information, there was one major drawback: The addressees had to be on the distribution list. This required that the user track down sources of desirable information and then get included in the distribution list for that information. It is more productive if users can get information of interest and value to them without having to know it is out there. Currently there are two options for doing this. The first option, bulletin board systems, or dumping grounds for related information (i.e., a bulletin board for upcoming events), is a low-tech, moderate-value, but

Exhibit A-3
A Relational Data Base Model Using an Automobile Components List

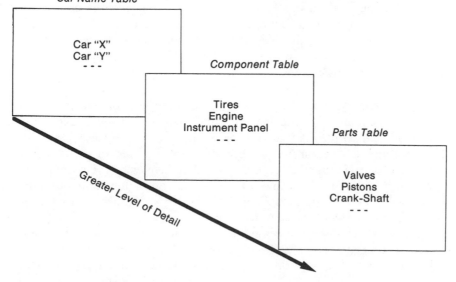

widely used solution to the problem. The second option, an intelligent email system, is a more technologically intensive solution with higher value but requires a longer time frame to implement. The advantage of the latter is that it requires no extra effort on the part of the addressee, and even less effort on the part of the addressor. Both options are explained below.

Bulletin board systems. Bulletin board systems have been the backbone of on-line communication among computer users for years. In fact, a whole subculture rich in etiquette and terminology has evolved. One of the most common terms for referring to these bulletin board systems (frequently abbreviated BBS) is SIG (special interest group). This term underscores the fact that individual BBS take on their own character and usually revolve around either one or a select set of topics which are freely discussed. All other subjects are taboo.

SIGs have a special significance for the collaborative dimension of the inquiry center. Organizations with email systems can quickly set up a series of SIGs for the discussion of "hot" topics or topics of ongoing concern. The topics are clearly defined, as are the goals of discussion. Thus, for those interested, the problem of getting on the right distribution list is eliminated. All mail that pertains to a specific topic can be put onto the proper bulletin board where it can easily be found by someone scanning a list of SIG topics.

In the short term, SIGs are clearly a low-cost answer. As time progresses, however, and people post ever-increasing amounts and types of information on bulletin boards, their functionality deteriorates. A balance is needed between how broadly a topic for an SIG is defined and how many SIGs people must wade through to find the information that interests them. In other words, the more narrowly defined the topic of a specific bulletin board, the higher its value to the user. As the number of types and the amount of information grow, either the number of topics will have to increase or each set of topics will have to be broadened. A list of more than thirty to fifty topics tends to frustrate the user, as does an individual topic that contains a large portion of useless information.

Intelligent email system. The solution to the problems of bulletin board systems can be found in an intelligent email system. Such a system allows the user to define a set of topics, words, or phrases that are of special interest. Whenever mail is sent out user-defined filters are invoked to see who gets what. If any word in the filter matches a word in the message, it is sent to the user's private mailbox. Users do not have to wade through voluminous topic lists or overpopulated topics looking for information. Addressors no longer have to figure out which topic to use. All is done by the computer.

The drawback to both systems—in fact, to any system where collaboration is encouraged—is that different people in different areas of a company will often view and refer to the same concept in different ways. (This is an aspect of the "two-communities" metaphor discussed in Chapter 6.) For example, a major computer firm had the name of one client stored in twenty-seven different ways in its data bases. Such disparity in something as common as a client's name made it impossible to collect all records on that client. To overcome the pseudo-language barriers found in a multicommunity environment, a simple data base of synonyms can be used. Synonyms intercede every time a request is made to find data. For example, a company that wants all information pertaining to the colors of its products might issue a search of its data something like, "Find all where description = 'color'." Without a synonym data base such a simple search might turn up nothing if it were performed by the British office of the same company, where "color" might be spelled "colour." In an environment with an active synonym data base function, both queries would yield the same result, despite the different spellings of the word.

Imagination/Creativity

The technologies that provide for the energy/collaboration dimension of the inquiry center provide only minimal support for the imagination/creativity dimension. All too often people are told to be creative in environments that breed conformity. Thus, the first step in facilitating imagination and creativity is to provide users with a conducive environment. In the following paragraphs we discuss the technologies that deal with system implementation issues.

Graphical user interface (GUI). The idea of a GUI was first proposed by Xerox Parc in the 1970s but did not gain widespread acceptance until some time after the introduction of the Macintosh computer in the mid-1980s. What made GUIs unique was that commands were issued in a symbolic manner, not in a command line. For example, in the command-line scenario, if you wanted to delete a file, a command would have to be typed that looked something like this: "del *filename* from *diskname/sub-directory*." In a GUI environment the user would point to a file with a pointing device and drag it to the trash can icon (or black hole) on the screen. Once the file was "thrown out," the trash can icon would change to that of a bulging one, symbolizing the fact that something was in it. To return the trash can to its normal state the user would choose the option "empty the trash" from a nearby menu. Copying files is another example. In a command-line environment the user would issue a command such as "copy *filename* from *diskname/sub-directory* to *diskname/sub-directory*." In a GUI environment the user drags the file icon from the icon of one disk to the icon of the other disk. There is no need to remember commands or their formats.

In such an environment human intuition takes over and users spend more time doing what they want to do instead of trying to figure out how to do it. In fact, the popularity of such interfaces has become so widespread that most major manufacturers of personal to mid-size computers are adapting to the framework. Large computers, like the mainframes of most major corporations, have not made this conceptual leap, however. Even the latest models of such machines have a human interface not fundamentally different from its predecessor of ten to twenty years. Thus, while GUIs need to exist to facilitate creativity, they cannot in most large companies. One solution is to divide the responsibilities of computing between the mainframe and the desktop computers. In other words, exploit the advantages of both. In today's environment this has not typically been the case. Usually only one or the other is utilized to its full potential. It is not uncommon to see a person using a $10,000 state-of-the-art PC to do the work of a $500 dumb terminal.

To solve this problem the computing industry has begun to embrace the concept of a "front-end/back-end" system.* A PC is used to perform all of the front-end tasks such as the user-interface issues for which it was designed. The mainframe does the back-end tasks such as number crunching or querying large data bases, functions for which it was designed. Products now exist that will facilitate this division of labor. These products were designed to let the user fully incorporate the output of the mainframes into PC applications such as word processors and spreadsheets for further analysis and presentation. Also, by using the PC as a front end, users only have to learn one interface through which to access many systems that may have different functions underneath but on the surface operate together. By allowing users to easily bring together disparate data, creativity can be greatly improved.

Multiprogramming. Multiprogramming is the ability to actively run more than one piece of software at a given time. This is closely related to the idea of bringing together disparate data. In other words, multiprogramming systems are necessary if the user is going to analyze different types of data simultaneously. Consider a situation in which a manager is making a case for a new-product program. In one window on the screen there might be a word

---

*A "front-end/back-end" system should not be confused with "distributed processing," which is a much more sophisticated concept. Distributed processing may incorporate a myriad of hardware in varying configurations from PCs to mainframes, although neither is required. The main difference between the two systems is that in a PC/mainframe combination running in a distributed processing scenario the division of labor between the two computers is blurred. In a front-end/back-end scenario the PC's function is mostly management of the interface in terms of screens, icons, and additional functionality not provided by the mainframe, whose function is to store, query, process, and package data for display and further use on the PC. To implement a true distributed system, all applications on all hardware must either be rewritten or replaced because of the complex communication that must occur between the different platforms. This makes the changeover to a distributed system painful and expensive. Meanwhile, a front-end/back-end system, while not being as powerful, will allow for improvement over old hard-to-use systems without having to replace them.

processor running in which the final report is being typed. In another window a spreadsheet might be running a forecasting model for the product's revenue potential over the coming years. In the third window is a mainframe data base of competitive analysis of products in the same market. Finally, in the fourth window, a news-retrieval service is keeping the analyst up-to-date on the progress of a congressional regulatory bill which could have a detrimental effect on the sales of the product. There are four different programs from three computers over two communications links using only one interface, some menus, and a pointing device. Data can also be exchanged between windows by simply selecting the data with the pointer, using a command to cut the data, positioning the pointer in the desired destination window, and using a command to paste the data. For example, the user might want to copy the final text of the regulatory bill into the final product proposal.

Hypertext linking. Multiprogramming systems bring together different forms of data "on-the-fly." Now let's go one step further and look at embedding these links in systems so that they can be recalled for viewing or editing at a later date. This is where the concept of hypertext linking comes into play. In a hypertext environment, text, or even objects (i.e., graphics), can be linked to other text or objects that have something in common or that provide more detail. Imagine a brochure for a new automobile. In a hypertext environment the introductory screen might contain just a picture of the car. To get more information on a specific aspect of the car the user would point and click on that region. For instance, to find out more about the interior the user would click on the door of the car. This would display the interior. The user would then click on the radio for more information about it or on the shift knob for more information on the transmission. At any point a word like "brakes" might appear in a description of something else. To get more information on brakes the user would simply click on the occurrence of that word. This is much quicker than searching the data base for the actual location of that data. All in all, this environment is much more flexible than most traditional systems where one must follow a linear path, usually within the constraints of a tree-structured hierarchy. Another advantage to this environment is that paths can be created dynamically as more connections are discovered, allowing further nurturing of the dimension of imagination and creativity.

Interactive video. Most data are flat: They lack emotion and perception. While in many cases this is the desired norm, it is quite the opposite when the data deal with the voice of the market. Much of the voice of the market is nonverbal, communicated more by the image customers project of themselves (i.e., the kind of car they drive, the neighborhood they live in, the clothes they wear, and so forth). Normal row/column data fall short of communicating such dimensions. Even if they could, it is not always the optimal way because different people have different needs in terms of the data they require. For example, cross-tabs may be what a market analyst needs but may be scorned by the designer, who is an artist and wants a more visually oriented stimulus. It is for the designer that interactive video may find its first use. This does not mean, however, that there are not benefits for the market analyst. Interactive video allows analysts to get closer to the customer whose needs they are trying to address. Without the visual dimension the customer is a series of numbers and summary statements that are easy to misunderstand. In the realm of the inquiry center one must understand data in a truly holistic sense. This is almost impossible when the visual dimension is absent.

CONCLUSION

In this Appendix I have given a brief glimpse of the technologies that allow—or will eventually allow—for the incorporation of data, information, intelligence, knowledge, and wisdom into everyday decision making. I have explained the technologies that support the three dimensions of the inquiry center and how those dimensions are useful in the weaving of a knowledge loom. Most of the technologies have a central concept in common: They are all people-involving. In other words, they were designed with the user in mind, the premise being that systems exist for the benefit of their users. Technologies developed for other purposes are doomed to failure. In simple economic terms, supply must equal demand. In this case, the supply is technology and the demand is represented by the voice of the manager. If the two are to meet an adjustment must occur. Otherwise managers will go elsewhere to meet their needs, thus ignoring the advances made possible by the technology.

Index